The Gostling Manuscript

The Gostling

Manuscript

Compiled by John Gostling

Foreword by Franklin B. Zimmerman

University of Texas Press, Austin & London

The original Gostling Manuscript is in the Humanities Research Center, the University of Texas at Austin.

The foreword to the Gostling Manuscript first appeared, in slightly modified form, in *Acta Musicologica*, vol. 41 (1969), fasc. I–II, pp. 55–70.

Library of Congress Cataloging in Publication Data
Gostling manuscript.
The Gostling manuscript.
Anthems, principally for solo voices and mixed chorus with string orchestra, orchestra, or continuo.
Reproduced in facsim. from a 17th–18th cent. ms. in the Humanities Research Center, University of Texas at Austin.
Includes indexes.
1. Anthems. 2. Choruses, Sacred (Mixed voices). I. Gostling, John, ca. 1650–1733. II. Zimmerman, Franklin B. III. Texas. University at Austin. Humanities Research Center. Library.
M1999.G67G7 783.4′5′2 77–1563
ISBN 0-292-72713-5

Printed in the United States of America

Foreword

The frustrating disappearance of the well-known Gostling Manuscript (also known to Purcell scholars as the W. Kennedy Gostling Manuscript) after a sale at Sotheby's in London on July 24, 1935, vexed music historians for more than three decades. Such a significant manuscript collection – considered the single most important source, aside from autographs, for some of the best anthems by Henry Purcell, John Blow, Jeremiah Clark, Pelham Humfrey, Matthew Locke, William Turner, and other composers of the Restoration period – remained the object of a search as diligent as that for the autograph of Purcell's semiopera, *King Arthur*, or for the original manuscript of his solo violin sonata. Therefore, the reappearance of the Gostling Manuscript in the middle of Texas in the late 1960s was an important musical event.

This handsome large folio volume might quite appropriately have been called the John Gostling Manuscript, since all its contents appear to have been copied by Purcell's highly musical contemporary, a close friend of the composer and his favorite, most brilliant bass soloist. Indeed, Gostling was one of the best-known performers of his time, and his great renown as a virtuoso moved John Evelyn to describe him as "stupendous" in a passage worthy of a modern-day publicity agent.[1] However, Gostling was such an assiduous col-

1. *Diary*, ed. E. S. de Beer, 6 vols. (Oxford: Oxford University Press, 1955), 28 Jan. 1684/5. John Hawkins attests to the friendship between Purcell and Gostling in the following anecdote from *A General History of the Science and Practice of Music*, 2 vols., 2d ed., 2:747: "The reverend Mr. Subdean Gostling played on the viol da gamba, and loved not the instrument more than Purcell hated it. They were very intimate, as must be supposed, and lived together upon terms of friendship; nevertheless, to vex Mr. Gostling, Purcell got some one to write the following mock-eulogium ["Of all the instruments that are"; Z263, Franklin B. Zimmerman, *Henry Purcell, 1659–1695: An Analytical Catalogue of His Music*, London: Macmillan, 1963] . . . which he set in the form of a round for three voices."

lector and copyist of contemporary music that a number of other manuscripts could be named after him with equal justice. Notably, these include two John Gostling manuscripts, at Canterbury and Gloucester cathedrals, respectively, and others at St. Paul's and elsewhere. The manuscript might also be called the William Gostling Manuscript from its bookplate, which identifies the singer's son (1696–1777), who inherited his father's library after the latter's death in July 1733. But a William Kennedy Gostling also owned the manuscript in the twentieth century, so this usage would produce more confusion.

Let us call it simply the Gostling Manuscript, remembering not to confuse it with the Gostling Part-books – now housed in the library at York Minster – which also contain a great number of sacred works by Purcell and his contemporaries. All eight books in this set as well as the so-called Bernard Manuscript books (London, Royal College of Music MSS 1045–51) bear the bookplate of William Gostling. William's own library, including many of the items bequeathed him by his father, was sold by William Flackton, a well-known musical antiquarian of Canterbury, who made the sale in 1778, according to the *Dictionary of National Biography*.[2]

In any event, it seems safe to assume that the Gostling Manuscript did not become separated from the Gostling estate in Flackton's sale. It apparently remained in the family until recent times, passing to William Kennedy Gostling and finally into the possession of a "Miss Gostling of 6, the Leas, Folkestone," its last-known English owner, as far as public knowledge was concerned. It was rediscovered in Austin, Texas. Meanwhile, its contents and their value were known only from vague, none too accurate accounts in the *Musical News*[3] and from the description in Sotheby's sale catalog:

> *The Property of Miss Gostling*
>
> 586 [PURCELL (Henry)] An important contemporary Manuscript of compositions by Henry Purcell and other members

2. However, J. A. Fuller-Maitland states that no record of the sale is found in the British Museum. Cf. *Grove's Dictionary of Music and Musicians*, 10 vols., suppl. vol. to 5th ed. (London: Macmillan, 1961), p. 191.

3. See especially the issues of 1903 for March 7, p. 222; April 11, p. 342; and May 23, p. 486.

> of the Chapel Royal, from the Library of William Gostling, for whom Purcell wrote "They that go down to the Sea in Ships", and other anthems included in this volume.
>
> The contents comprise sixty-four anthems, seventeen by Purcell, twenty-three by Blow, three by Lock, four by Pelham Humphreys, four by William Turner, and one by Child, one by Aldrich, three by Tudway, four by Clark, and a few others. Many of them bear dates and notes as to the circumstances in which they were written.
>
> This manuscript is probably the most important authority for the correct text of Purcell's anthems.[4]

So much for the known history, ancient and modern, of the Gostling Manuscript up to the time of its disappearance in 1935. Its more recent past still lies hidden behind the veil drawn by its anonymous purchaser from Sotheby's, a firm whose professional secrecy has helped keep the matter dark. The buyer also succeeded in taking the manuscript out of England and in keeping it hidden for a considerable period, probably somewhere in Texas, where scarcely anyone would have thought to look for it.

After an indeterminate number of years, during which the buyer remained anonymous and the seller silent in spite of all inquiries, the manuscript came into the hands of one James F. Drake – nobody seems to know how or when – and it was acquired, presumably from him, by the University of Texas Library. Thus, after more than thirty years, this unique and singularly helpful witness to English musical life in the late seventeenth and early eighteenth centuries again became accessible to scholars as a valuable research document in the Humanities Research Center.[5]

4. Actually, Purcell did not write for William Gostling but for John Gostling. Also, there are twenty-four anthems by Blow, counting "The Lord is King." The work is attributed to "I anonimous B," a jocular reference to Blow, to whom it is firmly attributed in *Grove's Dictionary*, 5th ed., 1:774. The anthems by Aldrich were actually written by Giacomo Carissimi, William Byrd, and Michael Wise. The one composer remaining to be mentioned is Francis Pigott, whose anthem is "I was glad."

5. For generous assistance and for gracious permission to use the collection, I am indebted to June Moll, former librarian of the Miriam Lutcher Stark Library. I must also thank Dr. Bryce Jordan, former President of Student Affairs, who brought the Gostling Manuscript to my attention.

For more than fifty years, musical scholars have testified to the importance of the Gostling Manuscript. In his preface to volume XIIIA of the Purcell Society Edition (1921), G. E. P. Arkwright wrote:

> Next in importance to Purcell's own autographs comes the very valuable MS book of anthems which once belonged to Purcell's bass singer, the Rev. John Gostling, and is now in the possession of his descendant, W. Kennedy Gostling, Esq. It is especially valuable, because some of the anthems in it are dated. Any information which this MS gives is above suspicion.

Nearly forty years later, Professors Anthony Lewis and Nigel Fortune referred to the manuscript, which by then had been listed as missing for several decades:

> With Vols. 28, 29 and 32 it is intended to complete the extant anthems of Purcell in this edition. . . . All the chief known sources of these anthems have been consulted by the present editors, with the exception of a volume originally belonging to the Rev. John Gostling, the famous bass singer and contemporary of Purcell. This passed into the possession of the late W. Kennedy Gostling and was sold on the 24th of July 1935; it is believed now to be in private hands, but it has proved impossible to trace.[6]

But surely the contents of the Gostling Manuscript itself speak most forcefully for its importance. A survey of the composers represented and the works it contains bears witness to the Reverend John Gostling's musical taste and editorial judgment, not to mention his skill as a copyist. Each composer is represented by some of his best works – Dean Aldrich, as usual, by the best works of others – and the most prominent composers of the time are represented, more or less in accordance with the stature of each, as measured by the relative number of anthems included for each. Obviously, such a quantitative measurement of quality is too crude to be completely depend-

6. *The Works of Henry Purcell* (London: Novello, 1960), 32 vols., 29:xi.

able. And in one instance it seems patently unsound, since Blow is represented by twenty-four anthems, Purcell by a mere seventeen.

Undoubtedly no highly sensitive musician would have taken Blow for the better composer. On this point, however, it is appropriate to explain that chronological range also played its part in the accumulation of works by any given composer. Blow's longevity, not the superiority of his compositions, brought about his numerical advantage, for he began composing at least a decade before Purcell's death. Therefore, his twenty-four anthems actually represent a creative period roughly twice as long as Purcell's.

By this same crude rule of thumb, all remaining composers seem to fall into place fairly, with the notable exception of Matthew Locke, who surely should have been at least on a par with Blow. Perhaps the shortness of Locke's career provides a reasonable explanation for the disparity. Or it may have been that his impolitic but very well publicized association with the foreign Catholic musicians active at Queen Catherine's "Popish" chapel at Somerset House may have diminished his popularity with the Anglican circle, for whom these anthems were written and performed. Otherwise, the Gostling Manuscript can be evaluated as an excellent, well-balanced anthology of masterful works, judiciously chosen from the large repertory available in Purcellian times – a period many consider to represent the apogee of the English anthem tradition.

The manuscript is impressive in size, running to over 418 pages, and handsome in appearance. Its large format – 29½ by 43½ centimeters – is enhanced by a beautifully preserved, still quite elegant paneled calf binding, the face of which bears the signature "Jo Gostling." From this, we may conclude that the contents of the manuscript remain almost exactly as John Gostling left them to be bound, probably about 1706 or shortly thereafter. (However, it seems that one page was removed after the binding was finished, as we shall see later.)

On the front paste-down, in a hand very like that of John Gostling, appears an alphabetical table of contents for the twenty-six anthems in the front end. (The words "front" and "reverse" are used here for convenience, as there is no easy way to differentiate the beginning from the end of the manuscript.) Like many Restoration scorebooks, this is double-ended, each end being reserved for one of two kinds of music – here the division is roughly between orchestral and choral anthems – a convenient way of sorting music for choral performance throughout the year. The reverse paste-down shows a similar list, once one has turned the book over and end for end, identifying the thirty-eight choral anthems which fill the remainder of the manuscript. A small sheet of paper tipped in on the recto of the reverse fly-leaf alphabetically lists forty-four other anthems which Gostling apparently had occasion to refer to from time to time. Apart from these, the only other item of interest in these prefatory pages is the bookplate of William Gostling, as shown on the front paste-down.

Altogether, then, there are sixty-four anthems fair-copied in full score. Those in the front end, which occupy over 205 pages, are anthems in the grand concertato style, mostly accompanied by strings but sometimes by other instruments as well. See, for instance, oboe d'amores in the accompaniment to John Blow's "Sing unto the Lord." The anthems in the reverse end, most either polyphonic or with thorough-bass accompaniment only, occupy over 213 pages. The chronological span of each end is clearly defined, and both represent about the same periods of time. The front end begins with Humfrey's "Like as the Hart," which dates from about 1670 to 1674, although it may have been copied into the manuscript four or five years afterward, and continues right on to 1706, the year in which Clark wrote his beautiful setting of Psalm 103, "Praise the Lord, O my Soul, and all that is within me." The reverse end begins with Blow's "O Lord I have sinned," composed shortly after January 3, 1670, for the funeral of General Monck, who was buried in Westminster Abbey shortly thereafter.[7] Like the front end, it also closes with an anthem by Clark, precisely described as a "Thanksgiving Anthem / Sept. 23, 1705 [performed] at / St. Paul's the Queen present / for the victory and success / in Flanders, in passing / the French lines / Composed by Mr. Jer: Clark / Organist of St. Paul's."

Chronological information afforded by inscriptions of this sort is quite useful in a few specific instances, and it frequently provides valuable evidence for dating various works, hence establishing

7. *Encyclopedia Britannica*, 14th ed. (London, 1929).

guidelines for dating some portions of the Gostling Manuscript itself. Watermarks are less helpful but are not to be overlooked, if only because they tend to confirm the time span sketched in above. Marks are fairly consistent throughout both parts of the volume, which may be taken as an indication that the pages of the manuscript were prepared for musical copy all at once, presumably some time in the 1670s. The even spacing of the chain lines throughout seems to corroborate this notion.

The watermark consistently appearing on the top half of the folios is one of the most common found in late seventeenth-century paper used in England for music copying. With only one minor variant, the mark is the usual fleur-de-lis inscribed in a crowned coat of arms, beneath which extends a long, pendant figure 4, its stem connecting at the bottom with the anagram WR, the initials of which are joined and on the slant. Even lower appear the letters I. I., which give way further along in the manuscript to the letters A. I. This upper watermark conforms in most details to Heawood's sketches numbered 1785, 1795, and 1801, all of which date from the 1670s and 1680s.[8] The watermarks on the lower half of the pages are less consistent. At the beginnings of both ends, under an elaborate cross inscribed within the symbol IHS, appear the letters PI, these being supplanted further in from each end by the letters (or number?) IV. Heawood lists these as items 1784 to 1786, dating them as belonging also to the 1670s and 1680s, or perhaps slightly later.

Other chronological evidence may be deduced from titles and miscellaneous biographical information appearing with various anthems. Even the placement of the anthems gives some indication regarding the date of origin of each, although nothing is nearly precise enough to support hard and fast conclusions. For instance, three of Humfrey's anthems appear at the beginning in the front end, and one appears near the beginning of the reverse end. But it seems obvious that these were copied into Gostling's manuscript quite some time after Humfrey died on July 14, 1674. Indeed, those in the front end are followed by anthems ascribed to Dr. John Blow, who was known as plain Mr. John Blow until December

8. Edward Heawood, *Watermarks, Mainly of the 17th and 18th Centuries* (Hilversum: Paper Publication Society, 1950), vol. 1.

1677, when the Archbishop of Canterbury conferred upon him the Doctor of Music degree.[9] These would not have been copied earlier than 1678, and their lateness suggests that Gostling may well have begun the manuscript after he had been appointed a Gentleman of the Chapel Royal early in 1679.[10]

On the other hand, William Turner appears as plain Mr. Turner throughout the body of the manuscript, but he has been granted his doctorate throughout the tables of contents. This merely means that the latter could not have been copied before November 23, 1696, when Turner became a Doctor of Music.[11] Probably, Gostling did not make up these lists until the manuscript was finished and bound, very likely in 1706. Finally, Jeremiah Clark's anthems all appear toward the ends of their respective sections, a placement quite in keeping with the general chronological order sketched so far.

In general, then, it appears that Gostling collected the music paper for his projected volume of anthems in the late 1670s and proceeded throughout the next three decades to copy works into his scorebook at a fairly steady rate. Some time after the last works had been copied in – that is, probably after 1706 – he had the entire manuscript bound, one suspects expensively, in paneled calf. This hypothesis is strengthened by two pieces of evidence which undermine my original theory that the pages were bound *before* the music was copied in. On page 40 in the reverse end, the beginnings of the first and second violin parts for Humfrey's "Like as the Hart" appear upside down at the bottom of the sheet. Apparently Gostling had made so many mistakes in copying the beginning of this first work at the front end that he decided to discard it, then later used it for copying in Blow's "O Lord thou hast searched me out." Also, after page 62 in the reverse end, an additional tenor part is bound into the manuscript. If the volume had already been bound at the time the addition was made – probably under Purcell's supervision, some time after 1688 – the extra sheet would have been tipped in rather than bound in. Finally, we may conjecture that some flaw existed even after the manuscript was stitched and bound, for frag-

9. *Grove's Dictionary*, 5th ed., 1:769.

10. Ibid., 3:722.

11. He is not to be confused with his near contemporary, the William Turner who wrote *Sound Anatomiz'd*. Cf. *Grove's Dictionary*, 5th ed., 8:614–615.

ments of a page that has been torn out remain between pages 140 and 141 in the front end. These indicate that pagination was carried out last of all, there being no missing page number, but the fragments give no hint as to the nature of the extirpated matter. As the reader will notice, Gostling's numbering was not always correct and consistent. For example, he repeated numbers 172 and 173 and assigned the number 107 to no less than three different pages. Although the manuscript is comparatively clean and free from stains and smudges, there are a few imperfections.

For further chronological evidence we must turn to the text of the manuscript, where numerous headings and appended annotations supply a wealth of information about dates and backgrounds of performances for various anthems and also shed some light on the chronological development of the Gostling Manuscript itself.

Franklin B. Zimmerman
University of Pennsylvania

Orchestral Anthems

	Behold I bring you glad Tidings Mr Purcell	94	1687 for Xtmass Day
	Be mercifull Dr Blow	176	87 For ye K. & Queen being ye [illegible]
B-	Blessed are they yt fear ye Lord. Mr Purcell	105	1687/8
	Bring unto ye Lord Dr Blow	185	
C —	Cry aloud Spare not. Dr Blow	17.	
G —	God sheweth me his Goodness plenteously Dr Turner	50.	
	I am well pleased Dr Aldrich	146	
I	It is a good thing to sing to sing praises Mr Purcell	68	
	I was Glad. Mr Purcell	44.	
	Like as ye Hart. Mr Humphreys	1.	
L.	Lord teach us to number or Dayes Mr Humpheys	12	
	O how amiable Dr Tudway	190	
	O Lord my God Mr Humphreys	6	
	O sing praises Dr Turner	138	
O	O sing unto ye Lord Dr Blow For Mr Wildon	153	
	O sing unto ye Lord, Dr Blow	36	
	O sing unto ye Lord Mr Purcell	124	1688
	Praise ye Lord O my Soul Mr Clark	198	
	Praise ye Lord O my Soul Mr Purcell	110	1687
P.	Ponder my words O Lord Dr Blow	172	
	Preserve me O God Dr Turner	86	
S. —	Sing unto ye Lord Dr Blow	24	
	They yt go down to ye Sea in ships. Mr Purcell	77	**
	Thy hands have made me Dr Blow	183	
T.	Thy mercy O Lord Dr Blow	59	
	Thy way O God Mr Purcell	119.	1687

In all. 26

Wm E. Gostling

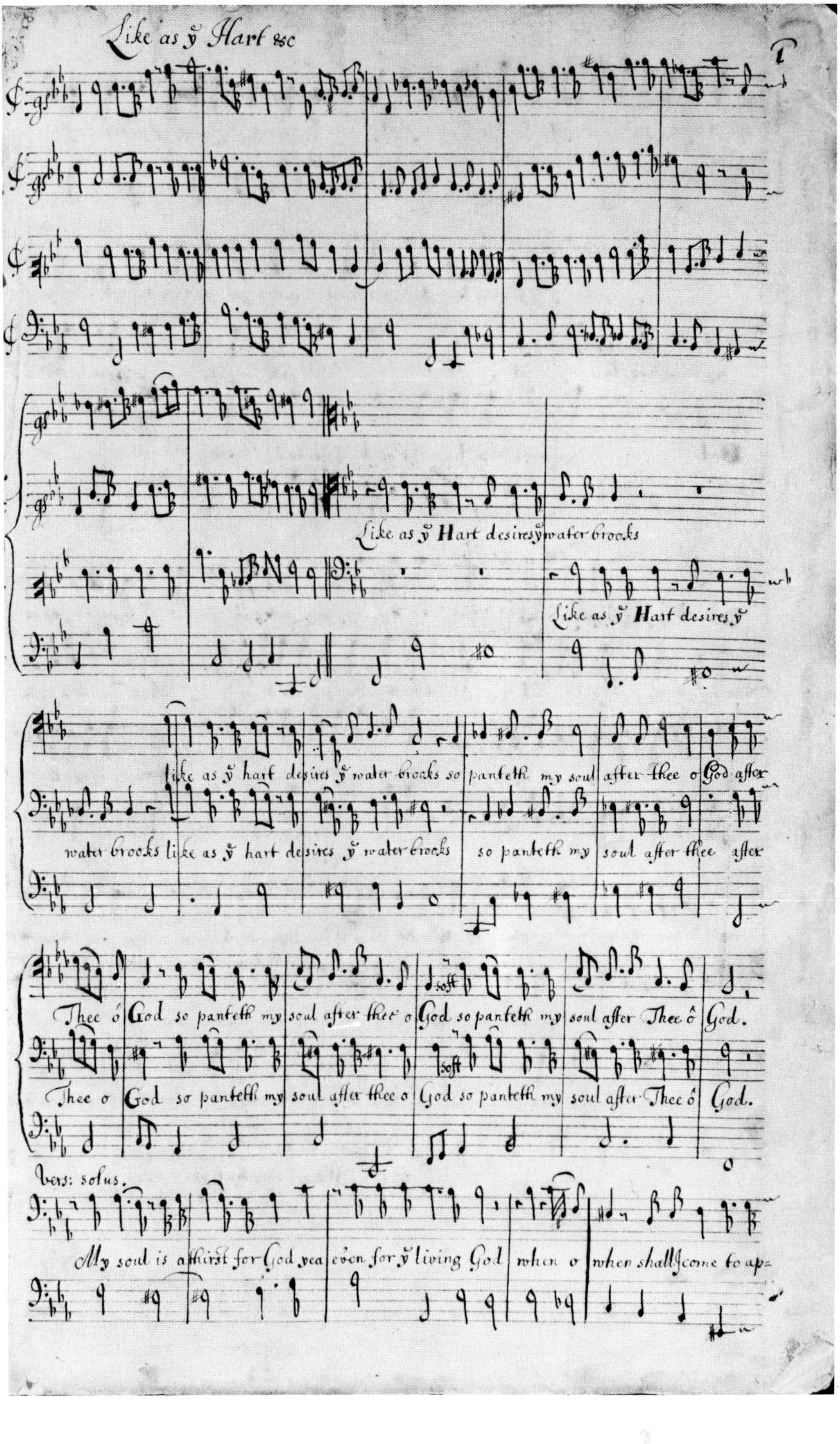
Like as ye Hart &c
Like as ye Hart desires ye water brooks
Like as ye Hart desires ye
like as ye hart desires ye water brooks so panteth my soul after thee o God after
water brooks like as ye hart desires ye water brooks so panteth my soul after thee after
Thee o God so panteth my soul after thee o God so panteth my soul after Thee o God.
soft
Thee o God so panteth my soul after thee o God so panteth my soul after Thee o God.
vers: solus.
My soul is athirst for God yea even for ye living God when o when shall I come to ap-

=pear before y Presence of God, when o when shall I come to appear before the Presence of
my tears have been my meat day & night my tears have been my
my tears have been my meat day & night my tears have
God my tears have been my meat day and night
6
meat day and night while they dayly say unto mee where is now thy god where
been my meat day and night while they dayly say unto mee where is now thy God
my tears have been my meat day & night while they dayly say unto mee where is now thy God
Cho
where is now thy god where where is now is now thy God. Where is now thy God where where is now is now thy God.
where is now thy God where where is now thy God. Where is now is now thy God where where is now is now thy God.
where is now thy God where where is now thy God. Where is now is now thy God where where is now is now thy God.
Cho:
Where is now thy God where is now thy God.
Symphony

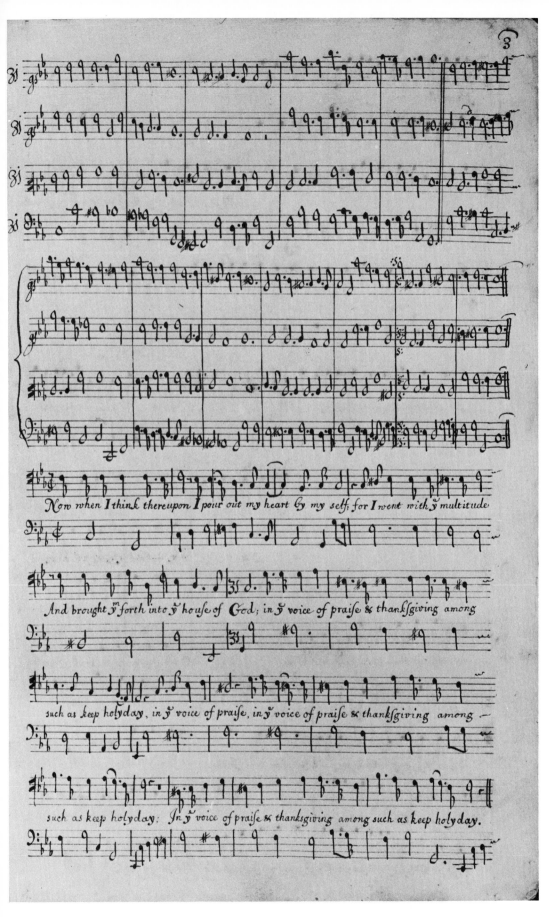

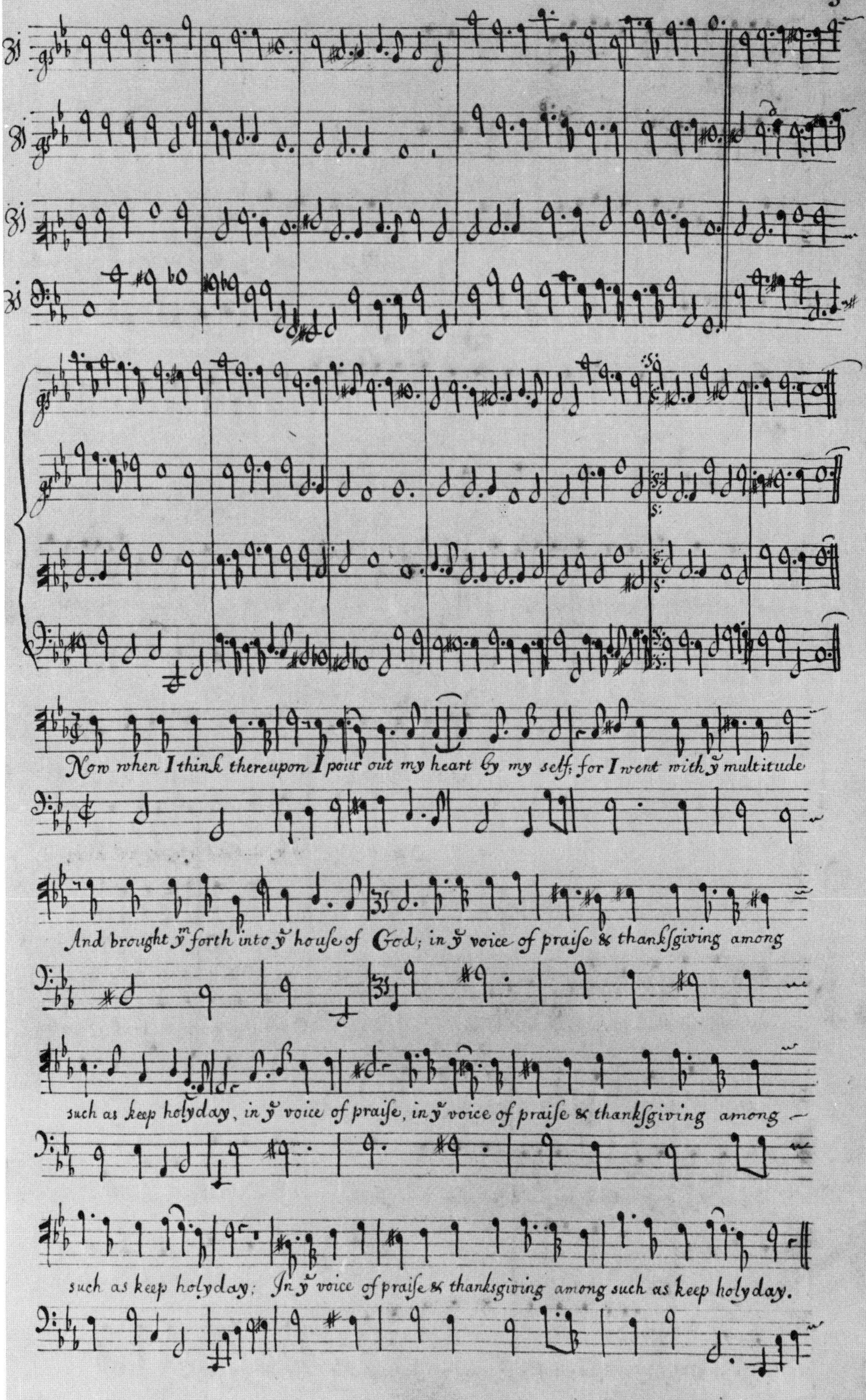
Now when I think thereupon I pour out my heart by my self; for I went with ye multitude
And brought ym forth into ye house of God; in ye voice of praise & thanksgiving among
such as keep holyday, in ye voice of praise, in ye voice of praise & thanksgiving among
such as keep holyday; In ye voice of praise & thanksgiving among such as keep holyday.

Ritornella
Verse
Why art thou so full of heaviness o my soul
o my soul, why why art thou so full of heaviness o my soul, & why art thou disquieted &
why art thou disquieted within me, o my soul, why why art thou disquieted o my soul
Vers a 4.
O put thy trust in God O put thy trust in God
O put thy trust in God O put thy trust in God
O put thy trust in God o
why why art thou disquieted within me
O put thy trust in God O put thy
O put thy trust in God for I will yet give him thanks for the help of his
O put thy trust in God for I will yet give him Thanks for I will yet give him
put thy trust in God put thy tr. in God for I will yet give him thanks for the
trust in God for I will yet give him Thanks for yͤ help of his Countenance for I will

countenance
for I will yet give him thanks for yͤ help of his countenance, I will
thanks give him thanks for I will yet give him thanks for yͤ help of his countenance I will
help of his countenance for I will yet give him thanks for yͤ help of his countenance, I will
yet give him thanks. I will
yet give him Thanks, I will yet give him thanks for yͤ help of his countenance.
yet give him Thanks I will yet give him thanks for yͤ help of his countenance.
yet give him Thanks I will yet give him thanks for yͤ help of his countenance.
yet give him Thanks, I will yet give him thanks for yͤ help of his countenance.
Cho:
O put yoͬ trust in God &c, as before in yͤ Verse.
Cho.
O put thy trust trust in God
Cho.
O &c
Cho.
O put thy &c as before in yͤ Verse
Mʳ Pel: Humphreys
exʳ

O Lord my God why hast Thou forsaken me: &c.

Verse solus.
O Lord my God why hast ye forsaken
me, o Lord my God why why hast thou forsaken me, & art so far from my-
health & from ye words of my Complaint o Lord my God why hast thou forsaken mee,
& art so far from my health & from ye words of my complaint, why hast thou forsaken
me & art so far from my health & from ye words of my complaint, why hast thou for=

-saken me & art so far from my health and from the words of my complaint
Symphony
soft
soft
soft
soft
Vers: 2 voc.
I am pou-red out am poured out like water all my bones are out of Joynt are
I am poured out like water am poured out like water all my bones are out of Joynt are
out of Joynt my heart
out of Joynt, my heart also in ye midst of my body is even like melting wax

also in yͤ midst of my body is even like melting wax my heart also in yͤ midst of my body in yͤ
my heart also in yͤ midst of my body in yͤ m: of my
midst of my body is even like melting wax my heart also in yͤ midst of my body is
body is even like melting wax, my heart also in yͤ midst of my body is even
Cho:
But be not
even like melting wax, my heart also in yͤ midst of my body is evn like melting wax. But be not
-n like melting wax my heart also in yͤ midst of my body is even like melting wax. But be not
Cho:
But be not
Thou far from me o Lord Thou art my succoͬ my succour, hast thee to Thou art my
Thou far from me o Lord Thou art my succoͬ my succour, hast thee to
Thou far from me o Lord thou art my succoͬ thou art my succour
Thou far from me o Lord thou art my succoͬ hast thee to help mee; thou art my succour.

9
help mee
succo^d hast thee to help mee. Thou art my succo^d hast thee to help me to help me.
help me. hast thee to help mee. Thou art my succo^d hast thee to help me to help mee.
hast thee to help me Thou art my succour hast thee to help me hast thee to help me to help me.
hast thee to help me, Thou art my succo^d hast thee to help me hast thee to help me to help me.
Thou art my succour hast thee to help me hast thee hast thee to help mee.
Thou art my succo^d hast thee to help mee hast thee to help - mee.
Thou art my succour hast thee to help me to help - mee
Thou art my succour hast thee to help - mee
The first Symphony again as before
Vers
For many dogs are come about me, & ye councell of y^e
wicked layeth siege against mee ye councel of y^e wicked laieth seige against me, They peirc'd my
They peirc'd my
hands & my feet I may tell all my bones, They peirc'd my hands & my feet I may
hands & my feet I may tell all my bones, They peirc'd my hands & my feet I may

tell all my bones
They stand
staring & looking upon me
tell all my bones
They stand
staring & looking upon me
They stand
staring & looking upon me
They part my
& cast lots upon my vesture
& cast lots upon my vesture
garments among ym
they part my garments among them
& cast lots upon my
Vesture.
Symphony
& cast lots upon my
Vesture.
& cast lots upon my
Vesture.
Symphony
Verse.
But be not ~

But be not thou far from me o Lord
hast thee to help me.
But be not thou far from me o Lord
hast thee to help mee.
thou far from me o Lord
Thou art my succour
Thou art my succour
hast thee to
help me o Lord.
Thou art my succour my succour
Thou art my succo
hast thee to help me o Lord
Thou art my succour
Thou art my
succour my succour
hast thee to help me o Lord
be not thou far from me o Lord.
Thou art my
succour
hast thee to
be not thou far from me o Lord
Thou art my succour my
succour thou art my
succour,
Thou art my
succour
Thou art my succo my
succour,
help me o Lord
Thou art my succour
hast thee to help me.
Chorus
hast thee to help me o Lord
Thou art my succour
hast thee to help me.
again
hast thee to help me o Lord
Thou art my succour
hast thee to help me.
as before.
Mr Humphrey.

Lord teach us to number or dayes.

Soft
Soft
Soft
Vers:
Lord teach us to number or dayes yt we may apply or hearts unto Wisdome
Lord teach us to number our dayes that wee may apply our hearts unto Wis=

Lord teach us to number or dayes y we may apply or hearts unto Wisdom, y we may apply &
soft
soft
=dom, Ld teach us to number or dayes y we may apply or hearts unto Wisdom y we may apply
vers a3
Turn thee again turn thee again o Lord, turn thee again o Lord at y last, & be
hearts unto wisdom, turn y again turn thee again o Lord turn y again o Ld at y last, & be
or hearts unto wisdom, turn y again o Lord turn y again o Ld o Lord turn y again o Ld at y last, & be
gracious be gracious unto thy servants Ritornella & be gracious be gracious unto thy
gracious be gracious unto thy servants & be gracious be gracious unto thy
gracious be gracious unto thy servants & be gracious be gracious unto thy
soft
servants & be gracious be gracious unto thy servants. Ritor
soft
servants & be gracious be gracious unto thy servants.
soft
servants & be gracious be gracious unto thy servants Ritor.

so shall we re=joice & be glad all ye dayes of or
O satisfy us wth thy mercy o satisfy us wth thy mercy. so shall we rejoice & be glad all ye dayes of or
so shall we rejoice & be glad all ye dayes of or
Life so shall we rejoice & be glad all ye days of or Life
Cho:
So shall we rejoice & be glad shall re=
Life so shall we rejoyce & be glad all ye dayes of or life.
So shall we rejoyce & be glad shall re=
Life so shall we rejoice & be glad all ye dayes of or Life
So shall we rejoice & be glad shall re=
So shall we rejoice & be glad shall re=
=joyce & be glad all ye days of or Life.
Symphony again.
Comfort comfort us again o
joice & be glad all ye dayes of or Life.
=joice & be glad all ye dayes of or Life
Symphony again.
Lord now after ye time ye thou hast
=joice & be glad all ye dayes of or Life.
and for ye years where=
plagued us; Comfort, comfort us again o Lord, o Lord after ye time ye thou hast plagud us

in we have suffred adversity
& for ÿ years where=
& for ÿ years wherein we have suffred adversity & for ÿ years where=
shew thy servants thy work & their children thy glory,
in we have suffred adversity shew thy servants thy work & their children thy glory & ÿ
= in we have suffred adversity shew thy servants thy work & their children thy glo=ry,
& ÿ glorious Majesty of ÿ Lord & God be up=
glorious Majesty of ÿ Lord & God be upon us
= on us & ÿ glorious Majesty of ÿ Lord & God
& ÿ glorious Majesty of ÿ Lord & God
& ÿ glorious Majesty of ÿ Lord & God be upon us, & ÿ glorious Majesty of ÿ Lord our

Cho
be upon us be upon us. Prosper thou ye work of or hands upon us prosper thou ye
be upon us upon us. Prosper thou ye work of or hands upon us, up: us, pr thou ye
God be upon us upon us. Prosper thou the work of or hands upon us, prosper thou ye
Prosper thou ye work of or hands upon us prosper thou ye
work of or hands upon us O prosper thou or han= =dy-
work of or hands upon us o prosper thou or handy work - O
work of our hands upon us o prosper thou or handy work o prosper thou or handy
work of or hands upon us O prosper thou or handy
work o prosper thou or handy work o prosper thou or handy work.
prosper thou or handy work or handy work o prosper thou or handy work or handy work.
work o prosper thou or handy work. O prosper thou our handy work.
work O prosper thou our handy work o prosper thou our handy work.
Mr Humphreys

Cry aloud & spare not.

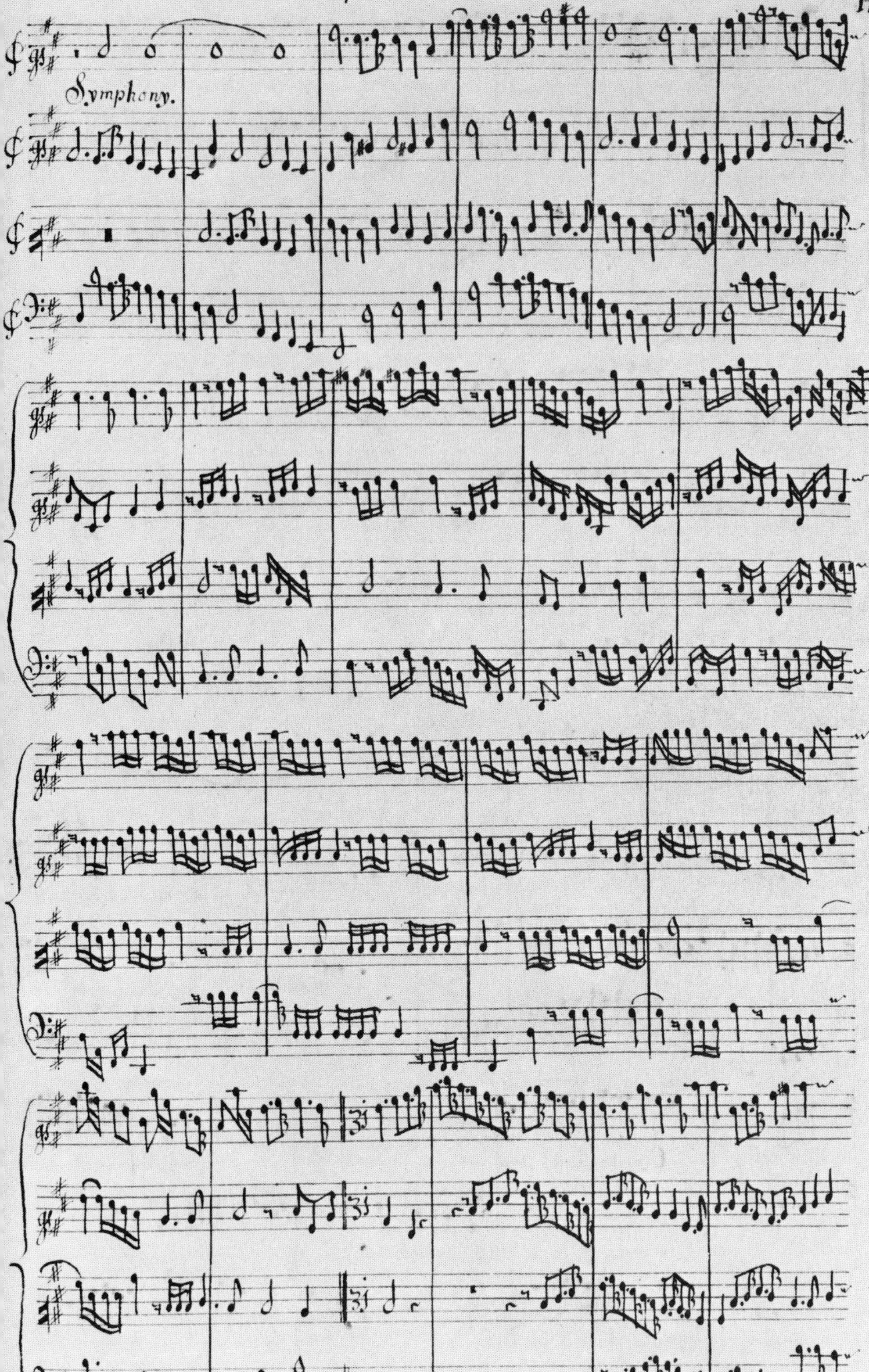
Symphony.

Verse, a3:
Cry aloud Cry aloud & spare not cry aloud &
Cry aloud
cry aloud cry aloud &
spare not
Cry aloud and spare not
Lift up thy voice like a trum=
spare not
Lift up thy voice like a trum===== pet
cry aloud cry aloud and spare not
Lift up thy voice like a trum=== pet like a

= = = = = pet. lift up thy voice like a trum = = = = = = = = = pet, & shew my people their trans=
lift up thy voice like a trum = = = = = = = pet, & shew my people their trans=
trum= lift up thy voice like a trum= pet, & shew my people their trans=
=gressions, & yͤ house of Ja = = = = = cob their sins yͤ house of Iacob their sins.
soft
Vers solus
=gressions & yͤ house of Jacob their sins yͤ house of Iacob their sins.
Ho!
=gressions & yͤ house of Jacob their sins & yͤ house of Iacob their sins.
evry one yͭ thirsteth come ye to yͤ waters & he yͭ hath no money come ye buy & eat; yea come buy
wine & milk without money and without price
where=
Cry aloud cry aloud & spare not cry aloud and spare not.
Cry aloud cry aloud aloud & spare not.

20.
=fore do ye spend yor mony for that wch is not bread, & yor labor for that wch satisfieth not.
Loud.
Lift up thy voice like a trum ========pet Lift up thy V. like a
Lift up thy voice like a trum====
Lift up thy V. like a
Lift up thy voice like a trum====pet like a trum=========pet. Lift up thy
soft
trum=========pet; hearken hearken unto me, & eat ye that which is good, and let your
trum ==========pet
voice like a trumpet
soul delight it self in fatness Encline yor ear & come unto me hear & yor soul shall live

loud
hear & yo soul yo soul shall live Cry aloud & spare not
Cry a=loud aloud & spare not lift up thy voice like a trum=
Cry aloud aloud & spare not lift up thy voice like a
lift up thy voice like a trum= = = = = = = pet, lift up thy voice like a trum= =
= = = = = = = pet lift up thy voice like a trum= =
trum= = = = = = = = pet like a trum= = = = = = = = pet, lift up thy voice like a
= = = = = = = = pet, and shew my people their Transgressions & the house of Jacob.
= = = = = = = = pet, & shew my people their Transgressions & ye house of Jacob
Trum= = pet, & shew my people their Transgressions, & ye house of Jacob

their Sins the house of Jacob their Sins
Cho: Cry aloud aloud and spare
their Sins ye house of Jacob their Sins.
Cho: Cry aloud and
their sins & ye house of Jacob their Sins
Cho: Cry aloud &
Cho:
Cry a-
not cry aloud aloud & spare not, lift up thy voice like a trum= = = pet, lift up thy voice
spare not aloud and spare not, lift up thy voice like a trum= = = pet lift up thy
spare not a= loud & spare not, lift up thy voice like a trum= = = pet like a trum=
=loud aloud and spare not; lift up thy voice like a trum=
like a trum= = = pet, & shew my people their transgressions
voice like a trum= = = pet, & shew my people their trans=
= = pet, lift up thy voice like a trum= = = pet, & shew my
= = pet, lift up thy voice like a trum= = = pet, and shew my people
& shew my people their transgressions & shew my people their transgressions &
=gressions & shew my people their transgressions and shew my people their transgressions and ye
people their transgressions shew my people their transgressions, & shew my people their transgress
their transgressions And shew my people their transgressions, & sh. my people their trans

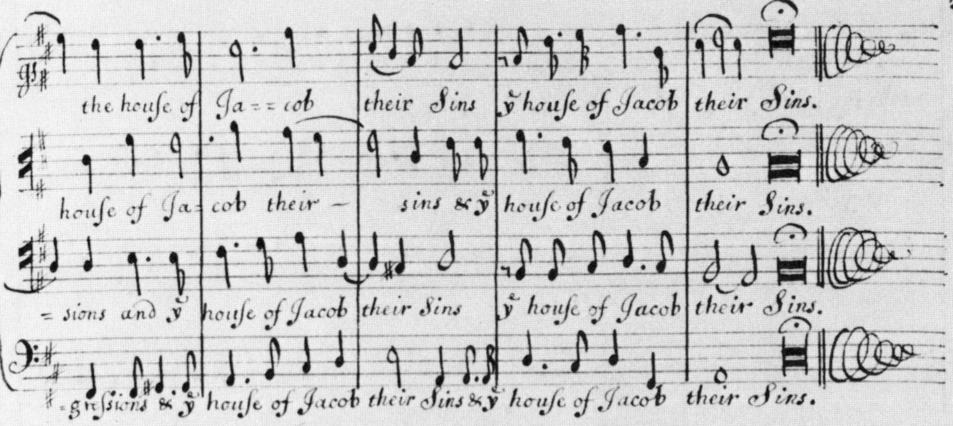
the house of Ja = = cob their Sins ye house of Jacob their Sins.
house of Ja = cob their - sins & ye house of Jacob their Sins.
= sions and ye house of Jacob their Sins ye house of Jacob their Sins.
= gressions & ye house of Jacob their Sins & ye house of Jacob their Sins.

Dr Blow.

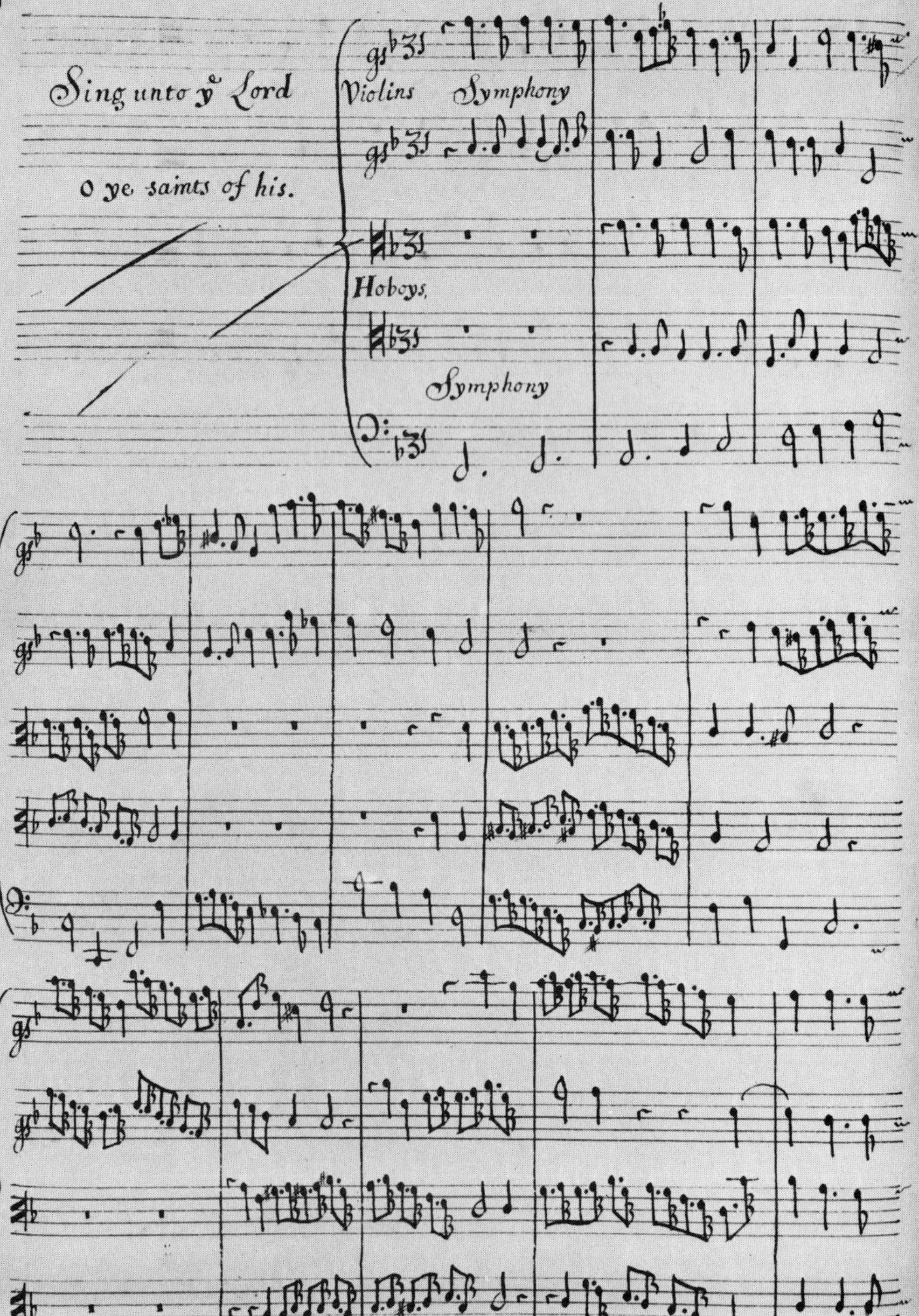
Sing unto ye Lord
O ye saints of his.
Violins Symphony
Hoboys.
Symphony

sing unto ye Lord o ye saints of his
sing unto ye Lord o ye saints of his
Sing unto ye Lord o ye Saints of his
sing unto ye Ld o ye saints of
sing unto ye Lord o ye saints of his
& give thanks for a remembrance of his holiness
sing unto ye
his
sing unto ye Lord o ye saints of his

Lord o ye Sts of his
& give
& give thanks for a remembrance of his holyness
sing unto ye Lord o ye Saints of
thanks for a remembrance of his holyness, & give thanks for a remembrance of his holyness
& give thanks for a remembrance of his holy=
Sing unto ye Lord o ye Sts of his & give thanks for a remembrance of his holy
his
& give thanks & give thanks for a re=membrance of his holy=
Symphony again as before
Symphony again
Symphony again
Symphony again
symphony again

on ye close of ye Symphony
For his wrath endureth but ye twinkling of an eye & in his pleasure is life in his
For his wrath endureth but ye twinkling of an eye & in his pleasure is life & in his
For his wrath endureth but ye twinkling of an eye
& in his plea=
pleasure is Life and in his Plea= sure is Life
pleasure is Life,
for his wrath endureth but ye twinkling of an Eye & in his
= sure is life,
For his wrath endureth but the twinkling
heaviness may endure for a night
and in his
and in his pleasure is Life heaviness may endure for a night.
plea - - - sure is Life
of an Eye
For his wrath endureth but ye twinkling
pleasure is Life & in his pleasure is Life heaviness may endure may endure for a night.
& in his pleasure is Life
heaviness
& in his pleasure is Life & in his pleasure is Life,
& in his plea= sure is Life.

heaviness may endure for a night But Joy cometh in ye morning but
may endure for a night But Joy cometh in ye morning but
heaviness may endure for a night But Joy
But Joy cometh in ye morning but
Joy cometh in ye morning But Joy, But Joy cometh in the
Joy cometh in ye morning But Joy But Joy cometh in ye
heaviness may endure for a night But Joy
Joy cometh in ye morning But Joy, But Joy cometh in
morning But Joy But Joy cometh in ye morning,
Flutes
morning but Joy But Joy cometh in ye morning,
heaviness may endure for a night But Joy But Joy cometh in ye morning
morning But Joy But Joy cometh in ye morning

Violin
Flute.
& in my pro=
And in my prosperity I said I shall never be remo= ved
=spirity I said I shall never be removed
Thou
Thou Lord of thy Goodness hast made my hill so
Lord of thy Goodness hast made my hill so strong thou Lord of thy Goodness hast made my
strong.
Thou Lord of thy Goodness hast made hast made my

hill so strong hast made my hill so strong
hill so strong hast made my hill so strong
Thou didst turn away thy face & I was troubled
Thou didst
Then
Then
thou didst turn away thy face & I was troubled
turn away thy face & I was troubled, thou didst turn away thy face & I was troubled
cry'd I unto thee ô Lord.
Then
cry'd I unto thee ô Lord
Then
Thou didst turn away thy face from me,
and I was troubled

cry'd I unto thee o Lord
gat me to my
cry'd I unto thee o Lord
& gat me to my Lord right
& gat me to my Lord right humbly.
and gat me to my Ld r: humbly
Lord right humbly and gat me to my Lord right humbly.
Symphony again on ye Close.
hum bly and gat me to my Lord right humbly.
Symphony again on ye Close.
& gat me to my Lord right humbly.
Symphony again on ye Close.
and gat me to my Lord to my Lord right humbly.
Symphony again on ye Close.
Verse on ye Close
What profit is there in my Blood when I go down I go down to ye Pit
What profit is there
What profit is there in my Blood w I go down I go

What profit is there in my blood when I go down I go
in my blood wn I go down I go down to ye Pit? When I go down I go down When I go
Down to the Pit? When I go down to ye Pit? When I go down I go
What profit is there in my blood wn I go down I go down to ye Pit?
Down to ye Pit? shall ye dust praise thee? or shall it declare thy truth or shall –
Down to ye Pit? or shall it declare thy Truth or shall it declare ~
Down to ye Pit? shall ye dust praise thee or shall it declare thy Truth de=
shall ye dust praise thee shall ye dust praise thee or shall it de~
it declare thy Truth?
shall it declare thy Truth?
=clare thy Truth?
=clare thy Truth?

Hoboy
Vers:
Thou hast turned my heaviness into Joy & girded me wth Gladness.
Thou hast turned my heaviness into Joy & girded me wth Gladness.
Thou hast tur: my heaviness
Thou hast turned my heaviness into Joy & girded me wth Gladness.
& girded me wth Gladness
and
& girded me wth Gladness
& girded me wth
into Joy
& girded me with Gladness
& girded me wth
& girded me with Gladness
Thou hast turned my heaviness into Joy

34.
girded me wth Gladness
Thou hast turned my heaviness
Thou hast tur: my heavi: into Joy &
Gladness, hast turned my heaviness into Joy
Thou hast tur: my heavi: into Joy &
Gladness wth Gladness;
Thou hast turned my heaviness,
Thou hast tur: my heavi: into Joy.
Thou hast turned my heaviness
Thou hast turn: my heavi: into Joy &
girded me wth Gladness & girded girded me with Gladness & girded girded me with Gladness.
Ritorn:
girded me wth Gladness & girded girded me wth Gladness & girded girded me wth Gladness.
Flutes:
& girded me girded me wth Gladness & girded me, girded me wth Gladness,
girded me wth Gladness, & girded me with Gladness & girded me with Gladness.

Cho:
Therefore shall evry good man sing of thy praise wthout ceasing, sing of thy praise of thy praise without
Therefore shall evry good man sing of thy praise wthout ceasing sing of thy praise without
Therefore shall evry good man sing of thy praise wthout ceasing sing sing of thy praise without
Therefore shall evry good man sing sing of thy praise wthout ceasing, sing of thy praise without
Violins
ceasing
Cho: Alleluia, Alleluia,
Vers:
Vers: O my God, I will give thanks unto Thee for ever & ever for ever & ever & ever
Cho: Alleluia, Alleluia,
Vers: O my God I will give thanks unto Thee for ever & ever for ever and ever & ever
Cho: Alleluia, Alleluia,
Vers: O my God I will give thanks unto Thee for ever & ever for ever & ever & ever
Cho Alleluia, Alleluia,
Dr Blow

36
O sing unto ye Lord a new Song.
O sing unto ye Ld a new Song
O sing unto ye Lord a new Song
sing unto ye Lord a new Song
O sing unto ye Ld a new Song
For he hath done done marvelous things wth his own right hand & with his holy
For he hath done done marvelous things wth his own right hand his own right hand & with his holy
For he hath done done marvelous things with his own right hand & with his holy —
For he hath done done marvelous things with his own right hand & with his holy —

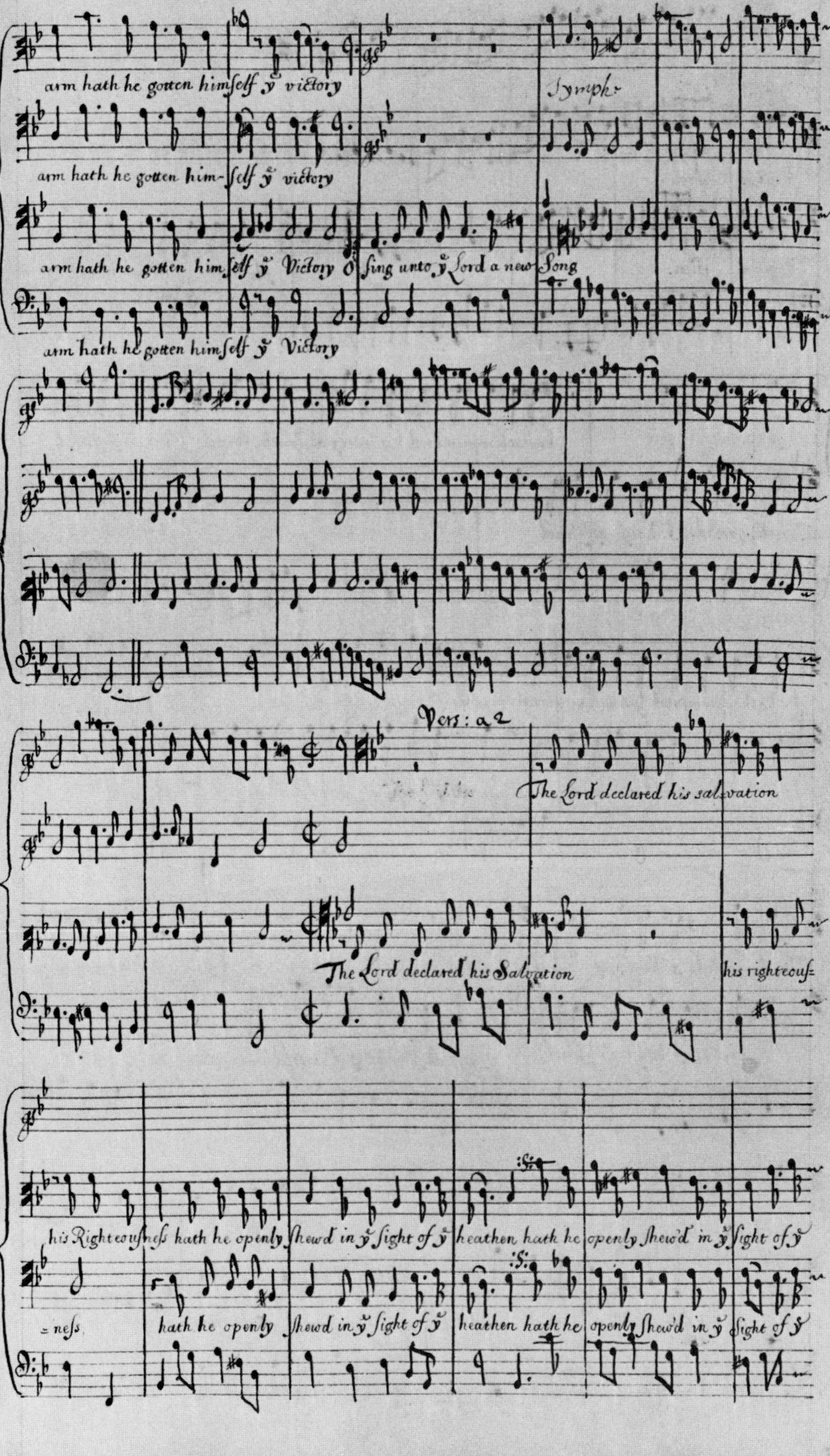
arm hath he gotten himself ye victory
Symph:
arm hath he gotten him- self ye victory
arm hath he gotten him self ye Victory O sing unto ye Lord a new Song
arm hath he gotten himself ye Victory
Vers: a 2
The Lord declared his salvation
The Lord declared his Salvation
his righteous=
his Righteousness hath he openly shew'd in ye sight of ye heathen hath he openly shew'd in ye sight of ye
=ness hath he openly shewd in ye sight of ye heathen hath he openly shew'd in ye sight of ye

hea= = = = then.
hea= = = then.
He hath remembred his mercy &
he hath remembred his mercy & Truth tow'rds ye house of Israel –
Truth tow'rds ye house of Israel
he hath remembred his mercy & truth tow'rds ye house of Israel, his mercy and
he hath remembred his mercy & truth tow'rds ye house of Israel, his mercy & Truth
Truth tow'rds ye house of Israel And all the ends of ye
tow'rds ye house of Israel, And all ye ends of ye world have seen
world have seen have seen seen ye Salvation of our God have seen ye Salv=
And all ye ends of ye world have seen have seen ye Salvation of our God, have seen ye Salv=

4 voc
Shew yo selves
=vation of o God
Shew yo selves
=vation of o God
Shew yo selves
joyfull unto ye Lord all ye Lands
sing sing sing rejoyce
joyfull unto ye Lord all ye Lands
sing
sing rejoyce
joyfull unto ye Lord all ye Lands
sing
sing rejoyce
Shew yo selves
joyfull unto ye Lord
all ye Lands
sing
& give Thanks
sing sing rejoyce & give Thanks,
& give Thanks
sing sing sing rejoyce & give
Thanks.
& give Thanks
sing
sing rejoyce & give
Thanks,
Sing
sing
rejoyce & give
Thanks.

Chorus,
Shew yo: selves joyfull unto ye Lord all yee Lands sing rejoyce and give Thanks
Shew yo: selves joyfull unto ye Lord all yee Lands sing rejoyce and give thanks
Chorus Shew yo: selves joyfull unto ye Lord all yee Lands
Shew yo: selves joyfull unto ye Lord all yee Lands sing rejoyce and give thanks,
sing rejoyce & give Thanks sing rejoyce & give thanks.
Symphony again
sing rejoyce & give Thanks and give thanks.
as before
sing rejoyce & give Thanks rejoyce and give thanks.
Symphony again
sing rejoyce & give thanks.
as before.
Bass solus.
O praise ye Ld. praise ye Ld. upon ye harp sing to ye harp wth a Psalm of thanksgiving sing to ye
soft
harp wth a Psalm of thanksgiving, Sing to ye harp with a Psalm of thanksgiving
wth
wth
soft
Trumpets

wth Trumpets wth Trumpets Also and Shawms O shew yo selves joyfull
Trumpets with trumpets wth Trumpets also & Shawms O shew yo
wth Trumpets also and Shawms O shew yo Selves
wth Trumpets O shew yo selves joyfull O
Shew yo Selves joyfull before ye Lord ye King.
selves joyfull be- fore ye Lord ye King.
shew yo selves joyfull be- fore ye Lord ye King.
Shew yo Selves joyfull be- fore ye Lord ye King.
The round world & they yt
Let ye Sea make a noise, let ye sea make a noise & all yt therein is

dwell therein
to=gether be joyfull to=
& let ye hills be joyfull be joyfull to=gether be joyfull to=
to=gether be joyfull to=
let ye floods clap yeir hands clap clap yeir hands
to=gether be joyfull to=
=gether before ye Lord let ye flouds clap ye floods clap clap yeir hands & let ye hills be joy=
=gether before ye Lord, let the floods clap, let ye Floods clap their hands.
=gether before ye Lord, let the Floods clap, let ye floods clap clap yeir hands.
=gether before ye Lord let ye flouds clap, let ye floods clap clap their hands.
full be joyfull, together to=gether before ye Lord.
and let ye hills be joyfull ye hills be joy==full together together before ye Lord, for he is
& let ye hills be joy=full together to=gether before ye Lord for he is
and let ye hills be joyfull be joy=full together to=gether before ye Lord for he is

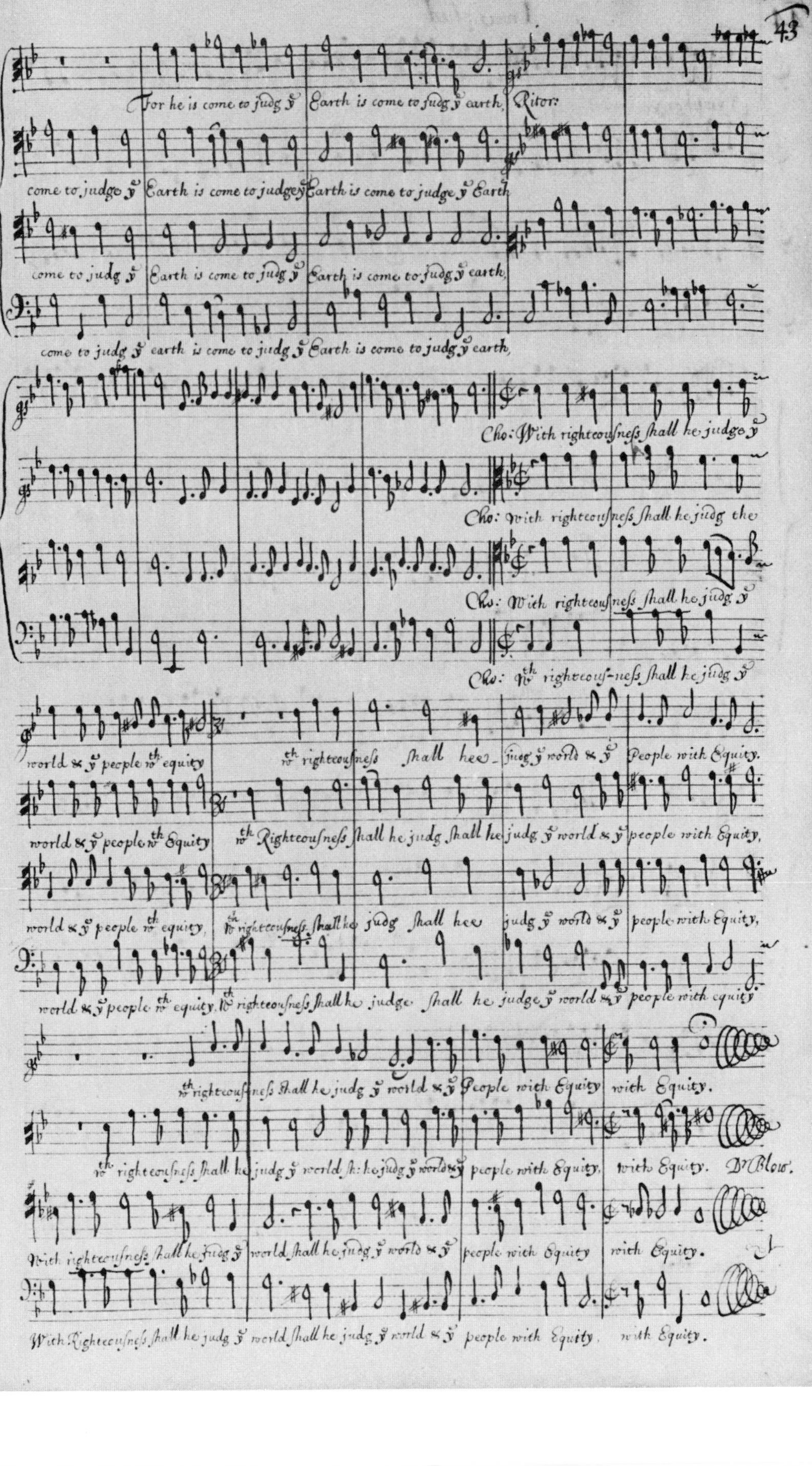
For he is come to judg ye Earth is come to judg ye earth, Ritor:
come to judge ye Earth is come to judge ye Earth is come to judge ye Earth
come to judg ye Earth is come to judg ye Earth is come to judg ye earth,
come to judg ye earth is come to judg ye Earth is come to judg ye earth,
Cho: With righteousness shall he judge ye
Cho: with righteousness shall he judg the
Cho: With righteousness shall he judg ye
Cho: wth righteous-ness shall he judg ye
world & ye people wth equity wth righteousness shall hee judg ye world & ye People with Equity.
world & ye people wth Equity wth Righteousness shall he judg shall he judg ye world & ye people with Equity,
world & ye people wth equity, wth righteousness shall he judg shall hee judg ye world & ye people with Equity,
world & ye people wth equity, wth righteousness shall he judge shall he judge ye world & ye people with equity
wth righteousness shall he judg ye world & ye People with Equity with Equity.
wth righteousness shall he judg ye world sh: he judg ye world & ye people with Equity. with Equity. Dr Blow.
With righteousness shall he judg ye world shall he judg ye world & ye people with Equity with Equity.
With Righteousness shall he judg ye world shall he judg ye world & ye people with Equity. with Equity.

I was glad

Symphony
I was
glad, I was glad, when they said unto me we will go we will go into ye house of ye Lord,
we will go will go into ye house of ye Lord, O Feet shall stand in thy Gates O O Jeru-salem

45
Our feet shall stand shall stand in thy gates
Jerusalem
Jerusalem
Jerusalem is built as a City yt is at unity in it self
For there ye tribes go up
For there ye
For
For there ye tribes go up for there ye tribes go up even ye tribes evn ye Tribes of ye Lord
Tribes go up for there ye tribes go up ye tribes go up evn ye tribes evn ye Tribes of ye Lord to
There ye tribes go up ye tribes go up go up evn ye tribes evn ye Tribes of ye Lord to

to testify unto Is - - - rael, And to give thanks unto ye name of the Lord,
testify unto Israel to testify unto Israel And to give thanks unto ye name of the Lord,
testify unto Israel to testify unto Israel And to give thanks unto ye name of ye Lord,
& to give thanks to give thanks unto ye name, give thanks unto ye name of ye
& to give Thanks & to give thanks to give thanks unto ye name give thanks unto ye name of ye
& to give thanks & to give thanks unto ye name give thanks unto ye name of ye
Lord.
Lord.
Lord.
soft
soft
soft
soft
For there is ye Seat of Judgmt. evn ye

Seat of yͤ house of David for there is yͤ Seat of Judgmᵗ evn yͤ Seat of yͤ house of David, evn yͤ
Seat of yͤ house of David
O pray for yͤ Peace of Jerusalem O pray, pray for yͤ peace
O pray pray for yͤ
O pray pray for yͤ

of Jerusalem They shall prosper shall prosper ye love thee shall pro=====sper ye love thee they shall
Peace of Jerusalem They shall prosper shall prosper ye love thee shall pro=====per ye love thee they shall
Peace of Jerusalem They shall prosper shall prosper ye love thee shall
prosper shall prosper ye love thee shall pro=====sper ye love thee shall pro=====sper that love thee
prosper shall prosper ye love thee shall prosp ye love ye ye love thee shall prosp shall per that love thee
prosper shall prosper ye love thee shall prosper shall prosper ye love thee shall prosp shall per that love thee.
Cho:
Peace be within thy walls peace be within thy Walls & Plenteousness within within thy Palaces and
Peace be within thy Walls peace be within thy Walls & Plenteousness within within thy Palaces &
plenteousness within within thy Palaces and Plenteousness within within thy Palaces.
Vers.
Plenteousness within within thy Palaces and Plenteousness within within thy Palaces

Vers:
For my Brethren & Companions sake I will wish thee prosperity For my brethren & companions sake I will
For my brethren & Companions sake I will wish will wish thee pro=
For my brethren & Companions sake I will wish will
wish will wish thee prosperity I will wish will wish thee Prosperity Peace be within thy Walls.
= perity will wish thee prosperity I will
wish will wish thee prosperity I will
wish will wish thee prosperity I will wish will wish Thee prosperity Peace be within thy Walls.
Cho:
Peace be within thy walls Verse: Peace be wth in thy walls & plenteousness within within
Peace be wth in thy walls
Peace be wth in thy walls
Peace be within thy Walls. Peace be wth in thy Walls Peace be wth in thy Walls & plenteousness within within
thy Palaces & plenteousness wth in wth in thy Palaces, & plenteousness within within thy Palaces.
thy Palaces & plenteousness wth in wth in thy Palaces & plenteousness within within thy Palaces.

Symphony.
Symphony
God
Sheweth
God Sheweth mee his Goodness plenteou
me his Goodness plenteously & God shall let me see my desire upon mine Enemies

God Sheweth me his Goodness plenteously and God shall
=ly and God shall let me see my Desire upon mine Enemies
let mee see my desire upon mine Ene mies.
God Sheweth mee his
God Sheweth mee his goodness plentiously God Sheweth mee his
God Sheweth me his Goodness his
God Sheweth mee his Goodness plenteously God Sheweth me his-
goodness plenteously & God shall let me see my desire upon mine Ene=mies & God shall let mee see, &
goodness plenteously. & God shall let mee see my desire upon mine Enemies, & God shall let mee see &
goodness plenteously, & God shall let me see my desire up-on mine Ene-mies & God shall let mee see, &
goodness plenteously & God shall let mee see my desire upon mine Enemies & God shall let mee see, &

Ritorn:
Ritorn:
God shall let me see my Desire upon mine Enemies.
God shall let me see my Desire up= on mine Ene= mies.
God shall let me see my Desire upon mine Ene= mies.
Ritorn.
God shall let me see my Desire upon mine Enemies.
Vers: solus
Slay ym not lest my people forget it but
scatter ym abroad among ye people but scatter ym abroad among ye people & put them down o

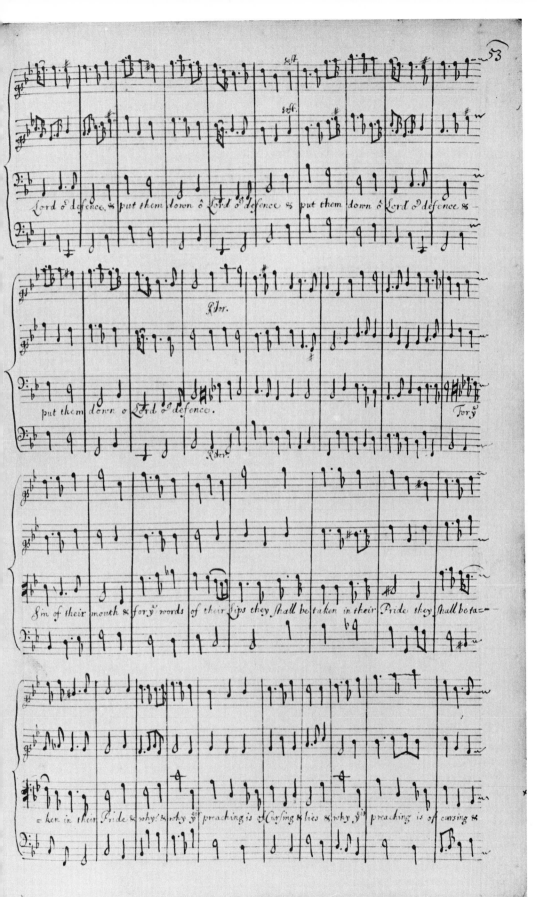

soft
soft
Lord o defence, & put them down o Lord o defence & put them down o Lord o defence &-
Ritor.
put them down o Lord o defence. For ye
Ritor.
Sin of their mouth & for ye words of their Lips they shall be taken in their Pride they shall be ta-
-ken in their Pride & why? & why ye preaching is of Cursing & lies & why, ye preaching is of cursing &

Symphony
Symphony.
Lies.
Symphony
Consume ym in thy wrath consume ym yt they may perish and
& know that it is
and know yt it is God and
know yt it is God yt ruleth in Jacob & unto ye ends of ye World
and

God that ruleth ye ruleth in Jacob & unto ye ends of ye world & know ye it is God ye ruleth in
know ye it is God ye ruleth in Jacob & unto ye ends of ye world & know ye it is God ye ruleth in
know ye it is God ye ruleth in Jacob & unto ye ends of ye world & know ye it is God ye ruleth in
soft
Ritor:
Jacob & unto ye ends of ye world & unto ye ends of ye world. Ritor:
soft
Jacob & unto ye ends of ye world & unto ye ends of ye world. Ritor:
soft
Jacob & unto ye ends of ye world & unto ye ends of ye world. Ritor.
As for Mee I will sing of thy Powr & will praise thy mercy be=
Vers: a 4 voc:
=times in ye morning.
as for mee I will sing of thy powr & will praise thy mercy thy mercy betimes in ye
as for me I will sing of thy powr & will praise thy mercy betimes in ye

56
as for mee I will sing of thy Powr & will praise thy mercy thy mercy be times in y morning
morning
morning
as for me I will
as for mee I will sing of thy Powr & will praise thy mercy betimes in ye morning
as for me I will sing of thy powr & will
as for me I will sing I will sing of thy powr & will
sing of thy powr & will praise thy mercy betimes in ye morning
& will
as for me I will sing of thy powr & will
faster
praise thy mercy betimes in ye morning. For thou hast been my defence & refuge in ye day of my
praise thy mercy betimes in ye morning. For thou hast been my defence & refuge in ye day of my
praise thy mercy betimes in ye morning For thou hast been my defence & refuge in ye day of my
faster
praise thy mercy betimes in ye morning For thou hast been my defence & refuge in ye day of my
Vers:
Trouble
For thou hast been my defence & refuge in ye day of my
Trouble
For thou hast been my defence & refuge in ye day of my
Trouble
For thou hast been my defence & refuge in ye day of my
Vers:
Trouble
For thou hast been my defence & refuge in ye day of my

Trouble in ye day of my Trouble Ritorn: Ver. For thou hast
Trouble in ye day of my Trouble. Ritorn Vers. For thou hast
Trouble in ye day of my Trouble. Ritor. Ver. For thou hast
Trouble in ye day of my Trouble. Ver. For thou hast
been my defence & refuge in ye day of my Trouble in ye day of my Trouble Ritor.
been my defence & refuge in ye day of my Trouble in ye day of my Trouble Ritor:
been my defence & refuge in ye day of my Trouble in ye day of my Trouble. Ritor.
been my defence & refuge in ye day of my Trouble in ye day of my Trouble. Ritor.
Cho:
Cho: For thou hast been my defence & refuge in ye day of my
Cho: For thou hast been my defence & refuge in ye day of my
Cho: For thou hast been my defence & refuge in ye day of my
Cho: For thou hast been my defence & refuge in ye day of my
Ritor:
Trouble in ye day of my Trouble. Cho: Unto
Trouble in ye day of my Trouble. Cho: Unto
Trouble in ye day of my Trouble Ritor: Cho: Unto
Trouble in ye day of my Trouble Cho: Unto

Ritor:
Cho:
Thee ô my Strength will I sing. Ritor
For thou ô my
Cho.
Thee ô my Strength will I sing. Ritor
For thou ô my
Cho.
Thee ô my Strength will I sing. Ritor
For thou ô my
Cho.
Thee ô my Strength will I sing.
For thou ô my
Cho: 6 pts
God art my Refuge & my mercifull God.
God art my Refuge & my mercifull God
For thou ô my God art my refuge my refuge & my mercifull
God art my Refuge & my mercifull God
For Thou ô my God art my refuge my refuge & my mercifull
God art my Refuge & my mercifull God
For Thou ô my God art my refuge my refuge & my mercifull
Cho: 6 pts
For thou ô my God art my refuge my refuge & my mercifull
For Thou ô my God art my refuge my refuge & my mercifull
God for Thou art my refuge & my mercifull God.
God for Thou art my Refuge & my mercifull God.
Mr Wm Turner.
God for Thou art my Refuge & my mercifull God.
God for Thou art my Refuge & my mercifull God.
God for thou art my Refuge & my mercifull God.

Thy Mercy ô Lord.

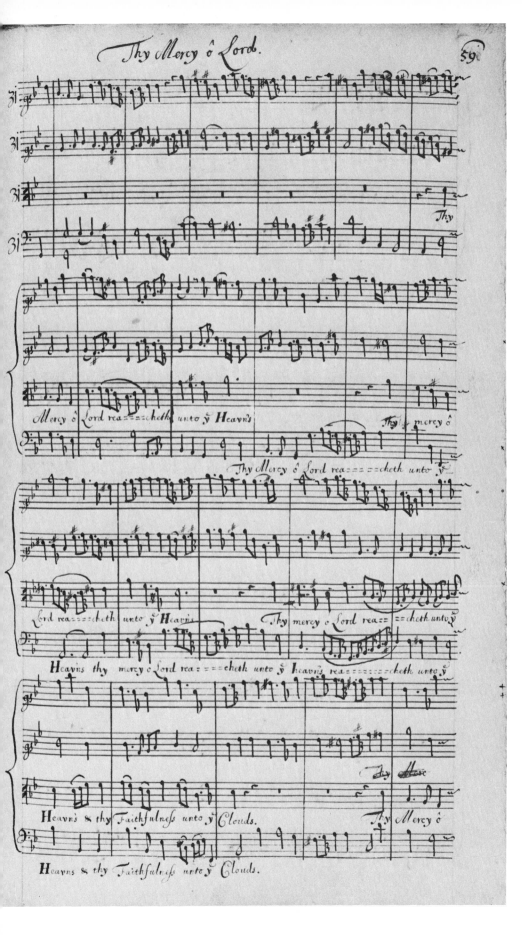

Thy
Mercy ô Lord rea====cheth unto ỹ Heavn's
Thy mercy ô
Thy Mercy ô Lord rea=====cheth unto ỹ
Lord rea====cheth unto ỹ Heavns
Thy mercy ô Lord rea== ==cheth unto ỹ
Heavns thy mercy ô Lord rea====cheth unto ỹ heavns rea========cheth unto ỹ
Heavn's & thy Faithfulness unto ỹ Clouds.
Thy Mercy ô
Heavns & thy Faithfulness unto ỹ Clouds.

Lord rea===cheth Thy mercy o Lord rea===cheth unto ye heavns rea======cheth
Thy mercy ô Lord rea===cheth Thy mercy o Lord rea=====cheth un-
unto ye heavns & thy Faithfullness unto ye clouds thy Faith============fulness unto ye
to ye heavns & thy Faithfulness unto the clouds thy Faith===========fulness unto ye
clouds thy Faith========fulness unto ye clouds
clouds thy Faith============fulness unto ye clouds
Thy Righteousness ô God ô

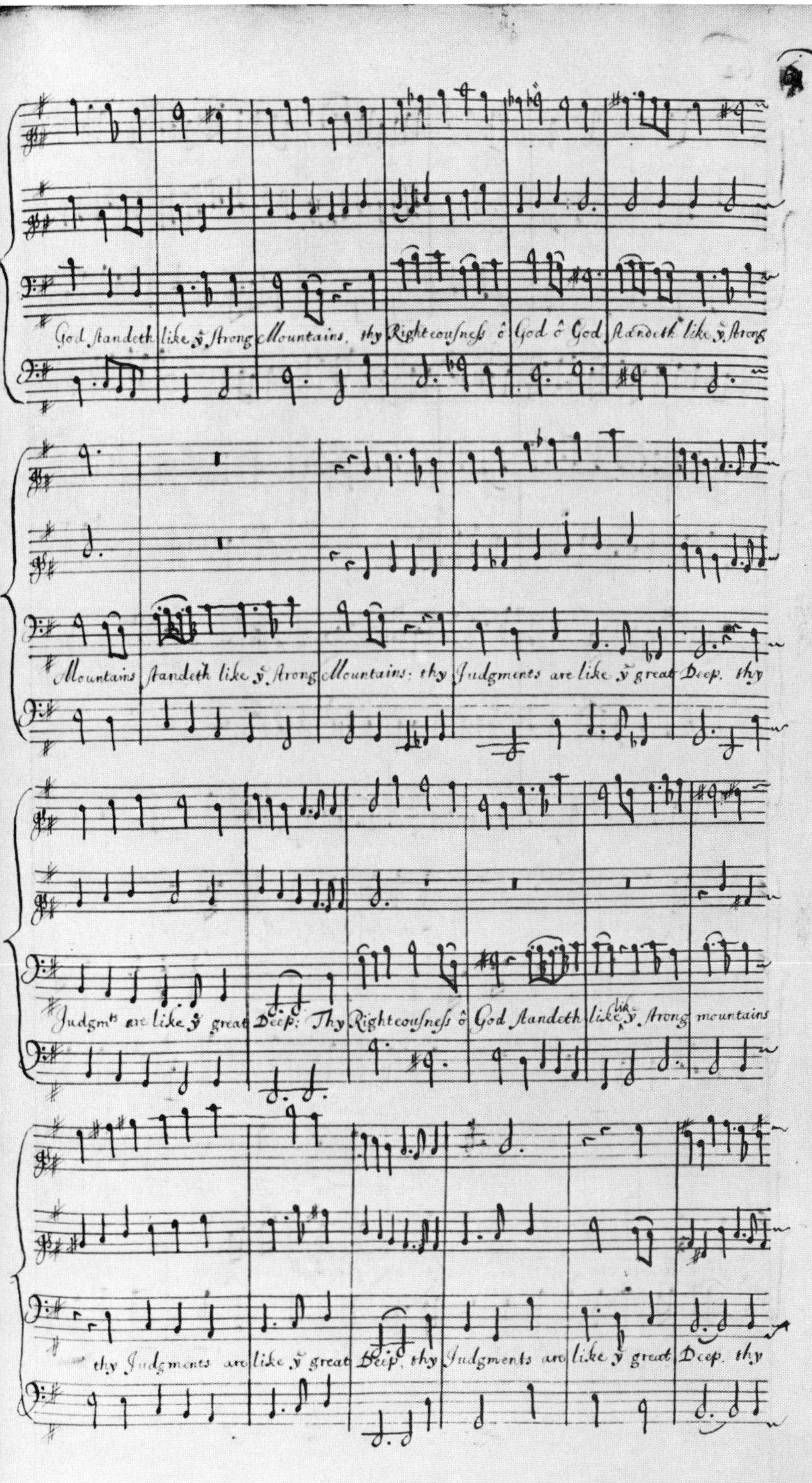
God standeth like yͤ strong Mountains, thy Righteousness O God O God standeth like yͤ strong
Mountains standeth like yͤ strong Mountains: thy Judgments are like yͤ great Deep. thy
Judgmts are like yͤ great Deep: Thy Righteousness O God standeth like yͤ strong mountains
thy Judgments are like yͤ great Deep: thy Judgments are like yͤ great Deep. thy

Judgmts thy Judgmts are like ye great Deep.
For in Thee is ye
Well of Life
& in thy Light shall we see Light
& in thy Light shall we see Light
& in thy Light shall we see
For in Thee is ye
For in Thee in Thee is ye well of
Light shall wee see Light; and in thy
Light shall we see Light
Well of Life & in thy Light shall we see Light
For in Thee in Thee is ye

Life & in thy Light shall we see Light shall we see Light
For with thee is the
And in thy Light shall we see Light shall we see Light & in thy Light
Well of Life
And in thy Light shall we see Light shall we see
well of Life
shall we see Light.
Light. For in Thee is y Well of Life & in thy Light shall we see Light shall we see
For in thee is y Well of Life.
For in thee is y Well of Life & in thy
Light For in Thee is y well of Life & in thy Light shall we see Light shall we see Light
& in thy Light shall we see Light & in thy Light in thy Light shall we see Light & in thy
Light shall we see light & in thy Light shall we see Light & in
& in thy Light shall we see Light shall we see Light & in thy
Light & in thy Light in thy Light shall we see Light.
thy Light shall we see Light
Light shall wee see Light shall we see Light.

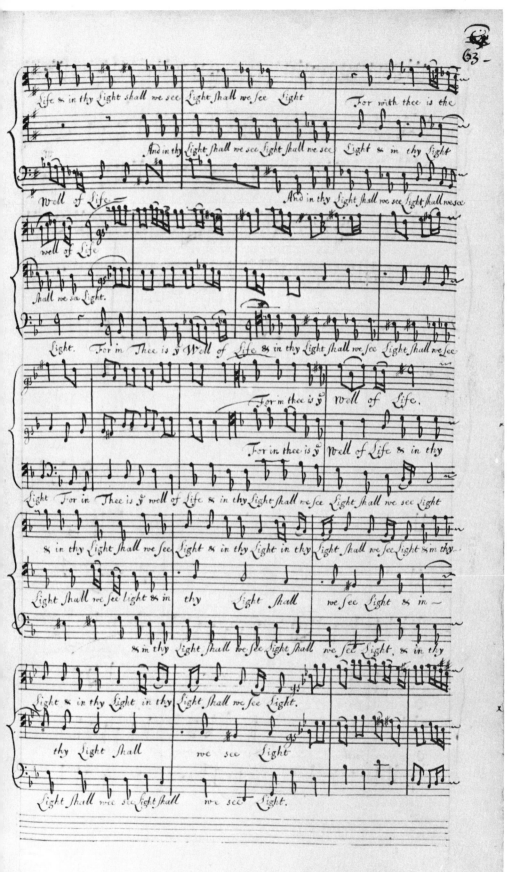

O continue forth thy lo==ving kindness unto ym yt know Thee yt know Thee
O continue forth Thy lo===ving
O continue forth thy lo===ving kindness unto ym yt know

continue forth thy Lo===========ving
kindness O O O continue forth thy loving kindness thy lo=====
Thee O O O continue forth Thy
Cho:
loving - kindness unto them yt know thee O O continue forth
lo====ving kindness unto them yt know thee. O O continue
lo==========ving kindness unto them yt know thee. O O continue
O O continue
forth Vers:
forth thy lo===============ving kindness thy lo=======================ing
forth Thy lo====ving kindness thy lo============ ing
forth Thy lo=============================ing loving

Cho:
Cho:
Cho:
Cho:
kindness unto ym that know thee. O O O continue forth thy lo====
kindness unto ym yt know thee O O O continue forth thy lo==ving
kindness unto ym yt know thee O O O continue forth continue forth
76
continue forth thy loving loving
=====ving kindness unto them to them that know thee continue forth continue
kindness thy lo===========ving kindness unto ym yt know thee continue forth, continue
thy loving loving kindness unto them to them that know thee continue forth, continue
kindness unto ym to ym yt know thee continue forth, continue
forth continue forth thy loving kindness unto ym yt know thee and thy Righteous=
forth continue forth thy loving kindness unto ym yt know thee, and thy righteous=
forth continue forth thy loving kindness unto ym yt know thee, & thy righteous=
forth continue forth thy loving kindness unto ym yt know thee, & thy righteous=

=ness unto ym yt are true of heart; & thy righteousness to ym yt are true of heart.
Dr Blow
=ness unto ym yt are true of heart, & thy righteousness to ym yt are true of heart.
=ness unto ym yt are true of heart & thy righteousness to ym yt are true of heart.
=ness unto ym yt are true of heart & thy righteousness to ym yt are true of heart.

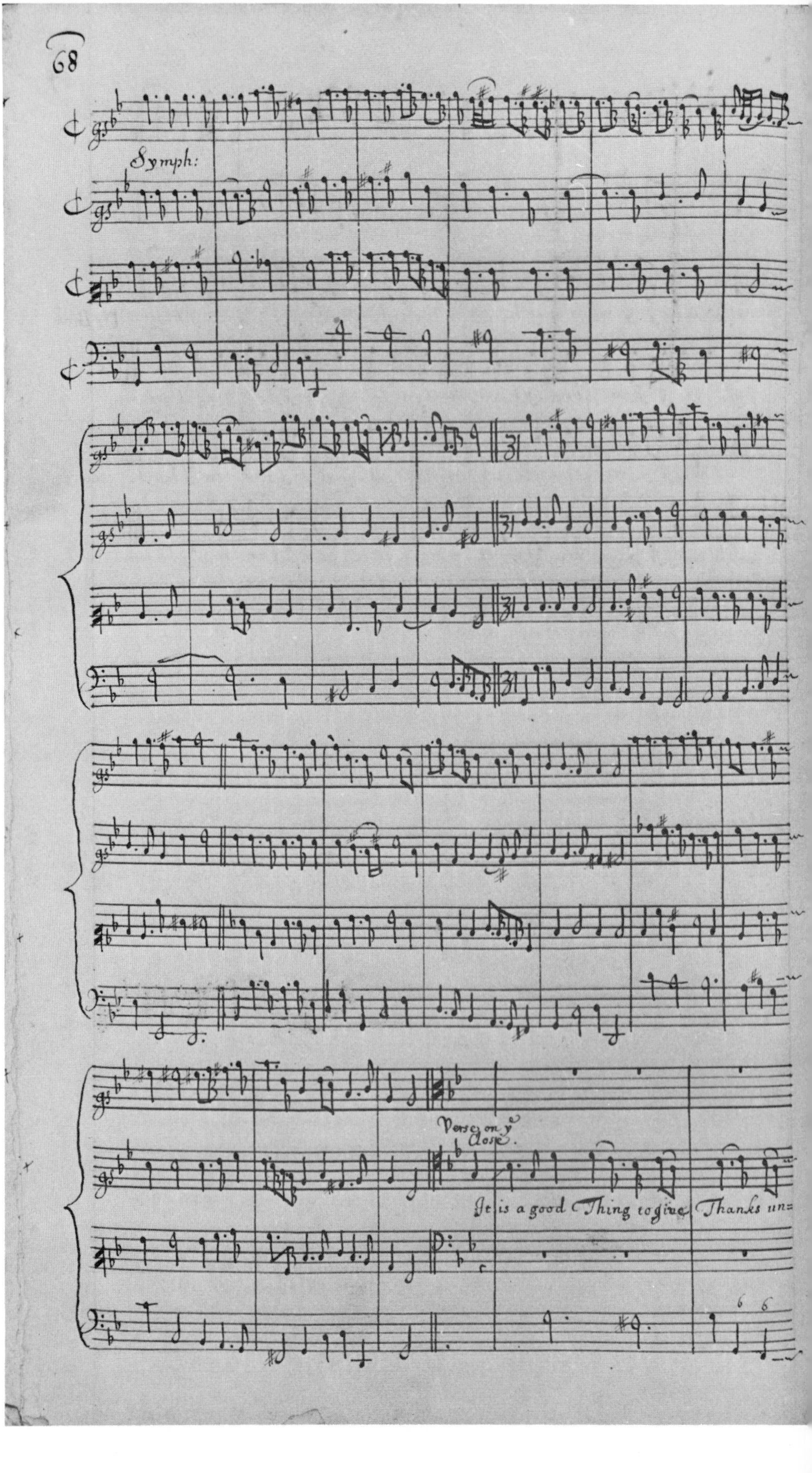
68
Symph:
Verse on ye Close.
It is a good Thing to give Thanks un=
6 6

it is a good thing to give Thanks unto ye Lord it
=to ye Lord it is a good
it is a good thing to give
is a good thing to give Thanks unto the Lord, and to sing praises unto thy
thing a good thing to give Thanks unto the Lord and to sing praises unto thy
Thanks unto the Lord unto the Lord and to sing praises unto thy
name O O thou most highest, and to sing praises unto thy name O O thou most
name O O thou most highest, and to sing praises unto thy name O O thou most
name O O thou most highest and to sing praises unto thy name O O thou most
highest. it is a good thing to give Thanks tis a good thing it is
soft
highest it is a good thing a good thing to give Thanks it is tis a good thing it is
soft
highest it is a good thing to give Thanks it is tis a good thing it is
soft

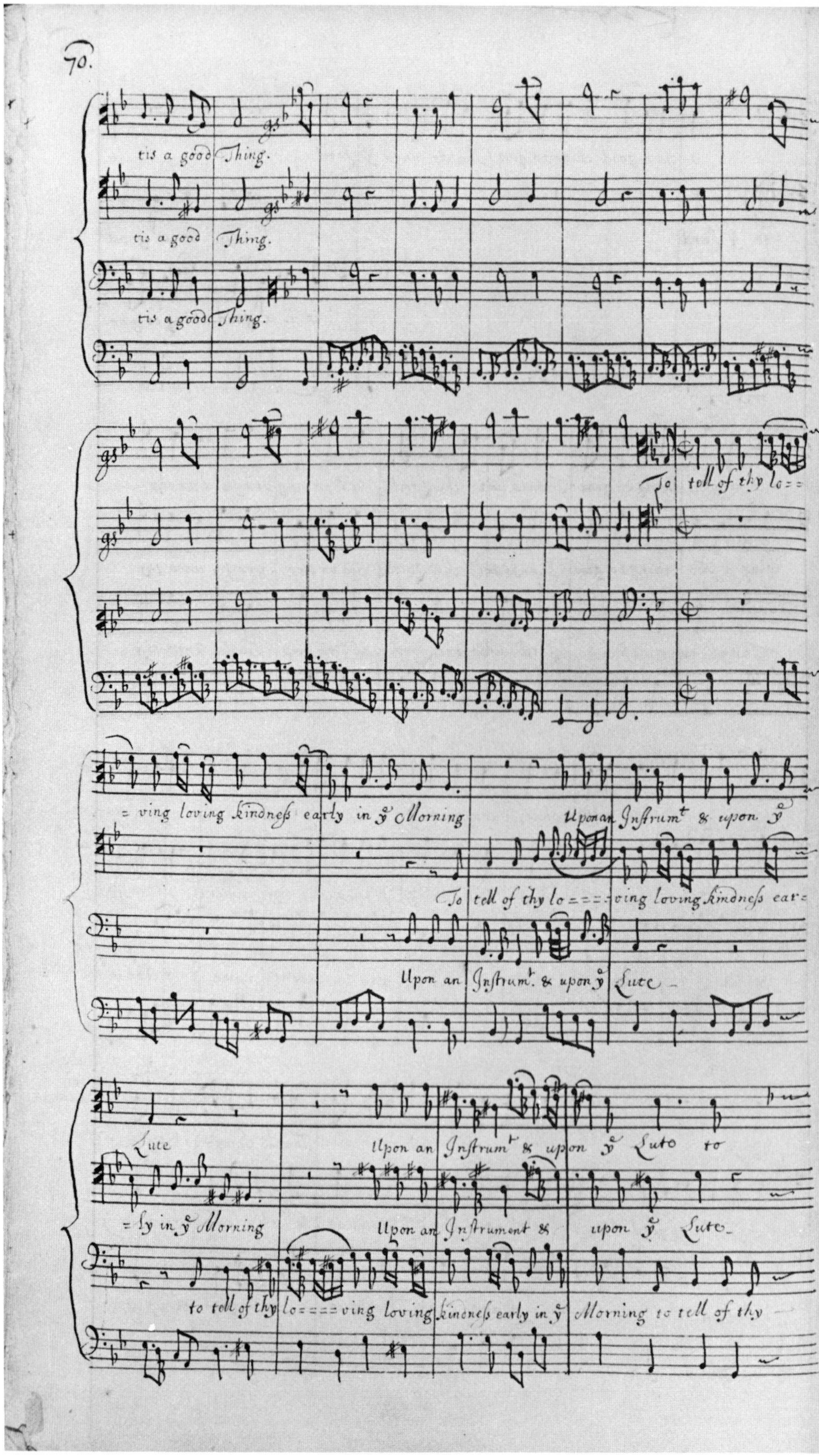
70.
tis a good Thing.
tis a good Thing.
tis a good Thing.
To tell of thy lo==
=ving loving kindness early in ye Morning
Upon an Instrumt & upon ye
To tell of thy lo====ving loving kindness ear=
Upon an Instrumt. & upon ye Lute
Lute
Upon an Instrumt & upon ye Luto to
=ly in ye Morning
Upon an Instrument & upon ye Lute
to tell of thy lo====ving loving kinedness early in ye Morning to tell of thy

tell of thy lo==== ving loving kindness upon an Instrumt. & upon ye Lute & upon ye
to tell of thy lo= === ving loving kindness upon an Instrumt & upon ye
lo====ving loving kindness early in ye Morning upon an Instrumt. and upon upon ye
Lute & of thy Truth & of thy truth in ye night season upon a loud
Lute and of thy Truth thy truth & of thy truth in ye nightseason upon a loud a loud
Lute & of thy Truth, & of thy Truth in ye night Season upon a loud upon a
a loud Instrumt & upon ye Harp upon a loud Instrumt &
upon a loud Instrument & upon ye harp upon a loud a loud Instrumt &
loud upon a loud Instrument & upon ye harp upon a loud Instrumt & up=
upon ye harp. Ritorn:
upon ye harp
on y harp
harp

72
For thou Lord hast made me glad thro thy works For thou Lord hast made mee
For thou Lord hast made me made me glad For thou Lord hast made me made me
For thou Lord hast made me glad hast made me
glad thro thy works, & I will rejoyce I will rejoyce in giving praise for yͤ operation of thy
glad thro thy works, & I will rejoyce I will rejoyce in giving praise for yͤ Operation of thy
glad thro thy works, & I will rejoyce I will rejoyce in giving praise for yͤ Operation of thy
hands & I will rejoyce I will rejoyce in giving prayse for yͤ operation of thy hands for yͤ
Soft.
hands & I will rejoyce I will rejoyce in giving praise for yͤ operation of thy hands for yͤ
hands & I will rejoyce I will rejoyce In giving Praise for yͤ Operation of thy hands for yͤ
operation of thy hands. The Triple of yͤ Symphony again.
operation of thy hands. The Triple of the Symphony again
Vers solus on yͤ Ʃiſe
operation of thy hands. The Triple of yͤ Symphony again.
O how glo… nous are thy

works & thy thoughts are very deep O Lord how glo--rious are thy works & thy thoughts are
very deep: an unwise Man doth not well consider it & a Fool doth not understand it O-
Lord how glo--rious are thy works & thy Thoughts thy Thoughts are very deep.
Vers: 3 voc:
For thou Lord hast made me made me glad thro thy works For thou Lord hast
For thou Lord hast made me made me glad ! For thou Lord hast made me
For thou Lord hast made me glad hast
made me glad thro thy works & I will rejoice I will rejoyce in giving Praise for ye opera:
made me glad thro thy works & I will rejoice I will rejoyce in giving praise for ye opera-
made me glad thro thy works & I will rejoice I will rejoyce in giving praise for ye opera:

-tion of thy hands. & I will rejoyce I will rejoyce in giving praise for ye Operation of thy
-tion of thy hands & I will rejoyce I will re-joyce in giving praise for ye Operation of thy
-ion of thy hands & I will rejoyce I will rejoyce in giving praise for ye Operation of thy
soft
hands for ye Operation of thy hands.
hands for ye Operation of thy hands alleluia alle-
hands for ye Operation of thy hands Alleluia alleluia alleluia alleluia
alleluia alleluia alleluia allelluia alleluia allelluia alle
-luia alleluia allelluia alleluia alleluia alle-luia alleluia allelluia alle-
alleluia alle-luia alleluia allelluia alle-
soft loud
-luia alleluia alleluia allelluia alleluia alleluia alleluia al-leluia alleluia alle-
-luia allelluia alleluia alle luia alleluia alle luia alleluia al-leluia allelluia alle-
-luia alle luia alleluia alle luia alleluia alle luia alleluia al-leluia alleluiah alle-

loud soft loud soft loud soft loud soft loud soft
luia alleluia alleluia alleluia alleluia
-luia alle luia alleluia alleluia alleluia
-luia alle luia alleluia alleluia alleluia.
It is a good thing to give Thanks unto y Lord
it is a good thing to give thanks unto y
Lord It is a good Thing to give Thanks unto y Lord & to sing
It is a good thing a good Thing to give thanks unto y Lord, & to sing
It is a good thing to give Thanks un to the Lord unto the Lord, & to sing
praises unto thy name O o thou most highest, & to sing praises unto thy name O o thou most
praises unto thy name O o thou most highest, & to sing praises unto thy name O o thou most
praises unto thy name O o thou most highest & to sing praises unto thy name O o thou most

highest
it is a good thing to give thanks tis a good thing it is tis a good
highest it is a good thing a good thing to give thanks it is tis a good thing it is tis a good
highest it is a good thing to give thanks it is tis a good thing it is tis a good
soft
thing
loud
Cho:
Alleluia alleluia alleluia alleluia alleluia alleluia alleluia
Alleluia
Alleluia
Alleluia
alleluia alleluia alleluia alleluia alleluia alleluia alleluia alleluia alleluia alleluia Alleluia.
H

They y^t go down to y^e Sea in Ships.

They that go
down to y^e Sea in Ships these these men see y^e works of y^e Lord & his wonders his

Wonders in the Deep for at his word ye stor - - - - - - my wind ariseth
for at his word ye Stor = = = = = = = = = = = = = = = my Wind ariseth wch lifteth up wch
lifteth up ye waves thereof they are carried up to Heavn & down again to ye
Deep. they are carried up to Heavn are carried up to Heavn & down again to ye

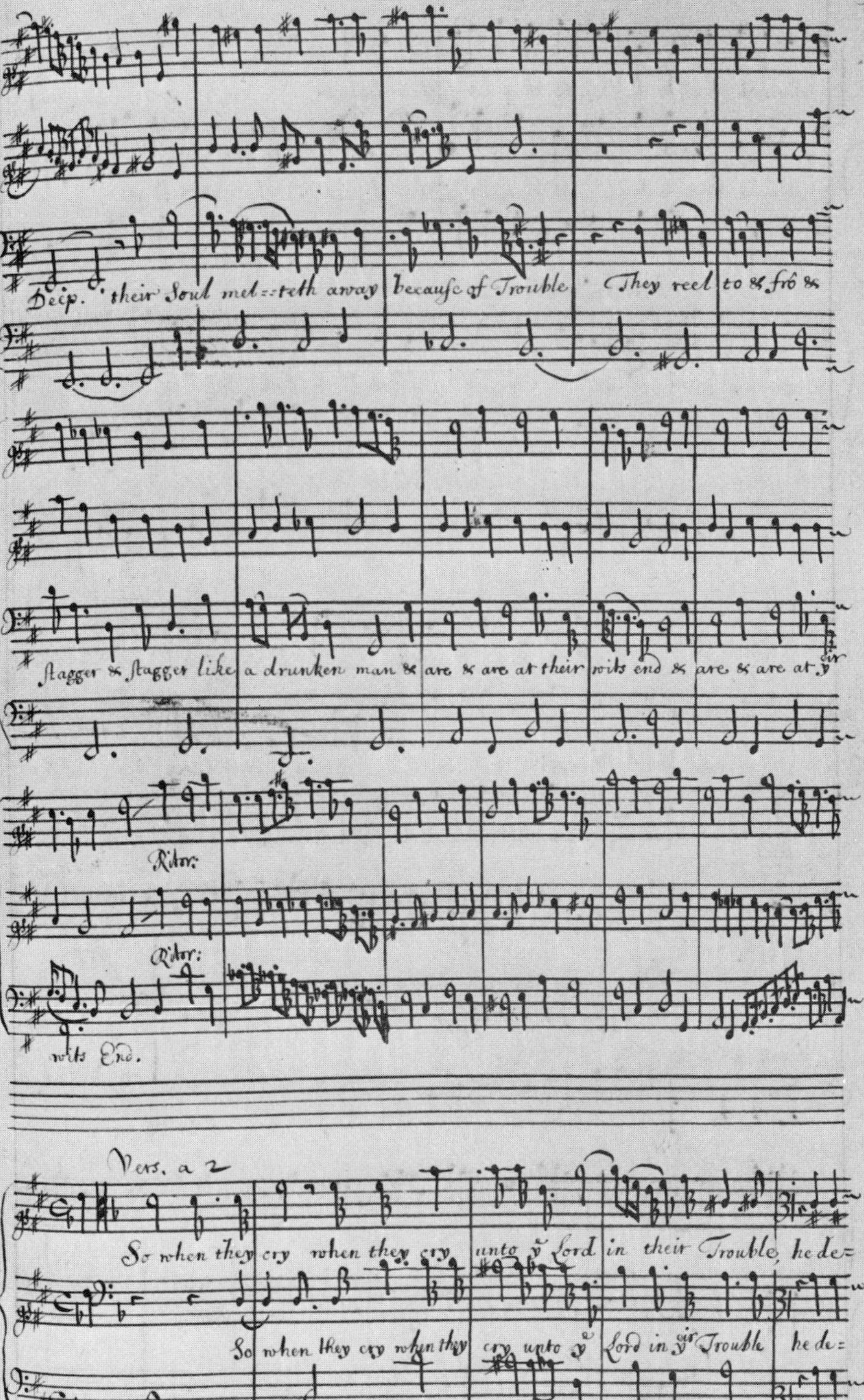
Deep. their Soul mel=-teth away because of Trouble They reel to & fro &
stagger & stagger like a drunken man & are & are at their wits end & are & are at
Ritor:
Ritor:
wits End.
Vers. a 2
So when they cry when they cry unto ye Lord in their Trouble, he de=
So when they cry when they cry unto ye Lord in yir Trouble he de=

-livereth them he de- livereth them out of their distress for he
-livereth them he de- livereth them out of their distress for he maketh ye Storm to
maketh ye storm — — to cease for he maketh he maketh ye Storm — — to cease
cease, for he maketh he maketh ye Storm to cease
soften by degrees.
so yt ye waves thereof are still still still so yt ye waves thereof are still
so yt ye waves thereof are still still still so yt ye waves there-of are still still still, ye
waves are still.

(violin soft)
verse
Then are they glad — because because they are at-
Then are they glad — are
Rest
Then are they glad be- cause they are at rest because be-
glad because they are at Rest, — Then are they glad because be
=cause they are at rest, & so he bringeth ym unto ye Hav'n where they would be & so he
=cause they are at rest & so he bringeth ym unto ye Hav'n where they would be & so he
bringeth ym unto ye Hav'n where they would be unto the Hav'n where they would —
bringeth ym unto ye Hav'n where they would be unto the Hav'n where they would —

82
Ritor
soft
soft
Verse O O yt men would therefore praise ye Lord O. O yt men would therefore praise ye
O, O yt men would therefore praise ye Lord O O yt men would therefore praise ye
Lord for his Goodness, & declare ye wonders, & declare ye wonders yt he doth for the
Lord for his Goodness, & declare ye wonders ye wonders yt he doth for the
children of men declare ye wonders, and declare ye wonders yt he doth for ye children of
children of men & declare ye wonders ye wonders yt he doth for ye children of
soft
men declare ye wonders yt he doth for ye Children of men, That they would exalt him
men declare ye wonders yt he doth for ye children of Men yt they would ex

ye they would exalt — — — — him also in ye Congregation of ye
=alt him, ye they would ex alt him they would exalt him also in ye Congregation of ye
people & praise him and praise him in ye Seat and praise him in ye seat praise him in ye seat of ye
people & praise him and praise him. m ye Seat and praise him in ye seat ye seat of ye
Elders, & praise him & praise him in the seat and praise him in the seat praise him
Elders, & praise him in the seat and praise him in ye seat praise him in ye seat ye
in ye seat of the Elders, and praise him in ye seat praise him in ye seat of ye Elders.
seat of ye Elders, & praise him praise him in ye seat ye seat of ye Elders

Cho:
O O praise ye Lord O, O praise ye Lord praise ye Lord for his Goodness & declare ye
O, O praise ye Lord O, O praise ye Lord praise ye Lord for his Goodness & declare ye
Cho: O, O praise ye Lord O, O praise ye Lord praise ye Lord for his Goodness & declare ye
O, O praise ye Lord, O, O praise ye Lord praise ye Lord for his Goodness
Wonders and declare ye wonders ye he doth for ye children of men declare ye wonders
Won-=ders the wonders yt he doth for ye children of Men & declare ye
wonders ye Won- -ders yt he doth for ye children of Men declare ye wonders ye
& declare ye wonders ye wonders yt he doth for ye children of Men & declare ye
and declare ye Wonders yt he doth for ye Children of Men.
wonders the wonders yt he doth for ye Children of Men. Hen: Purc
Won- - - -ders yt he doth for ye Children of Men.
Wonders the Wonders ye he doth for the Children of Men.

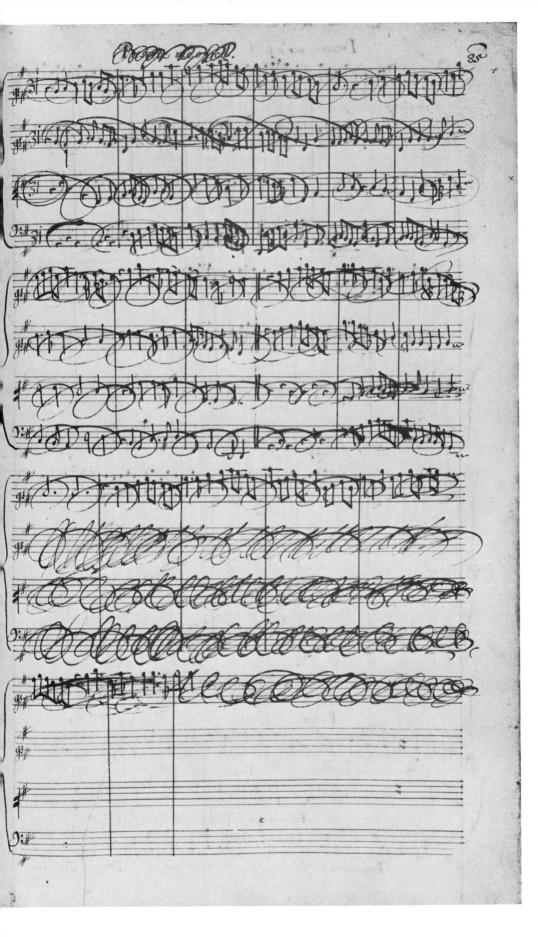

86
Preserve me o God
Symphony
vers:
Pre serve me o God.
for in Thee have I
vers: a 4
Pre- serve me ô God
Pre serve me o God for in
Thee in Thee have
Preserve me ô
God preserve me ô
God for in Thee have
Preserve me ô God
preserve me ô God for in
Thee in Thee have

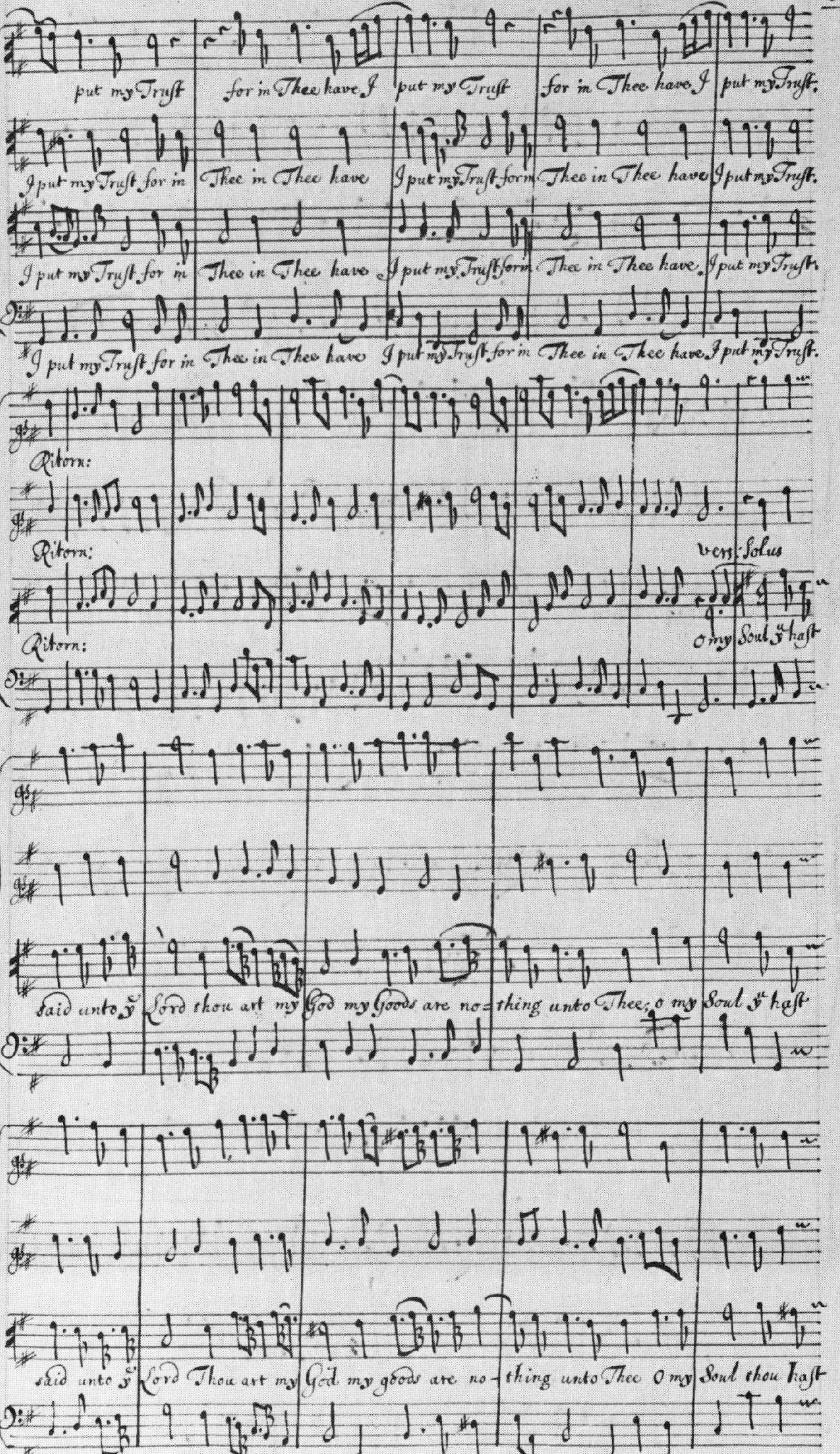
put my Trust for in Thee have I put my Trust for in Thee have I put my Trust.
I put my Trust for in Thee in Thee have I put my Trust for in Thee in Thee have I put my Trust.
I put my Trust for in Thee in Thee have I put my Trust for in Thee in Thee have. I put my Trust.
I put my Trust for in Thee in Thee have I put my Trust for in Thee in Thee have I put my Trust.
Ritorn:
Ritorn:
vers: Solus
Ritorn:
O my Soul yu hast
said unto ye Lord thou art my God my Goods are no= thing unto Thee; O my Soul yu hast
said unto ye Lord Thou art my God my goods are no- thing unto Thee O my Soul thou hast

88.
:aid unto ye Lord thou art my God my Goods are nothing unto Thee my Goods are nothing unto
vers:
Ritor.
Ritor:
vers: Solus.
Thee.
All my delight is upon ye Saints yt
Ritor.
are in ye Earth, all my delight is upon the Saints yt are in ye Earth & upon such as excell in
Ritorn:
Ritor:
Vertue, & upon such upon such as excell in Vertue.
Rit:

Vers: a 4
But they y run–
after another God
Shall have great Trouble.
But they y run–
after a– nother God shall have great
But they y run
after a– nother God But they y
But they y run– –
after a– nother God
shall have great
after another God
But they y run
after another God–
shall have great
Trouble shall have great
Trouble But they y
run–
after a–
run
after another God
after another God– shall have great.
Trouble shall
have shall have great
Trouble shall have shall
have great Trouble shall–
Trouble shall
have shall have great
Trouble shall have shall
have great Trouble shall
– nother God
shall have shall have great
trouble shall have shall
have great Trouble shall
Trouble shall have shall have great
Trouble shall have shall
have great Trouble shall–
Vers a 4.
have shall have great
Trouble.
Symphony again
Come in upon y Close
have, shall have great
Trouble.
as at first.
of y Symph: I have set–
have shall have great
Trouble.
Symphony again
Vers: I have set God
have shall have great
Trouble.
as at first.

90
I have set God always before me for he is on my right hand
God always before me for he is on my right hand for he is
always before me for he is on my right hand, for he is on my right hand
I have set God always before me for he is on my right
for he is on my right hand therefore I shall not fall. I shall not fall.
on my right on my right hand therefore I shall not fall therefore I shall not fall
for he is on my right- hand therefore I shall not I shall not fall therefore I shall not fall.
hand. therefore I shall not fall therefore I shall not I shall not fall.
therefore I shall not fall, therefore I shall not fall. Ritor:
therefore I shall not fall therefore I shall not fall. Ritorn:
therefore I shall not fall therefore I shall not fall. Ritorn:
therefore I shall not fall therefore I shall not fall. Retorn:
Vers:
Wherefore my Heart was glad wherefore my heart was glad & my

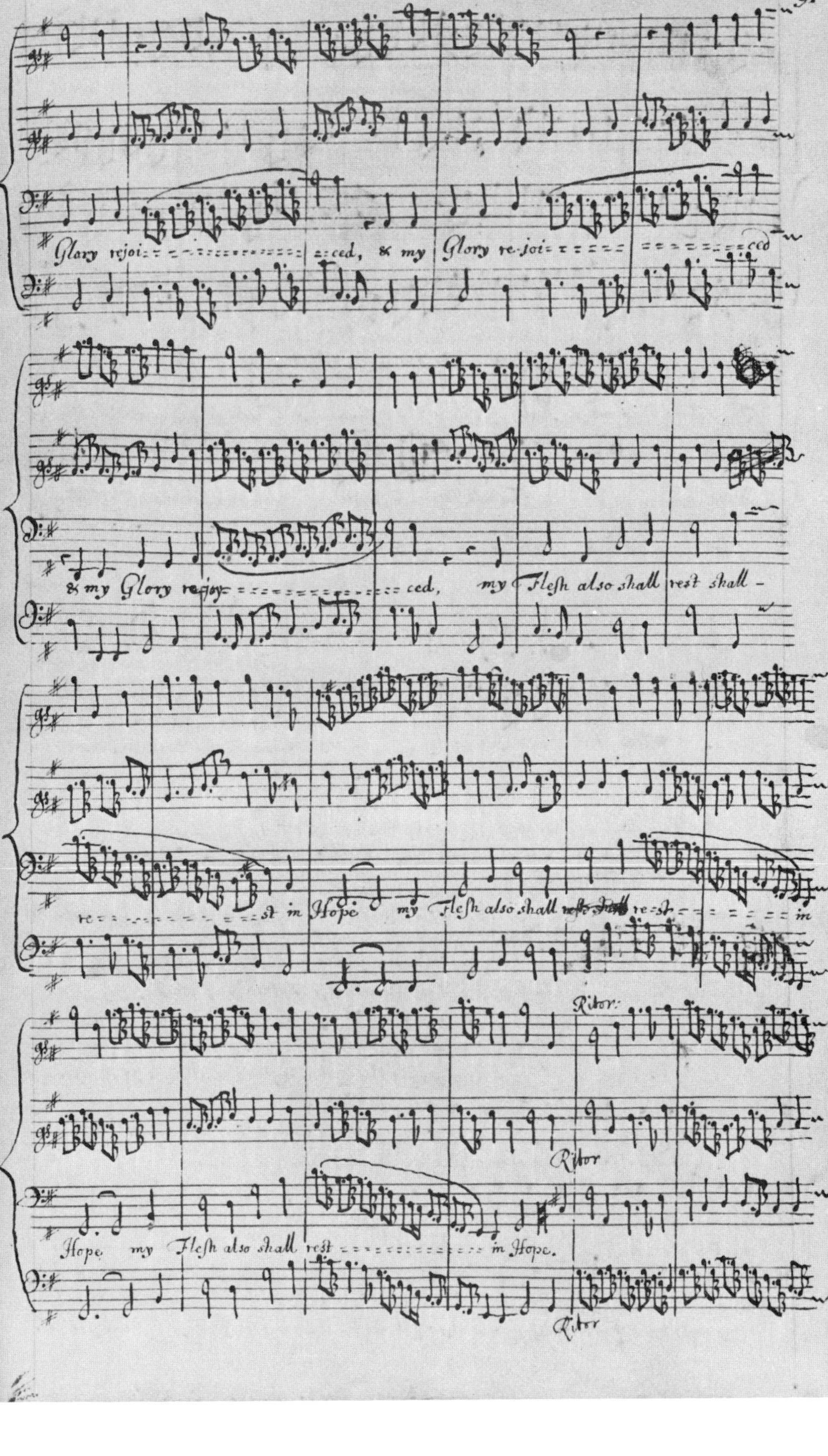
Glory rejoi- - - - - - - - - - - - ced, & my Glory re-joi - - - - - - - - - - - ced
& my Glory rejoy- - - - - - - - - - - - ced, my Flesh also shall rest shall -
re- - - - - - - - - - st in Hope my Flesh also shall rest shall re-st - - - - - - - in
Ritor:
Ritor
Hope my Flesh also shall rest - - - - - - - - - - in Hope.
Ritor

Vers: a 4
Thou shalt shew me ye Path of Life in thy presence is ye Fullness of Joy the Fullness of
Vers. a 4.
Thou shalt shew me ye path of Life in ye presence is ye Fulness of
Vers: a 4.
Thou shalt
Thou shalt shew me ye path of
Joy. Thou shalt shew me ye Path of Life in thy Presence is ye fulness of Joy.
Joy in thy Presence is ye Fulness of Joy in thy Presence is ye Fulness ye Fulness of Joy.
shew me ye Path of Life in thy Presence is ye Fulness of Joy ye Fulness of Joy, & at thy right
Life in thy Presence is ye fulness of Joy in thy Presence is ye Fulness ye Fulness of Joy — &
& at thy right hand there is pleasure there is Pleasure for ever=
& at thy right hand there is pleasure for ev==er=== more. &
hand ye is pleasure, ye is Pleasure & at thy right hand there is pleasure there is pleasure for ever=
at thy right hand there is Pleasure & at thy right hand there is Pleasure for ever for ever=

more & at thy right hand there is pleasure there is pleasure & at thy right hand there is pleasure there is
at thy right hand there is pleasure there is pleasure and at thy right hand there is pleasure y^e is pleasure for
more. And at thy right hand there's pleasure there is pleasure for
more — & at thy right hand there is Pleasure there is pleasure for evermore there is
Pleasure for ever more, & at thy right hand there is pleasure there is pleasure for ever more.
ever for ever more & at thy right hand there is pleasure there is pleasure for evermore.
ever for ever more & at thy right hand there is pleasure there is pleasure for evermore
pleasure for ever more & at thy right hand there is pleasure there is pleasure for evermore.
Ritor:
Ritor:
Ritor:
Cho: And at thy right hand there is pleasure there is
Cho: And at thy right hand there is pleasure there is
Cho: And at thy right hand there is pleasure there is
Cho: And at thy right hand there is pleasure there is

94
Rit
Cho:
Pleasure for evermore
at thy right hand there is
Pleasure for evermore.
Pleasure for evermore.
Pleasure for evermore.
Ritor:
Pleasure there is pleasure for evermore.
Cho: And
at thy right hand there is pleasure there is pleasure for evermore, and at thy right
hand there is pleasure there is pleasure for evermore.
Composed by
Mr. Wm Turner
Aug: 24th. 1686.

Behold I bring you glad Tidings. For Christmas day. Luke. ch:2. ve: 10. 11. 14

Symphony.
very slow:
quick

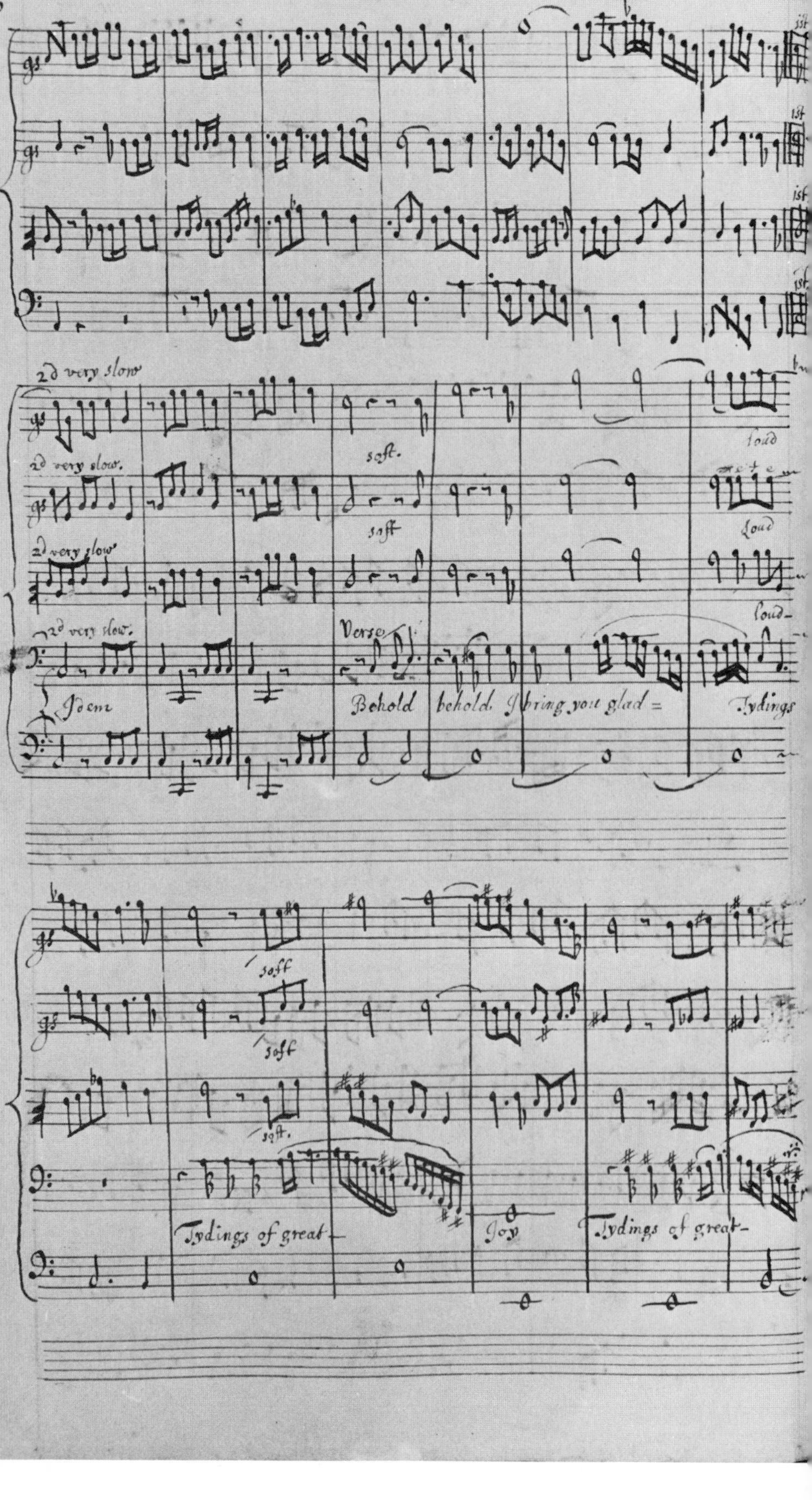

1st
2d very slow
soft
loud
Verse
Idem
Behold behold I bring you glad =
Tydings
Tydings of great-
Joy
Tydings of great-

Joy which shall be to all People for unto you this day is born a Saviour,
For unto you this day is born a Savio^r wch is C^t y^e Lord. Behold behold, I bring you glad
Tidings For unto you this day is born a savio^r wch is C^t y^e Lord wch is C^t y^e

glad Tidings glad — Tidings
Glad Tidings glad — Tydings
Tidings of great —
Lord.
Tidings of great — Joy glad Tidings glad Tydings
Tidings of great — Joy glad Tidings glad Tidings
Joy. glad Tidings glad Tidings
glad Tidings of great Joy wch shall be to all people.
glad Tidings of great — Joy wch shall be to all people.
glad Tidings of great Joy wch shall be to all people.
glad Tidings glad Tidings of great Joy which shall —
glad Tidings glad Tidings of great Joy wch shall —
glad Tidings of great — Joy which shall

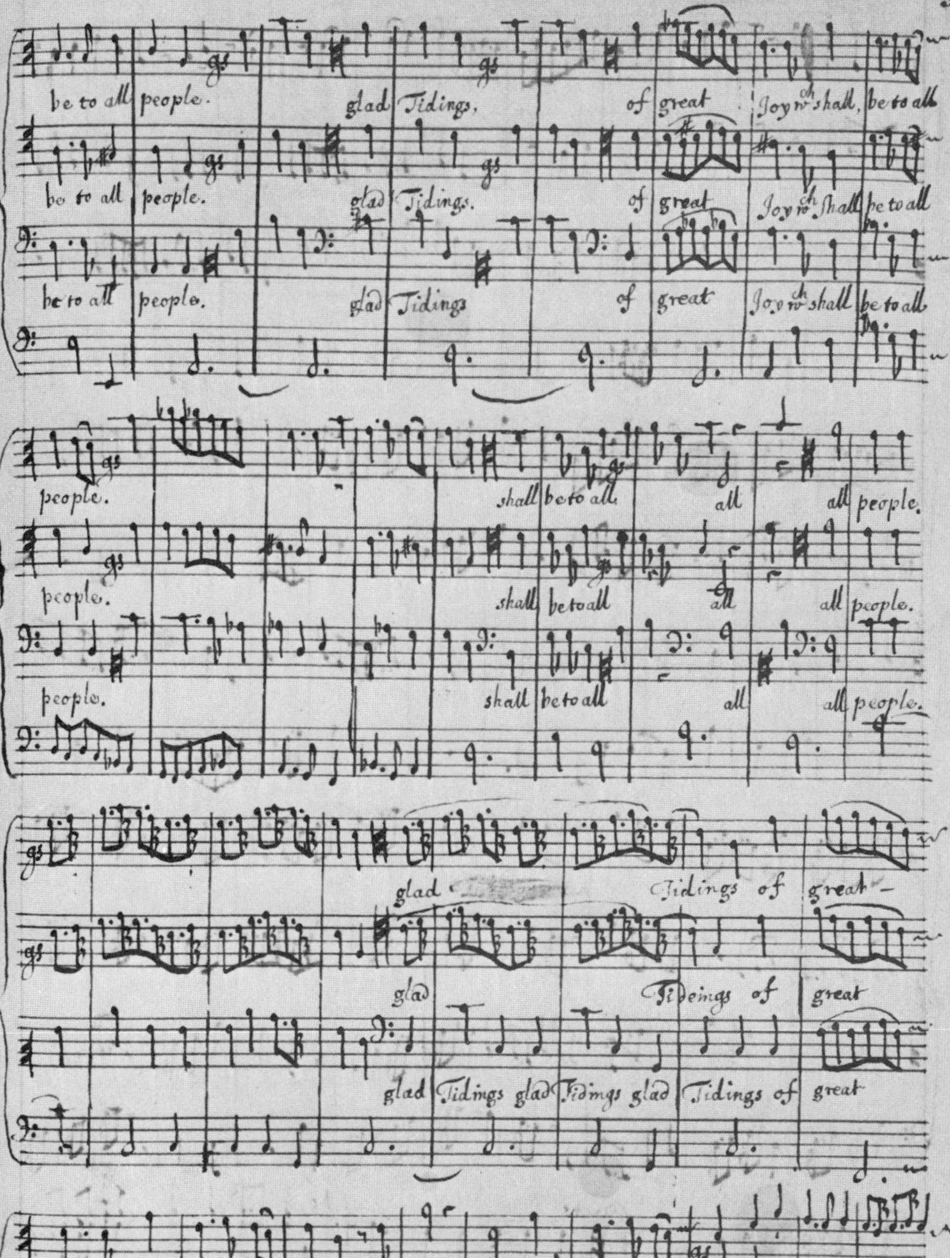
be to all people. glad Tidings, of great Joy wch shall, be to all
be to all people. glad Tidings. of great Joy wch Shall be to all
be to all people. glad Tidings of great Joy wch shall be to all
people. shall be to all all all people.
people. shall be to all all all people.
people. shall be to all all all people.
glad Tidings of great
glad Tideings of great
glad Tidings glad Tidings glad Tidings of great
Joy wch shall be to all people to all all shall be to all people.
Joy wch shall be to all people to all all Shall be to all people.
Joy wch Shall be to all people to all all Shall be to all people.

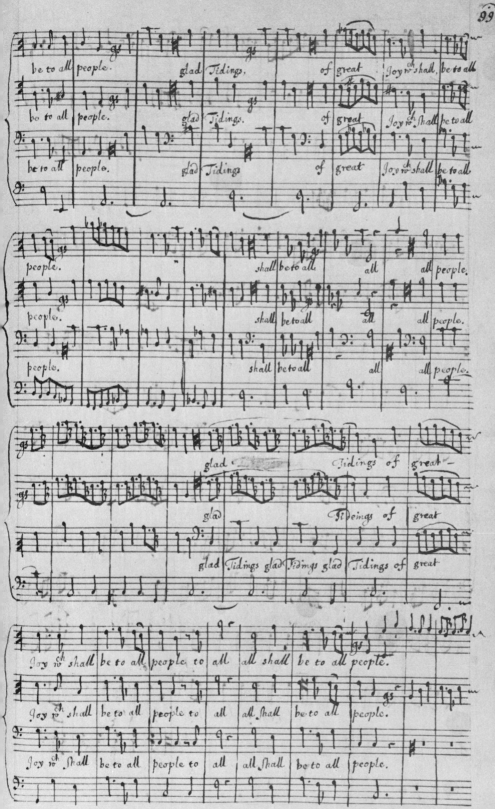

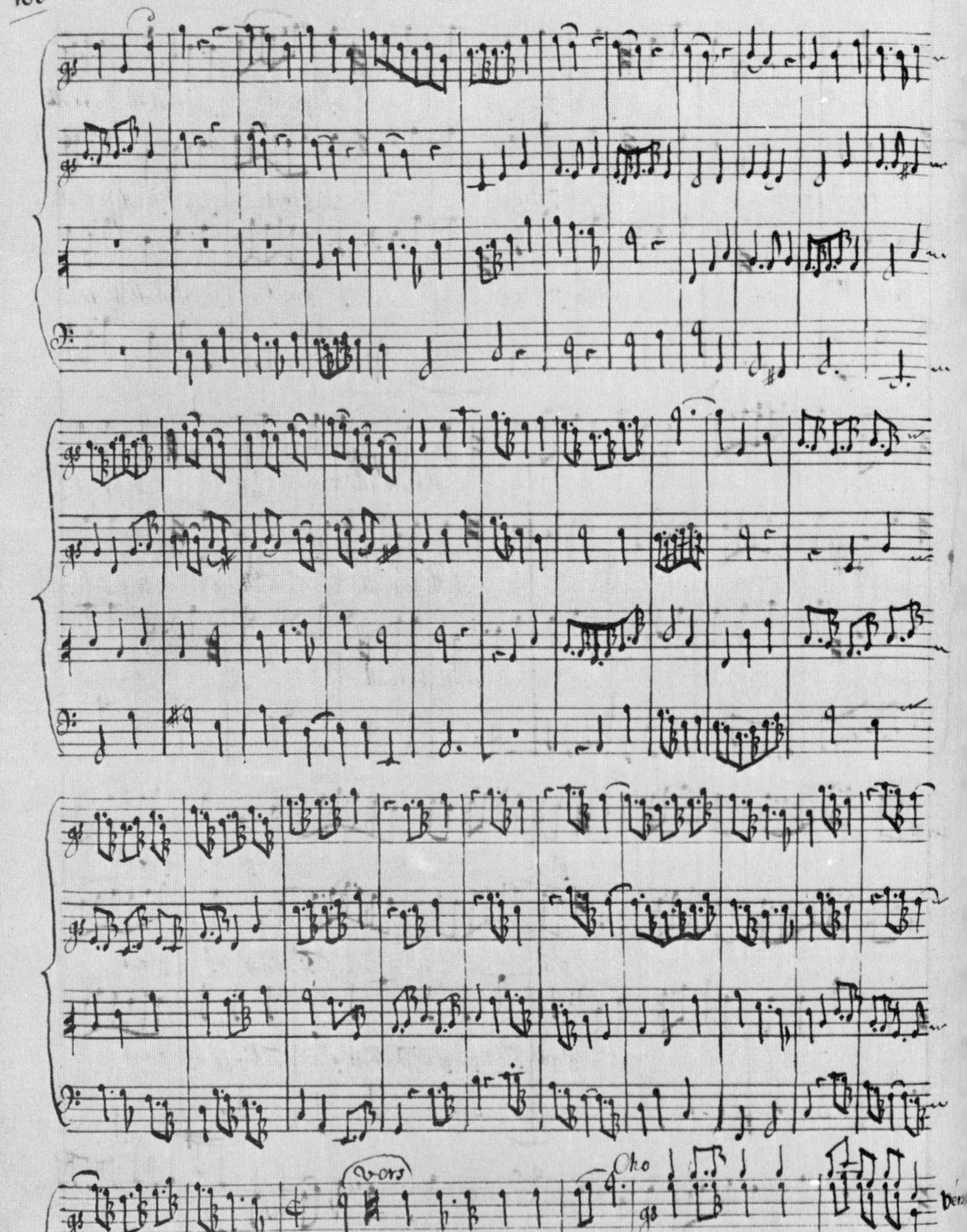
Vers
Glory to God on high
Cho
Cho:
Glory to God on high
Glory to God on high.
Cho
Glory to God on high.
Vers:
Cho
Glory to God on high
Glory to God on high.

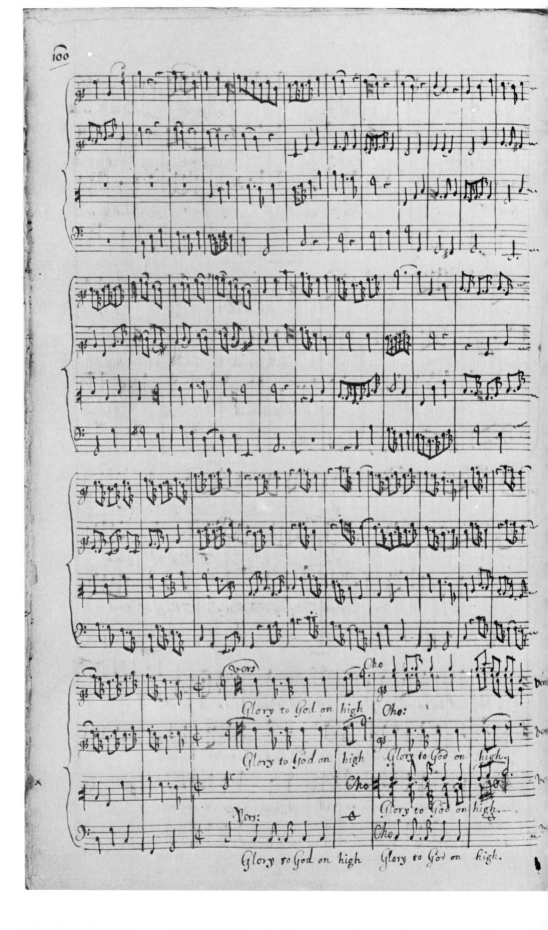

vers:
And on Earth Peace, Peace good-Will towards Men
And on Earth Peace peace good-Will towards Men.
And in Earth Peace peace good-Will towards Men,
Cho:
Glory to God on high
vers:
And on Earth
Cho: Glory to God on high
And on Earth
Glory to God on high.
And on Earth
peace peace good-will towards Men.
peace peace good will towards Men.
peace peace good will towards Men
Cho:
vers:
Glory to God on high.
Cho:
Glory to God on high
vers
And on Earth Peace
Cho:
Glory to God on high.
Cho
Glory to God on high
And on Earth Peace
Cho:
vers:
Glory to God on high
And on Earth peace

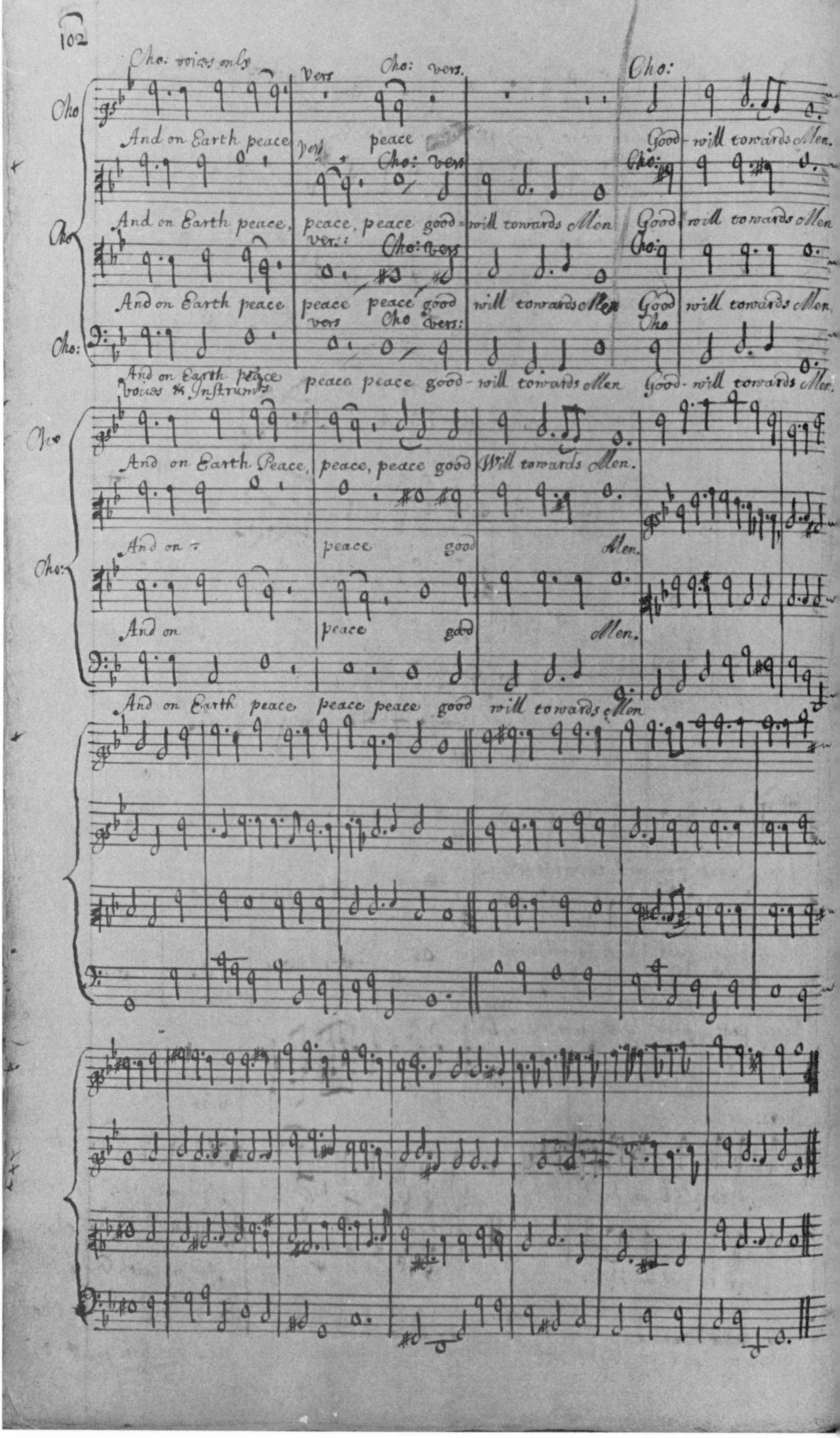

102
Cho: voices only
Vers
Cho: vers.
Cho:
And on Earth peace
peace
Good-will towards Men.
And on Earth peace, peace, peace good-will towards Men Good-will towards Men
And on Earth peace peace peace good will towards Men Good will towards Men.
And on Earth peace peace peace good-will towards Men Good-will towards Men.
voices & Instruments
And on Earth Peace, peace, peace good Will towards Men.
And on
peace good Men.
And on Earth peace peace peace good will towards Men

vers:
Alleluia, Alleluia, alleluia alleluia alleluia alleluia alleluia
Alleluia alle-
Alleluia alle- luia alleluia alle- luia alleluia alle- luia alleluia
Alleluia alleluia alle- luia alleluia alle- luia alle- luia alle- luiah alle-
Alle- luia alle- alle- luiah alle-
Alle- luia alleluia alle- luia alleluia Alleluia Alleluia alleluia alle
luia alleluia alleluia alleluia alle-
luia alle luia alleluia alle luia alle-
luia alle luia alleluia alle luia alle-
luia alleluia alleluia alle- luia alleluia alleluia alle-
luia alle- luia alleluia alle- luia alleluia alleluia alle-
luia alle- luia alleluia alle- luia alleluia alleluia alle-

Drag
luia alleluia alle-luia alleluia alle-luiah alleluia alle-luia allelu-ia.
Cho
Drag
luia alleluiah alle luia alleluia alle luiah alleluia alle luia alle luia
Cho:
Drag
luia alleluia alle lu
luia alle luia
Cho:
Drag
Cho:
Ritor
Cho:
Cho:
Glory to God on high.
violin
Cho Glory to God on high.
Amen
Cho:
Glory to God on high.
Cho Glory to God on high
Amen
Cho:
Glory to God on high.
Ritor:
Cho: Glory to God on high:
Cho:
Glory to God on high.
Ritor.
Cho: Glory to God on
Cho

Composed by Mr Henry Purcell

For Christmas day

1687.

al:
.8

Anthem for ye Thanksgiving appointed Jan: 15th 1688 for ye Queens being wth child

1st
2d
vers
1st
2d
vers
1st
2d.
vers
1st
2d
vers.

Verse
Blessed, blessed are they that fear that fear the Lord, blessed blessed are they ye
Vers. Blessed blessed are they ye fear that fear the Lord blessed blessed are they ye
Vers. Blessed blessed are they that fear that fear the Lord blessed blessed are they ye fe
Vers. Blessed blessed are they that fear that fear the Lord blessed blessed are they ye fe
fear ye Lord ye fear ye fear ye Lord. & walk in his ways &
fear ye Lord ye fear ye fear ye Lord & walk in his ways & walk in his
fear the Lord ye fear ye fear ye Lord, & walk in his ways & walk & walk in his
fear the Lord ye fear ye fear ye Lord & walk in his ways walk — in his —
walk in his ways and walk in his ways & walk
ways & walk in his ways & walk in his ways & walk in his ways &
ways walk — in his ways & walk in his ways & walk in his ways and —
ways & walk in his ways & walk in his ways walk

Ritor:
in his ways and walk in his ways & walk in his ways.
walk in his ways & walk in his ways & walk in his ways.
Ritor
walk & walk in his ways walk in his ways & walk in his ways.
Ritor:
in his ways & walk in his ways.
Ritor
For thou shalt eat ye
O well is thee O well is Thee
O well is thee O well is thee
Labors of thine hands for thou shalt eat ye labors of thine hands
&
76
happy happy happy & happy shalt thou be & hap py shalt thou

O well is thee O — — well is thee,
O well is thee O well is thee,
be
Thy wife shall be as yᵉ fruit = = full Vine thy
Vers
O well is thee O
O well is thee. O
Wife shall be as yᵉ fruitfull Vine upon yᵉ Walls of thine House
well is thee
well is thee
Thy children like yᵉ Olive branches round — — — — — — — — about thy
O well is thee O well is thee (Violins soft)
O well is thee, O well is thee
Table
The Ld. thy God from out of Sion shall so-

bless thee The Lord thy God from out of Sion shall bless Thee ỹ thou shalt see Je=
=rusalem ỹ thou shalt see Jerusalem in prosperity all thy Life long all
Vers:
O well is thee O well is thee
O well is thee O well is thee
Yea thou shalt
thy Life long
see thy childrens children shalt see thy childrens children & peace peace shall be shall

be upon Israel, yea thou shalt see shalt see thy childrens children & peace peace shall be
be upon Israel peace peace shall be, & peace peace shall be shall - - - be upon
O well is thee, O well is thee & happy happy, & happy happy, and
O well is thee O well is thee & happy happy & happy happy and
Israel. O well is thee O well is thee O well is thee and happy happy
O well is thee O well is thee O well is thee and happy happy
happy happy shalt thou be. O well is thee & happy happy shalt thou be lo!
happy happy shalt thou be O well is thee & happy happy shalt thou be lo
& happy shalt thou be O well is thee and happy shalt thou be lo.
and happy shalt thou be O well is thee & happy shalt thou be lo

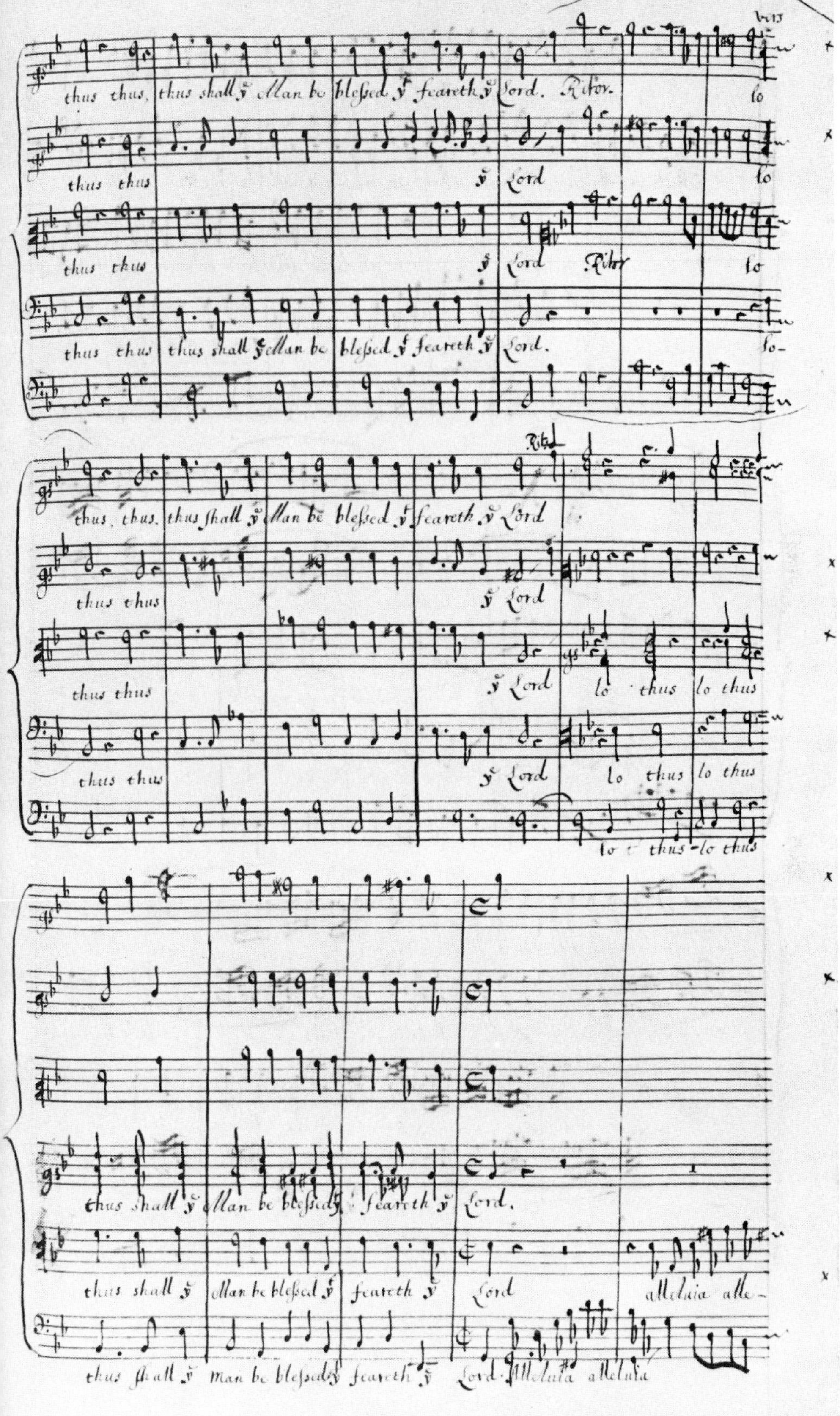
thus thus, thus shall ye Man be blessed yt feareth ye Lord. Ritor.
lo
thus thus
ye Lord
thus thus
ye Lord Ritor
thus thus thus shall ye Man be blessed yt feareth ye Lord.
thus, thus, thus shall ye Man be blessed yt feareth ye Lord
lo thus lo thus
thus shall ye Man be blessed yt feareth ye Lord.
Alleluia alleluia

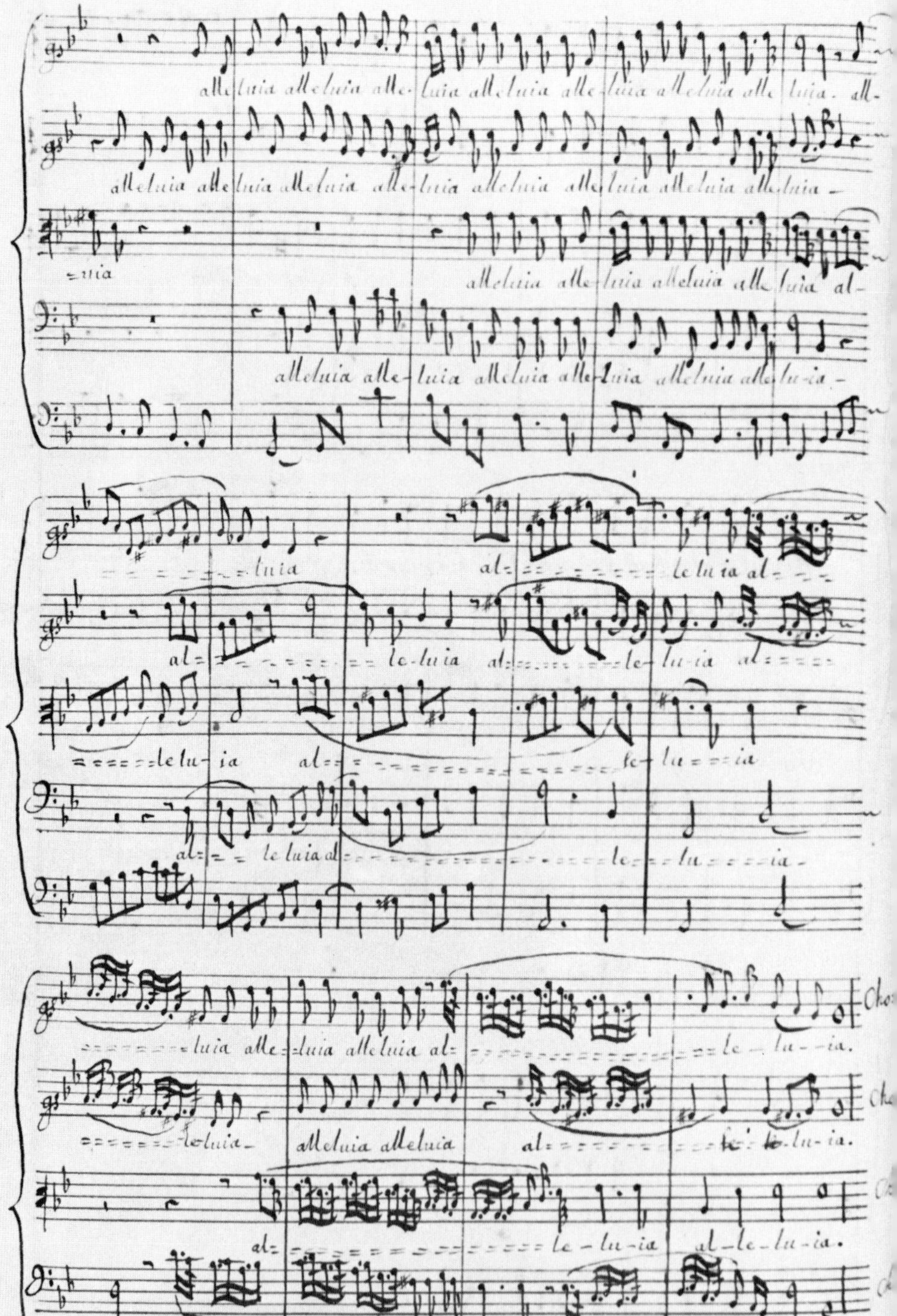
alleluia alleluia alle-luia alleluia alle-luia alleluia alle-luia. al-
alleluia alle-luia alleluia alle-luia alleluia alle-luia alleluia alle-luia -
-luia
alleluia alle-luia alleluia alle-luia al-
alleluia alle-luia alleluia alle-luia alleluia alle-lu-ia -
luia
al le-lu-ia al
al le-luia al le-lu-ia al
le-lu-ia al le-lu-ia
al le luia al le-lu-ia
luia alle-luia alleluia al le-lu-ia.
le-luia alleluia alleluia al le-lu-ia.
al le-lu-ia al-le-lu-ia.
al luia alle lu-ia al le-lu-ia
Cho

Alleluia Alleluia Allelu- ia
Alleluia Alle- luia Allelu- ia.
Alleluia Alle- luia Allelu- ia.
Alleluia Alle luia Allelu- ia.

Composed by Mr Henry Purcell. Jan: 12. 1687. For ye Thanksgiving Appointed in London & 12 miles round, upon her Majesties being wth Child. & on ye 29 following over England.

Praise the Lord ô my Soul.

Symphony
76
Vers: Solus.
Praise the Lord o my Soul.

O Lord my God, Thou'rt become exceeding glo- - - - - - - - - - - -vious thou art clothd with
Majesty & Hono.r thou deckest thy self with Light as it were wth a Garment & spread- -est
out ye Heavens like a Curtain, Who layeth ye Beams of his Chambers in ye Waters and
maketh ye Clouds his Chariot & walk-eth upon ye Wings of ye Wind, & walk-eth upon ye
Wings of ye Wind. He laid ye Foundations of ye Earth yt it never it
never should move at any Time, Thou coveredst it wth ye Deep, like as wth a Garment the
Waters stand, stand, stand in ye Hills at thy Rebuke they flee, at thy rebuke they
flee at ye Voice of thy Thun- - - - - -der they are afraid they go up as high as ye

Hills & down to ye valleys beneath, even to ye place wch thou hast appointed for them even to ye
place wch thou hast appointed for them; even to ye place which thou hast appointed
soft
Ritor:
He bringeth forth
vers.
vers.
for ye
Grass for ye Cattel & green herb for ye Service of Men & green
Hee bringeth forth Grass for ye Cattle he bringeth forth Grass for ye
Herb for ye Service of Men he bringeth forth Grass for the Cattle & green
Cattel & green herb for ye Service of Men he bringeth forth Grass for ye
herb for ye Service of Men and green herb for ye Service of Men, ye he may bring
Cattel & green herb for the Service ye Service of Men

food out of yᵉ Earth
yᵗ he may bring food
yᵗ he may bring food out of yᵉ
That he may bring food out of yᵉ Earth
yᵗ he may bring food
yᵗ he may bring
Earth and Wine and Wine yᵗ maketh glad
yᵉ heart of Man & Wine and
Food out of yᵉ Earth out of yᵉ Earth and Wine and
Wine yᵗ maketh glad yᵉ heart of
Wine yᵗ maketh glad
yᵉ heart of Man & Wine & Wine
Man and Wine & Wine yᵗ maketh glad
yᵉ heart of Man & Wine and
that maketh glad
yᵉ heart of Man.
Wine yᵗ maketh glad
yᵉ heart of Man.
He appointed yᵉ Moon for

certain Seasons he appoint ed ye Moon for cer- tain Seasons
& ye Sun knoweth his go- ing down & ye Sun knoweth his go- ing down
soft
loud
he made Darkness yt it may be Night, he made Darkness yt it may be Night and ye Sun
knoweth his go- ing down, his going down, & ye Sun knoweth his go- ing, down
Ver. a 2.
O Lord, O Lord, how manifold are thy Works, O Lord how manifold are thy
O Lord, O Lord how manifold are thy Works, O Lord how manifold are thy
works in wisdom in wisdom hast thou made them all, O Lord in wisdom, in wisdom hast thou
works in wisdom in wisdom hast thou made them all O Lord in wisdom in wisdo hast thou

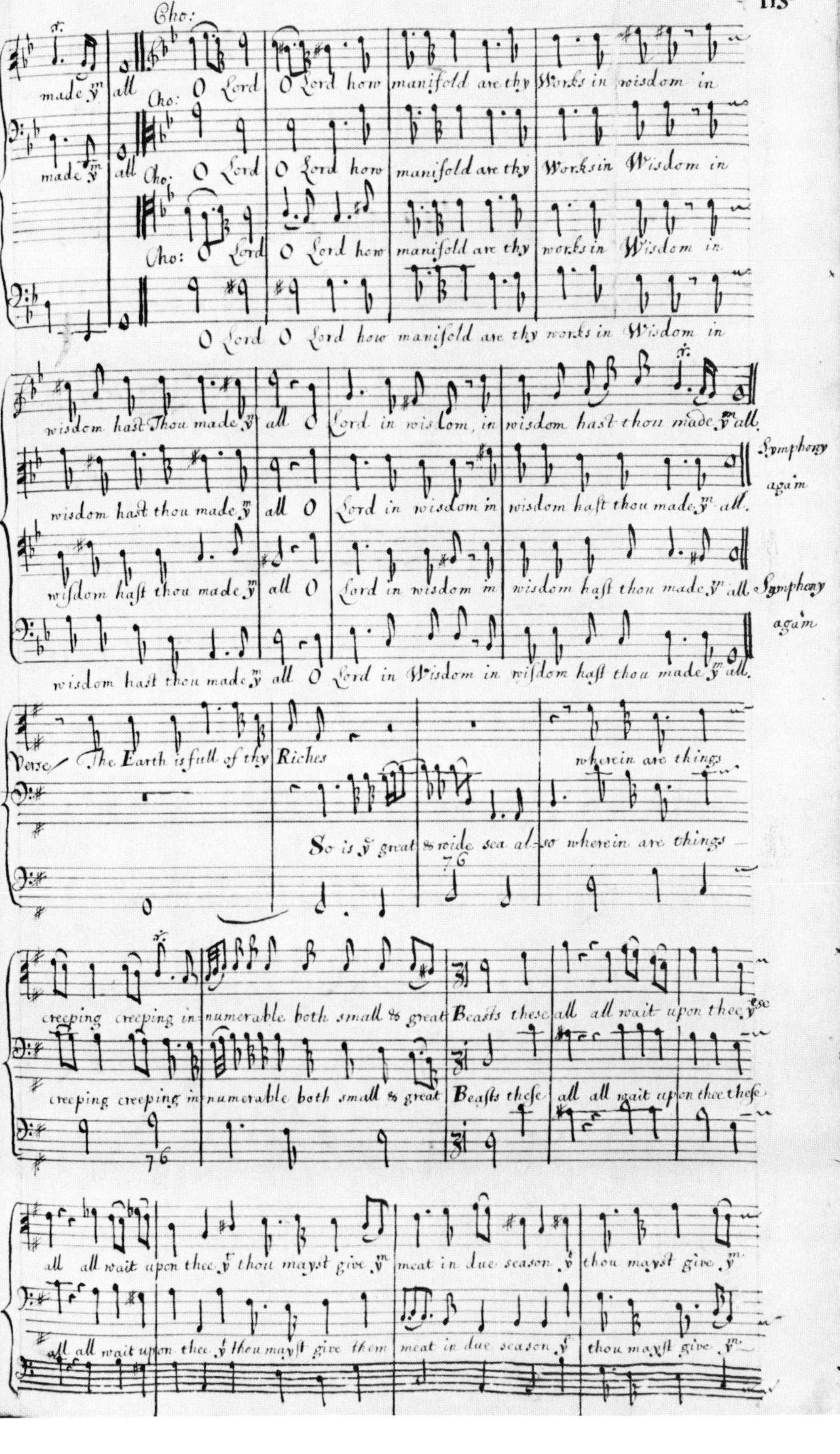
Cho:
made yᵐ all
O Lord O Lord how manifold are thy Works in wisdom in
Cho:
made yᵐ all
O Lord O Lord how manifold are thy Works in Wisdom in
Cho:
O Lord O Lord how manifold are thy works in Wisdom in
Cho:
O Lord O Lord how manifold are thy works in Wisdom in
wisdom hast Thou made yᵐ all O Lord in wisdom, in wisdom hast thou made yᵐ all.
wisdom hast thou made yᵐ all O Lord in wisdom in wisdom hast thou made yᵐ all.
Symphony again
wisdom hast thou made yᵐ all O Lord in wisdom in wisdom hast thou made yᵐ all
Symphony again
wisdom hast thou made yᵐ all O Lord in Wisdom in wisdom hast thou made yᵐ all.
Verse The Earth is full of thy Riches wherein are things
So is yᵉ great & wide sea al-so wherein are things
76
creeping creeping in-numerable both small & great Beasts these all all wait upon thee, yᵗ
creeping creeping in-numerable both small & great Beasts these all all wait upon thee these
76
all all wait upon thee, yᵗ thou mayst give yᵐ meat in due season yᵗ thou mayst give yᵐ
all all wait upon thee yᵗ thou mayst give them meat in due season yᵗ thou mayst give yᵐ

meat in due season when thou givst it them they
meat in due season when thou givst it ym they gather it when thou givst it them they
gather it wn thou opnest thyne hand wn thou opnest thine hand they are filled wth
gather it. wn thou opnest thine hand they are fill=====ed with
good good good are fil=====led wth good.
good they are fil=====led wth good good good are filled wth good.
When thou
When thou
hidest thy Face they are trou==bled wn thou takst away their breath they dy they
hidest thy Face they are trou==bled, when thou takst away their Breath they dy they

dy and are turned again to their Dust. When thou lettest thy Breath go
dy and are turned again to their Dust When thou lettest thy Breath go
forth they shall be made And thou shalt renew the Face of ye
forth they shall be made & thou shalt renew ye Face of ye Earth, and thou shalt re-
Earth & thou shalt re-new ye Face of ye Earth re-new ye Face of ye Earth.
Ritor:
-new ye Face of ye Earth & thou shalt re-new ye Face re-new ye Face of ye Earth
Ritor:
Ritor:
slow
Ritorn:
The Glo-
Ritorn:
The Glo-
-rious Majesty The glo-rious Majesty of the
-rious Majesty The glo-rious Majesty of ye

Lord shall endure endure for ever ye Lord shall rejoice in his works the Ld shall re=
=joyce in his works shall rejoyce in his works shall re=
=joyce in his Works.
Cho: O Lord O Lord how manifold are thy Works in
Wisdom in wisdom hast thou made ym all O Lord in wisdom in wisdom hast thou made ym all.
Composed by Mr. Hen: Purcell. 1687.

Thy way ô God is holy. &c Psa:

Verse.
Thy way ô God ô God is holy Thy
Thy way ô God O God is
Way ô God o God thy way is holy who who is so great a God as our God –
holy thy way ô God ô God is holy.
Who – Who –
Who is so great a God who is so great a God so great a God as oʳ God who –
is so great a God as oʳ God who who is so great so great a God as oʳ God who
is so great a God so great a God as oʳ God.
is so great a God so great a God as oʳ God.

Thou art ye God yt doth wonders, Thou art ye God yt doth wonders
Thou art ye God yt doth wonders Thou art ye God yt doth wonders
Thou hast mightily delivred hast mightily hast mightily delivred thy people thou
Thou hast mightily de- livred hast mightily hast mightily delivred thy people thou
art ye God yt doth wonders, thou hast mightily hast mightily delivred thy People.
art ye God yt doth wonders, thou hast mightily hast mightily delivred thy People.
The waters saw thee o God ye Depths also were troub==led the Depths also were
The waters saw thee O God the Depths also were trou
troubled ye Clouds pour==red out water. The Air thun== dred.
==bled ye Clouds pour====ed out water. The Air thund==

The Air Thun-dred & thine Arrows went a-broad & thine Arrows went a-
-dred & thine Arrows went abroad and thine Arrows went abroad.
-broad ye Air thun-dred & thine Arrows went abroad, & thine Arrows went a-
soft.
soft.
The air thun-dred & thine Arrows went abroad & thine Arrows went a-
-broad thy Way ô God ô God is holy Thy way ô God ô God thy way is
-broad. Thy way ô God ô God is holy thy way ô God ô God is
holy who who is so great a God as oʳ God Who is so great a- God who
holy. Who who is so great a God as our God who-
is so great a God so great a God as our God who is so great a God so great a God as oʳ God.
Who is so great so great a God as oʳ God who is so great a God so great a God as oʳ God.
Symphony again as before
Symph: again as before.

122
Vers:
The voice of thy Thun==der was heard round about the voice of thy
The voice of thy thu=nder was heard round– about y^e voice of thy Thun=
Thun===der was heard round about y^e Lightnings shone upon y^e Ground y^e Earth was
=der was heard round a bout y^e Lightnings shone upon y^e Ground y^e Earth was
mo==ved & shook withall y^e Earth was mo==ved & shook w=
mo==ved & shook withall y^e Earth was mo==ved & shook w=
=all
=all
Vers.
Thou art y^e
Thou art y^e
God y^t doth Wonders, Thou art y^e God y^t doth wonders, Thou hast mightily delivred hast
God y^t doth wonders Thou art y^e God y^t doth wonders Thou hast mightily delivred hast

mightily hast mightily delivred thy people Thy Way ô God ô God is holy Thy
mightily hast mightily delivred thy people Thy Way ô God ô God is
way ô God ô God thy way is holy who who is so great a God as ô God who is so great a
holy thy way ô God ô God is holy Who who is so great a God as ô
God who is so great a God so great a God as ô God who is so great a God so great a-
God who who is so great so great a God as ô God who is so great a God so great a
Cho:
Cho: Alleluia Alle luia alleluia alle luia alleluia alle luia alleluia alle-
God as ô God Cho: Alleluia alleluia alleluia alle luia alleluia alle luia alleluia alle
Godas ô God Alleluia alle luia alleluia alle luia alleluia alle luia alleluia alle
Alleluia alleluia alleluia alleluia alleluia alle-luia alleluia alle-
-luia alleluia alle luia Alleluia.
Composed by
-luia alleluia alle luia Alleluia.
Mr Hen: Purcel
1687.
-luia alleluia alle luia Alleluia
-luia alleluia alle- lu-ia.

O Sing unto ye Lord.
Symphonia

Vers: upper Base.
O sing unto ye Lord sing unto ye Ld, sing unto ye Ld a new song sing unto ye Ld a new song.
8 above
2d Treble
Cho:
Alle-luia Al-le-lu-ia Alle-lu-ia Alle-luia
Alle-lu-ia Alle-lu-ia Alleluia Alleluia Alle-lu-ia Alle-lu-ia
Alle-lu-ia Alleluia. Alle-lu-ia Alleluia Alleluia Al-le-lu-ia
Alle-lu-ia Al-le-lu-ia, Al-le-lu-ia, Al-le-lu-ia, Al-le-lu-ia, Al-le-lu-ia, Al-le-lu-ia

Verse
Sing unto yͤ Lord all all yͤ whole Earth, Sing unto yͤ Lord all yͤ whole Earth
Cho: Violins
Cho:
Cho:
Cho:
Cho: Alle-lu-ia, Alle-lu-ia. Alle-luia, Alle-luia. Alle-luia. Alle-luia Alle-lu-ia
Cho: Alle-luia. Alle-luia Alleluia Alleluia Alleluia Alleluia Alle-lu-ia
Cho: Alle-luia, Alle-luia Alle-luia Alle-luia Alle-luia Alle-luia Alle-lu-ia
Alle-luia. Alleluia. Alleluia Alleluia. Alleluia. Alleluz-ia Al-le-lu-ia

Verse.
Sing unto ye Lord sing — un-to ye Ld. & praise his name & praise &
Sing unto ye Ld sing — unto ye Lord unto ye Lord,
Verse
Sing unto ye Ld sing
Verse
Sing unto ye
Vers.
praise his name Sing unto the Lord sing — & praise his
Sing unto ye Lord sing unto ye Lord & praise his name & praise
unto the Ld & praise his name & praise his name & praise his name prayse
Lord sing — unto ye Ld & praise his name & praise —
Name & praise his Name from day to day from day to day from day to
his name be telling of his Salvation from day to day be-
his name from day to day be telling of his salvation from
his name be telling of his sal-

day from day to day be telling of his Salvation
telling of his sal-vation from day to Day from day to day from day to
Day to day from day to day from day to - Day - be-
-vation be telling of his Salva--tion from day to day from day to-
from day to day from day to day be telling of his sal---va---tion
Day from day to day be telling of his Salvation from day to day from day to
telling of his sal---va---tion be telling of his sal---va---tion-
---day---be telling of his Salvation from day to day from day to
Soft
from day to day from day to day from day to day.
Day be telling of his Sal--vation from day to day.
from day to day from day to day from day to day.
Solo
day from day to day. Declare his

Hono declare his Hono his hono unto ye Heathen declare his hono
declare his hono unto ye heathen & his Won===ders his Won===ders unto all people
Cho:
Cho:
Cho:
Cho:
Cho.
Cho:
Cho: Glory & worship are before him Glory & worship are before him.
Cho: Glory & worship are before him Glory & worship are before him
Cho: Glory & worship are before him Glory & worship are before him
Cho: Glory & worship are before him Glory & worship are before him

Pow'r & hono:r, Pow'r & hono:r are in his Sanctuary.
Pow'r & hono:r Pow'r & hono:r are in his Sanctuary.
Pow'r & hono:r Pow'r & hono:r are in his Sanc= = = = = tuary.
Pow'r & hono:r Pow'r & hono:r are in his San= ctuary
Vers: 2. voc.
The Ld is great The Ld is great & cannot
The Ld is great is great The Ld is great great & cannot
worthily be praised. The Ld is great he is more to be feared is more to be
worthily be praised he is more to be feared be feared is more to be
feared be feared than all than all Gods as for all ye
feared be feared than all than all Gods as for all ye Gods ye

Gods of ye heathen they are they are but Idols but it is ye Lord ye made ye Heavns it
Gods of ye heathen they are they are but Idols but it is ye Lord ye made ye Heavns it
is – ye Lord ye made ye Heavn's ye made ye Heavns
soft
2d Tr. 6
Ritor.
is ye Lord ye made ye Heavns
Ritor.
Ritor
soft
loud

Soft
Soft
Soft
Verse
O worship ye Lord
Verse
O worship ye Lord
Ver: O worship ye Lord O O
Ver: O worship ye Lord O O
Cho:
worship ye Lord in ye beauty of holiness. O worship ye Lord O O worship ye
Cho:
worship ye Lord in ye beauty of holiness. O worship ye Lord O O worship ye
Cho:
worship ye Lord in ye beauty of holiness. O worship ye Lord O O worship ye
Cho
worship ye Lord in ye beauty of holiness. O worship ye Lord O O worship ye
Cho

Lord in ye beauty of holiness let ye whole earth stand in aw of him.
Lord in ye beauty of holiness let ye whole earth stand in aw let the
Lord in ye beauty of holiness let ye whole earth stand in aw let ye
Lord in ye beauty of holiness let ye whole earth stand in aw let ye whole earth
let ye whole earth stand in aw of him, let ye whole earth stand let
whole earth stand in aw of him, let ye whole earth stand in
whole earth stand in aw of him let ye whole earth Stand in aw let ye
stand in aw of him let ye whole earth Stand in aw let ye
ye whole earth stand in aw of him.
aw of him let ye whole earth stand in aw of him.
whole earth stand in aw of him in aw of him. Vers:
whole earth stand in aw of him Tell it out among ye heathen that ye Lord is

134
First Treb
2 Treb
Cho:
The Lord is King The Ld is King is King ye Lord is King.
The Lord is King The Ld is King is King ye Lord is King.
The Lord is King The Ld is King is King ye Ld is King.
verse
King The Lord is King The Ld is King is King ye Ld is King, & ye it is he who hath
made ye round world so sure ye it cannot be
tis he tis he tis he who hath made ye round world so sure ye it cannot be moved
tis he tis he who hath made ye round world so sure ye it cannot be moved
tis he tis he who hath made ye round world so sure ye it can=not be moved
moved tis he tis he tis he who hath made ye round world so sure ye it cannot be moved &
Vers

how y^t he shall judg y^e people righteously & how y^t he shall judg shall judg y^e people righteous=
Cho:
Cho: He shall judg y^e people righteously shall judg y^e people righteously shall judg y^e people righteously
Cho: He shall judg y^e people righteously shall judg y^e people righteously shall judg y^e people righteously.
Cho: He shall judg y^e people righteously shall judg y^e people righteously shall judg y^e people righteously
=ly Cho: He shall judg y^e people righteously shall judg y^e people righteously shall judg y^e people righteously.
Cho:
Vers
Alle=lu= ia Al=le=lu=ia Al=le=lu=ia.
Alle=lu= ia Al=le=lu=ia. Alle
Cho:
Vers Alle=lu=ia Al=le=lu=ia Alle=lu=ia Alle=luia Al=le=lu=ia.
Cho:
Alle=lu=ia Al=le=lu=ia Alle=luia Alle=lu=ia.

Cho:
Alle= lu= ia Alle= lu= = ia Al= = le= lu= ia Alle luia Al= = le= lu= = ia.
lu= ia Alle= = = lu= ia Alle= lu= = ia Alle= lu= = ia Alle- lu= = ia.
Alle= lu= = ia Alle= = luia Alle= luia Al= le= lu= = lu= ia
Alle= lu= = ia Al= = le = lu= = ia Alle lu= = ia Alle= = = lu= = = ia
Alle lu= = ja Alle
Alle= lu= =
Alle-

lu= ia Al= le= lu= ia Alle= lu= = ia Alle= lu= = Al= = = le= lu= ia Alle=
ia Alle= = lu= = = ia, Alle= = lu= = = ia
Alle= lu= ia Alle= lu= = = = ia Alle= = lu= = = ia Alle
lu= ia Alle= lu= = = = ia, Alle= = lu= = = ia Alle= = lu=
lu= = ia Al= = = le= lu= ia. Amen.
Alle= = lu= = = ia Alle= = = lu= = = ia. Amen.
=luia Alle= = lu= = = ia. Amen.
=ia Alle= = lu= = = ia Alle= = lu= = = ia Amen.
Composed by
Mr Purcell.
1688.

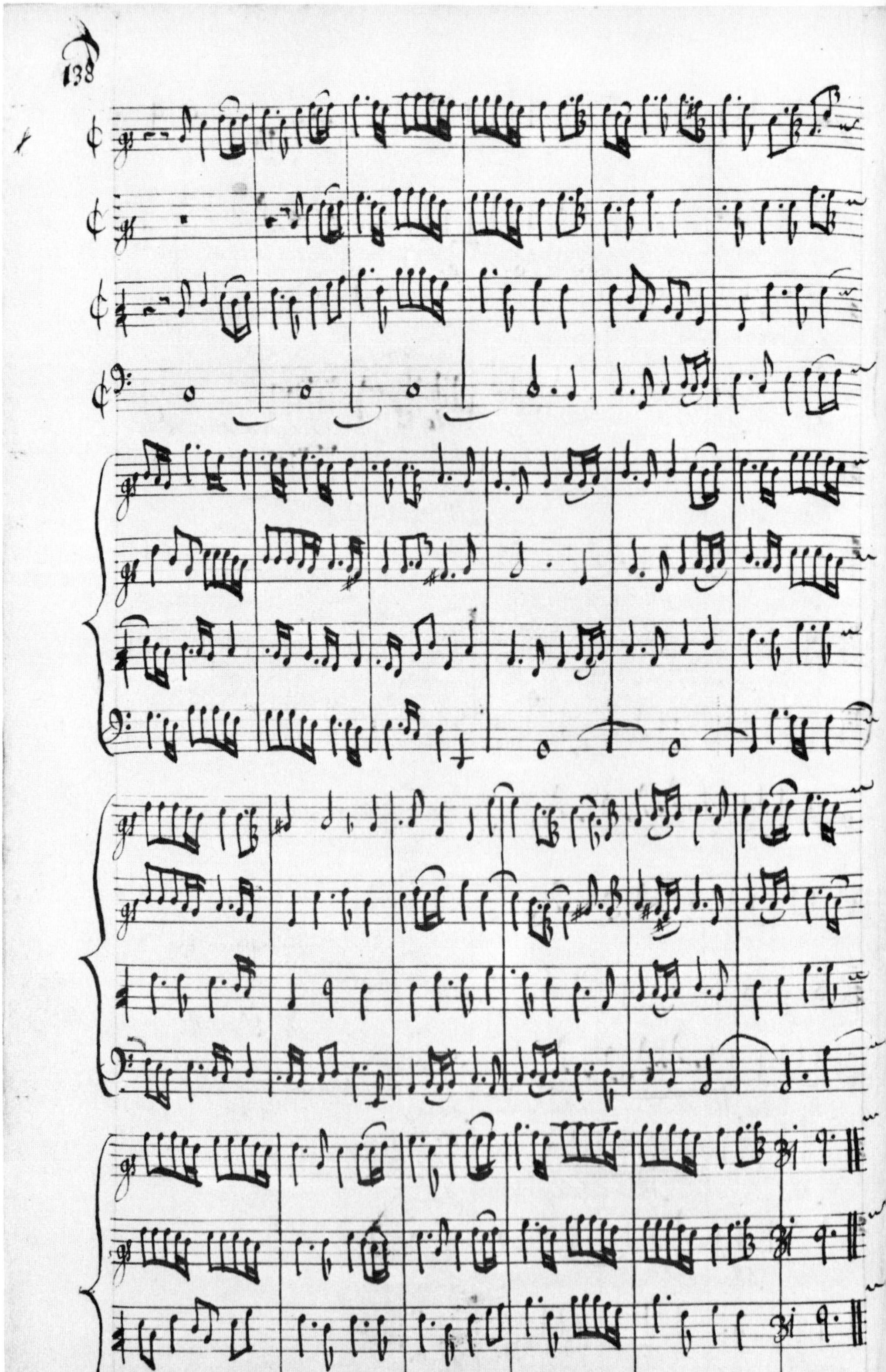

Symphony.
Symphony
Symphony.
Symphony.
Vers a 4
Vers: O sing
Vers: O sing
Vers: O sing
Vers: O sing
Praises sing Praises unto o^r God, O sing Praises sing Praises unto our King.
Praises sing Praises un-to o^r God O sing Praises sing Praises unto our King.
Praises sing Praises un-to o^r God O sing Praises sing Praises unto our King.
Praises sing Praises unto o^r God O sing praises sing Praises unto o^r King.
Retor:
Vers: a 2.
Retor:
God is gon
Retor:
God is gon up gon
Ground

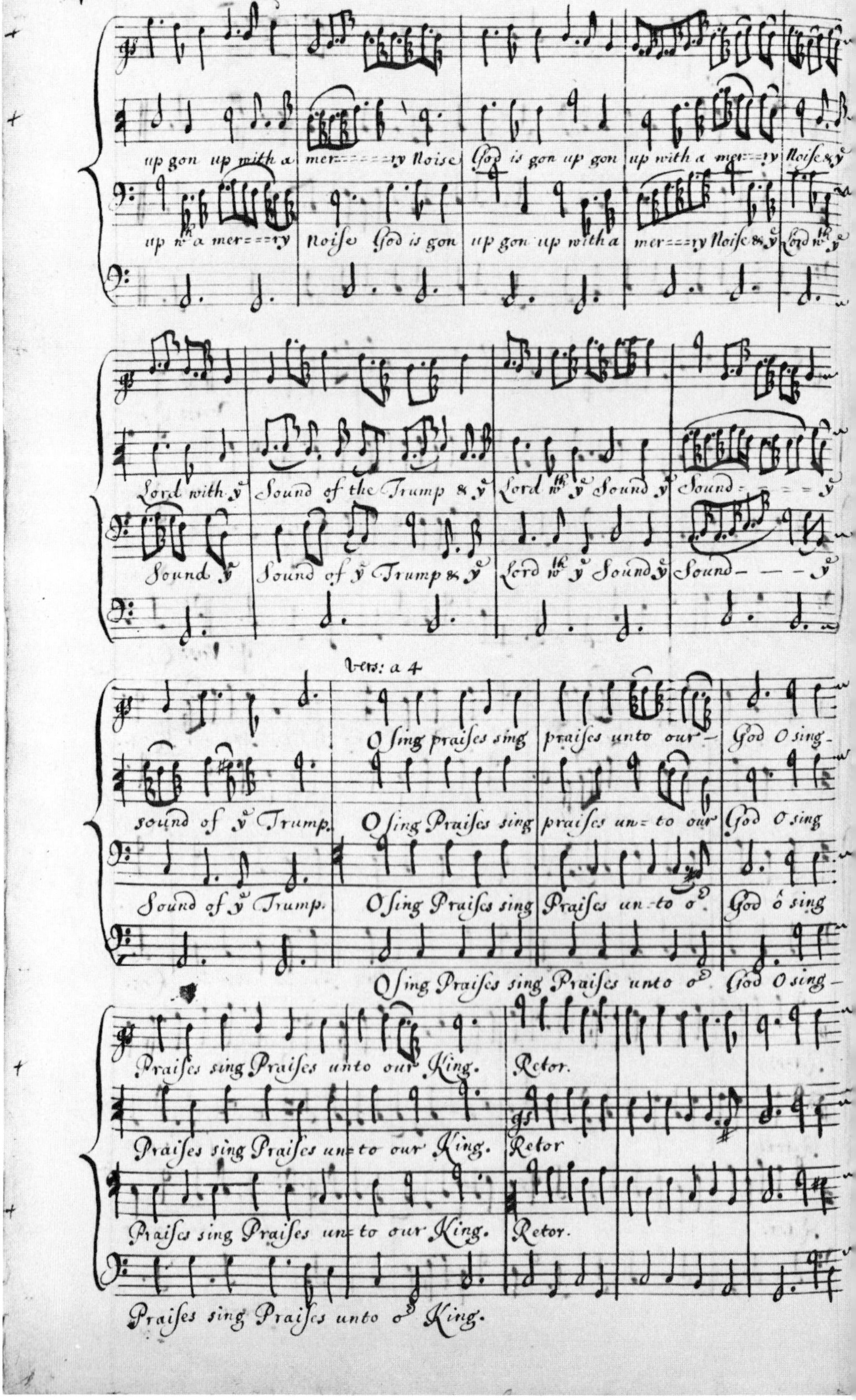
up gon up with a mer====ry Noise God is gon up gon up with a mer===ry Noise & ye
up wth a mer===ry Noise God is gon up gon up with a mer===ry Noise & ye Lord wth ye
Lord with ye Sound of the Trump & ye Lord wth ye Sound ye Sound= = = = ye
Sound ye Sound of ye Trump & ye Lord wth ye Sound ye Sound— — — ye
Vers: a 4
O sing praises sing praises unto our— God O sing-
sound of ye Trump. O sing Praises sing praises un= to our God O sing
Sound of ye Trump. O sing Praises sing Praises un-to or God o sing
O sing Praises sing Praises unto or God O sing-
Praises sing Praises unto our King. Retor.
Praises sing Praises un=to our King. Retor
Praises sing Praises un=to our King. Retor.
Praises sing Praises unto or King.

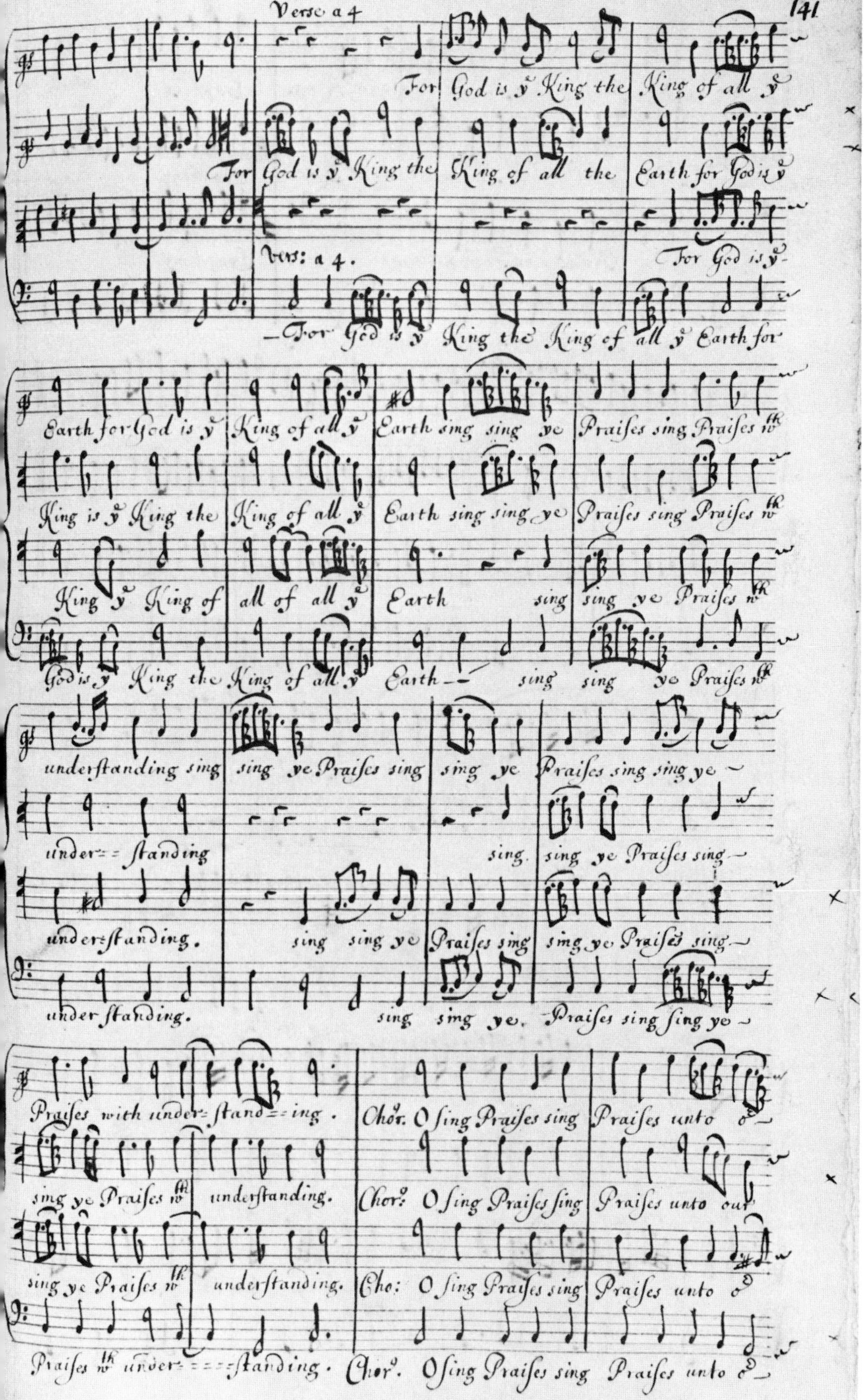
Verse a 4
For God is yͤ King the King of all yͤ
For God is yͤ King the King of all the Earth for God is yͤ
Vers: a 4.
For God is yͤ
For God is yͤ King the King of all yͤ Earth for
Earth for God is yͤ King of all yͤ Earth sing sing ye Praises wᵗʰ
King is yͤ King the King of all yͤ Earth sing sing ye Praises wᵗʰ
King yͤ King of all of all yͤ Earth sing sing ye Praises wᵗʰ
God is yͤ King the King of all yͤ Earth sing sing ye Praises wᵗʰ
understanding sing sing ye Praises sing sing ye Praises sing sing ye
under==standing sing. sing ye Praises sing.
under=standing. sing sing ye Praises sing sing ye Praises sing.
under standing. sing sing ye. Praises sing sing ye
Praises with under=stand==ing. Chor. O sing Praises sing Praises unto oͬ
sing ye Praises wᵗʰ understanding. Chor: O sing Praises sing Praises unto our
sing ye Praises wᵗʰ understanding. Cho: O sing Praises sing Praises unto oͬ
Praises wᵗʰ under====standing. Chor. O sing Praises sing Praises unto oͬ

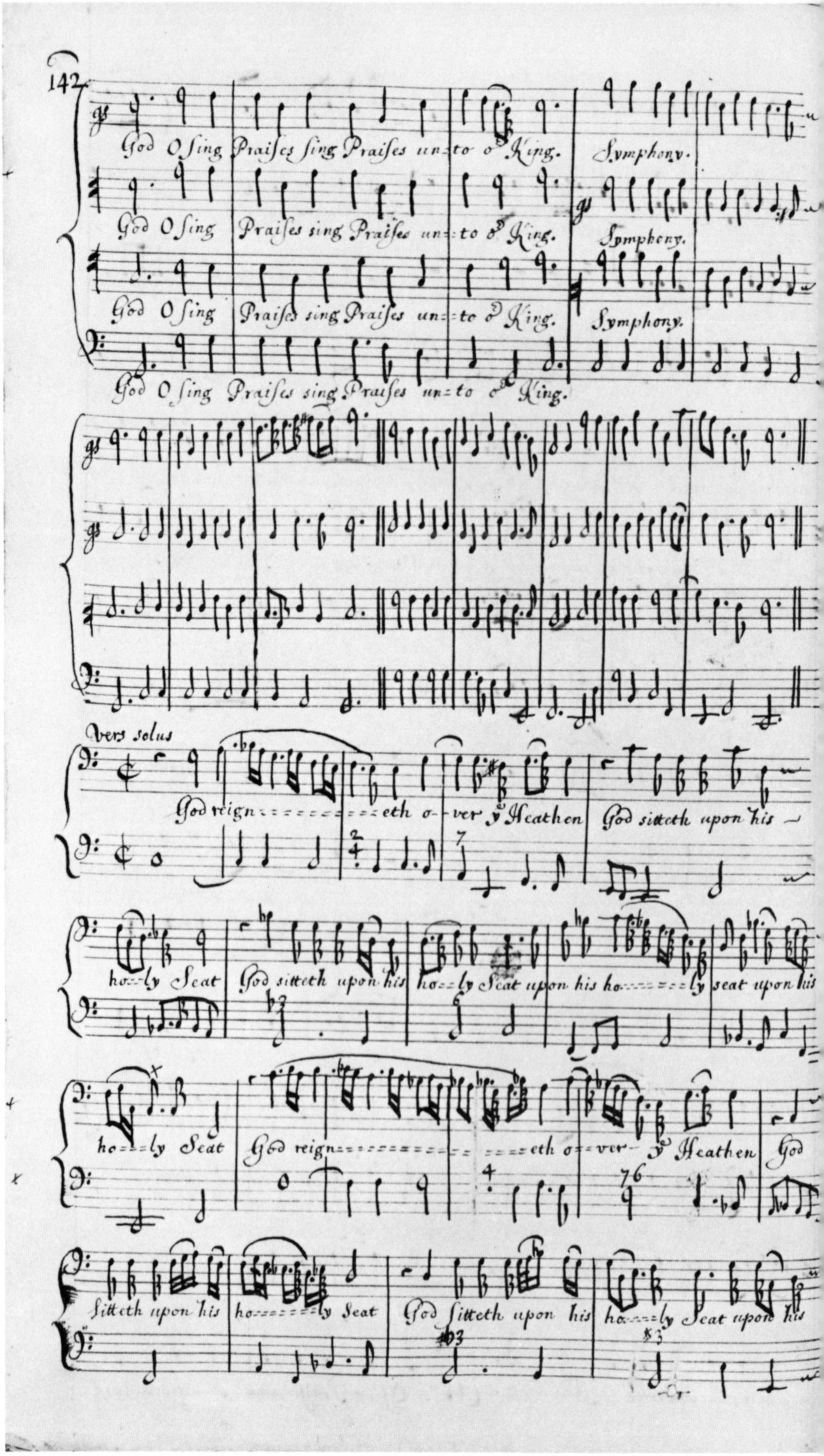
142
God O sing Praises sing Praises un-to o^r King.
Symphony.
God O sing Praises sing Praises un-to o^r King.
Symphony.
God O sing Praises sing Praises un-to o^r King.
Symphony.
God O sing Praises sing Praises un-to o^r King.
Vers solus
God reign-eth o-ver y^e Heathen God sitteth upon his
holy Seat God sitteth upon his holy Seat upon his ho-ly seat upon his
holy Seat God reign-eth o-ver y^e Heathen God
sitteth upon his ho-ly Seat God sitteth upon his ho-ly Seat upon his

ho-ly Seat upon his ho- ly Seat upon his ho- ly Seat.
Vers. a 4
O sing Praises sing praises unto our God O sing praises sing praises un- to our King.
O sing Praises sing Praises un-to our God O sing Praises sing praises un- to our King
O sing praises sing praises unto our God O sing praises sing praises un- to our King.
O sing praises sing praises unto our God o sing praises sing praises unto our King.
Retor:
Vers: a 4.
Retor:
Vers: Halleluia Halle-
Retor.
Vers. a 4.
Halleluia Hal-le- luia halleluia halle- luia
-luia Halleluia halle- luia
Hallelu-
Halleluia Halle- luia Halleluia Halle- luia
Halleluia Halle- luia Halleluia Halle- luia Halleluia Halle- luia

144
Halleluia Hallelu-ia Hallelu-ia Halleluia
-ia Halleluia Hallelu-ia Halleluia Hal-
Hallelu-ia Halleluia Halleluia Hallelu-ia Hal-le-lu-
Halleluia Hallelu-ia
Halleluia Hal-le-lu-ia Hal-le-lu-ia Hal-le-lu-ia Hal-
-lelu-ia Hal-le-lu-ia Hal-le-lu-ia Hal-le-lu-
-ia Hallelu-ia Halleluia Hal-
Hal-lelu-ia Hal-le-lu-
le-lu-ia Halleluia Hal-le-lu-
-ia Hal-leluia Halle-luia Hal-lelu-ia.
le-lu-ia Halleluia Hal-le-lu-ia Hal-
-ia Hal-le-lu-ia Halle-lu-ia Hal-

ia Hal-le-lu-ia Hal-le-lu-ia Hal-le-lu-
Hal-le-luia Hallelu-ia Hal-le-lu-
-le-lu-ia. Hal-le-lu- Halle-luia Halle-luia Hallelu-ia Hal-le-lu-ia Hal-
ia. Hal-le-lu-ia: Cho: Halleluia Halleluia Halleluia Hal-
ia Hal-le-lu-ia Cho: Halleluia Halle-luia Halleluia Hal-
le-lu-ia Cho. Halleluia Halle-luia Halleluia Halle-
le- ia: Cho: Hal-le-lu-ia Halle-
Chorus
-le-lu-ia Halle-luia Hal-le-lu-ia.
-le-lu-ia Hal-le-lu-ia
-luia Halle-lu-ia Hallelu-ia
-luia Halleluia Halle-luia Hallelu-ia
Composed by
Mr Turner
1687

I am well pleasd
Organ
I am well pleasd I am well pleasd
That ye Ld hath heard ye voice of my prayr
I am well pleasd
That ye Ld hath heard ye voice of my prayr
That he hath inclind his

That he hath inclin'd his ear unto me Therefore will I call up=
ear unto me- Therefore will I call up= on him, Therefore will I call up=
That he hath inclin'd his ear un= to me Therefore will I call up=
=on him. Therefore will I call up on him as long as I live.
=on him. Therefore will I call up= on him as long as I live.
Therefore will I call up= on him up= on him as long as I live.
The snares of death com= =passed me round about. And ye pains of Hell gat hold up=
on me gat hold upon me I have found trouble & heaviness & I did call upon ye name of ye Lord-
O Lord I be= seech thee de= li= ver my soul O Lord I beseech Thee I be= seech Thee de=
liver my soul
Turn over
Turn over.

=liver my Soul. Gracious is ye Lord & righteous yea or God is mercifull The Lord pre=
Gra=cious is ye Lord & righteous yea or God is merci=full The Lord pre=
Gra=cious is ye Lord & righteous yea or God is merci=full The Lord pre=
=serveth ye Sim=ple when I was in misery he de=livered me.
serveth ye Simple, when I was in misery he de=livered me he de=livered me when I
serveth the Simple wn I was in misery he de
76 98 #64 63
when I was in misery he de=livered me
was in misery he de=livered me when I was in misery he de=livered me. Turn turn again then un=
=livered me when I was in misery he de=livered me he de=livered me.
76 765 987
=to thy rest o my soul
For ye Lord hath rewarded thee he hath rewarded Thee
For he hath delivered my

Turn turn again then turn a = gain unto thy Rest o my
Turn turn a = gain then turn a = gain unto thy Rest o my
soul from death mine eyes from tears my feet from fal = ling: turn turn a = gain then turn a gain unto thy rest o my
soul for ye Ld hath rewarded thee he hath rewarded Thee. For he hath delivred my soul my
soul for ye Ld hath rewarded thee he hath rewarded ye for he hath de = livred my soul my soul from death mine
For ye Lord hath rewarded Thee For he hath delivred my soul my soul from
Soul from death my feet from fal = = ling For he hath de = livred my soul for he hath delivred my
eyes from tears my feet from fal = ling for he hath delivred my soul for he hath delivred my soul my soul fro
Death my feet from fall = = ling For he hath delivred my soul for he hath delivred my soul my
Soul my soul from death my feet from fal = ling
Death mine from tears my feet from fal = ling I shall walk I shall walk before the Lord in ye
soul from death mine eyes from tears my feet from falling

Land of the li- - ving.
I shall walk I shall
Land of the li- - ving
I shall walk I shall walk before the Ld in ye Land of ye li- - ving
walk before the Ld in ye land of ye li- - - ving
For he hath delivred my soul my
For he hath de livred my soul my soul from death mine
For he hath delivred my soul my soul from
soul from death my feet from fal- ling. Turn turn again thou turn again unto thy rest O my-
eyes from tears my feet from fal- ling. Turn turn a- gain thou turn a- gain unto thy rest O my
death my feet from fal- ling. Turn turn a- gain thou turn a- gain unto thy rest O my
soul for ye Ld hath rewarded thee he hath rewarded Thee
For he hath delivred my soul my
soul for the Ld hath rewarded thee he hath rewarded thee for he hath de- livred my soul my soul fro death mine
soul, For ye Lord hath rewarded thee For he hath delivred my soul my soul fro

soul from death my feet from fall = = ing, For he hath de- livred my soul for he hath delivred my
eyes from tears my feet from fal = ing for he hath delivred my soul for he hath delivred my soul my soul from
death my feet from fal = = = ing for he hath delivred my soul for he hath delivred my soul my
soul my soul from death my feet from fal = = = = = - ing For he hath delivred my soul my soul from
death mine eyes from tears my feet from fal = For he hath delivred my soul my soul fro=
soul from death mine eyes from tears my feet from falling he hath delivred my soul from death mine eyes from
death mine eyes from tears my feet from fall = ing. I will pay my vows unto the Lord.
death mine eyes from tears my feet from fall = ing. I will pay my vows unto the Lord –
tears my feet from fall = ing. I will pay my vows unto the Lord
in ye sight of his people. in ye courts of ye Lords house even in ye midst of thee O Je = rusa =
in ye sight of his people in ye courts of ye Lords house even in ye midst of thee O Jerusal =
in ye sight of his people in ye courts of ye Lords house even in ye midst of thee O Jerusa =

Cho:
Alleluia.
Dr Aldrich

Prelude.
Anthem. Dr Blow.
153
Sing
Mr Howel
O Sing unto ye Lord Sing unto ye
Mr Barns
O Sing unto ye Lord a new Song sing unto ye Lord a new Sing unto ye
Sing-
Sing Sing unto ye
Mr Williams
O Sing unto ye Ld a new Song Sing unto ye Lord
Mr Edwards

unto ye Ld a new Song, Sing unto ye Lord Sing unto ye Lord unto the Ld all-
Lord Sing unto ye Lord a new Song, Sing unto the Lord Sing unto the Lord
Lord Sing unto ye Lord all the whole earth, Sing unto ye Lord Sing unto the
Sing unto ye Lord all ye whole earth Sing unto ye Lord Sing unto ye Lord all-
Lord Sing un- to the Lord all the whole earth, Sing unto the Lord Sing unto ye Lord all
Sing unto ye Lord unto ye Ld a new Song Sing unto ye Lord Sing unto the Lord all
all the whole Earth. alleluia alle-
Lord all ye whole Earth. alleluia allelu- ia alle- lu-
all. all ye whole Earth
all the whole Earth allelu- ia allelu- ia alleluia alle-
all the whole Earth allelu- ia allelu- ia alle-

lu = = ia
Sing unto the Lord & praise his name
alleluia
alleluia Sing unto ye Lord and praise his name
Sing unto ye Lord & praise his name.
allelu = ia, allelu = ia
lu = ia Sing unto ye Lord & praise his name alleluia
alleluia allelu =
lu = ia allelu = ia alleluia allelu = ia alleluia Sing
lu = ia alleluia alleluia allelu = alleluia allelu = = ia allelu =
allelu allelu = ia alleluia al = le = lu = ia
allelu = ia alleluia allelu ia allelu = ia alleluia al = le = lu = ia
alleluia allelu ia allelu ia alleluia allelu = ia allelu =
ia Sing un = to ye Lord & praise his name alleluia. allelu = ia alleluia al = le = lu
Sing unto the Lord & praise his name allelu ia allelu =

Slow.
allelu= ia sing unto ye Ld & praise his name be telling of his sal= vation from day to
sing unto ye Ld & praise his name alleluia, be telling of his salvation from
Bem.
iah sing unto ye Ld & praise his name Be
Bem sing unto ye Ld & praise his name
76
Day from day to day be telling of his sal= vation from day to day be telling of his sal=
day to day from day to day be telling of his sal= va= tion be=
telling of his salvation from day from day to day from day to day be telling of his sal=
be telling of his sal= vation from day to day be telling of his sal= vation from day to

ration from day to day
be telling of his Sal=
ration from day to
day.
telling of his salvation from
day to day from
day to
day.
=ration from day to
day from day to day from
day to=
day
day be
telling of his salvation from
day to
day
Vers: Mr Barnes
De=
clare declare his
Mr Church
Declare de=
=clare declare his
honour his hono un=
=to ye heathen
hono his hono un=
=to ye heathen
And his
Mr Williams
Declare de=
clare his hono his
hono declare his
hono unto the—

& his won=ders his won=ders & his wonders his wonders unto all people & cannot
won==ders his wondzers his won=ders and his wonders unto all people for ye Lord is great & cannot
heathen declare declare his hono unto the heathen for the Lord is great
cannot cannot worthily be praised. & cannot cannot & cannot cannot cannot worthy=
cannot cannot worthily be praised. & cannot cannot & cannot cannot can=not
For ye Lord is great & cannot cannot cannot worthily be
=ly be praised he is more more to be feared to be feared ye all all Gods For ye Lord is
worthily be praised he is more more to be feared to be feared ye all all Gods For ye Lord is
praised he is more more more to be feared to be feared than all Gods for ye Lord is great
great & cannot cannot & cannot cannot cannot cannot worthily be praised he is
great & cannot cannot & cannot cannot worthily be prai==sed he is
& cannot cannot & cannot cannot cannot worthily be praised he is more

more more to be feared is more to be fear= =ed than all Gods
more more to be feared, is more to be fear= ed than all - Gods.
more more to be feared is more to be feared to be feared than all Gods
Glory and worship Glory and worship Glory, Glory and worship are before him.
Mr Howell Glory and worship Glory and worship Glory & worship are be- -fore him.
Mr Barn Glory and worship Glory and worship Glory Glory and worship are be= fore him.
Glory and worship Glory and worship Glory Glory and worship are be fore him.
Glory and worship Glory and worship Glory Glory and worship are be= fore him.
Glory & worship Glory and worship Glory and worship are be= fore him.

160
Glory & worship Glory and worship pow'r and hono' pow'r & hono' are
Glory & worship- Glory and worship pow'r and hono', pow'r & hono' are
Idem-
Glory & worship- Glory & worship- pow'r and hono' pow'r & hono' are
Glory & worship Glory & worship pow'r and hono', pow'r & hono' are
in his sanctu- ary- Glory and worship, pow'r and honour pow'r and
in his sanctu- ary- Glory and worship pow'r and honour, pow'r and
Idem
In his sanctu- ary- Glory and worship, pow'r and honour, pow'r and
in his sanctu- ary, Glory and worship, pow'r and honour, pow'r and,

hono are in his Sanctu- ary Glory & worship pow'r and hono pow'r & hono are
in his Sanctu- ary.
Alleluia alleluia allelu- ia
Allelu- ia allelu- ia allelu-
Allelu- ia allelu-

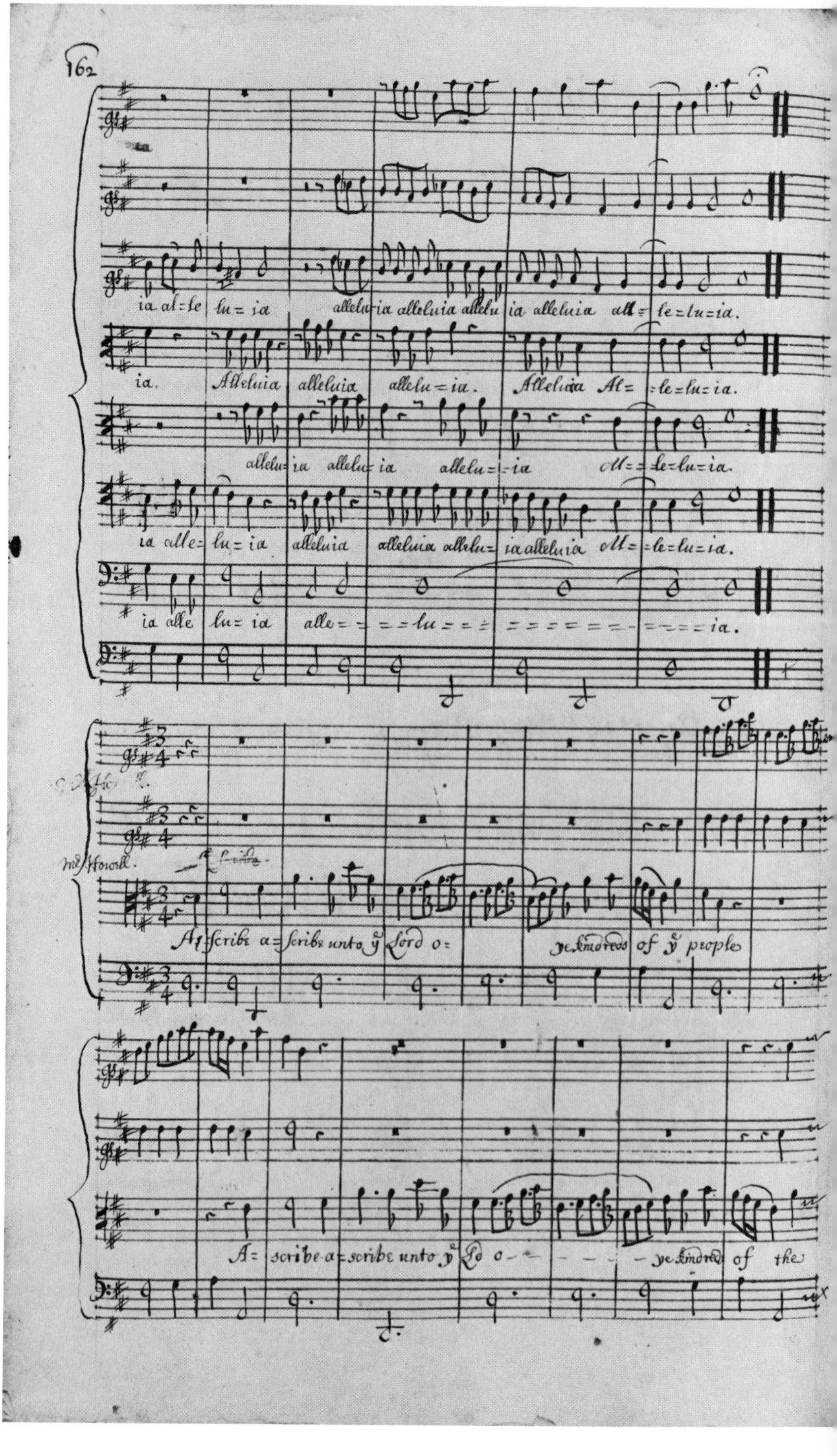
162
ia al=le lu=ia alleluia alleluia alleluia alleluia all= le=lu=ia.
ia. Alleluia alleluia allelu=ia. Alleluia Al= =le=lu=ia.
allelu=ia allelu=ia allelu=ia All= =le=lu=ia.
ia alle=lu=ia alleluia alleluia allelu=ia alleluia All= =le=lu=ia.
ia alle lu=ia alle=lu= ia.
Mr Howell.
Ascribe a=scribe unto ye Lord o= ye kindreds of ye people
A= scribe a=scribe unto ye Lo o ye kindred of the

people
A= scribe unto ye Lord wor= ship wor= ship ascribe unto ye
Lord wor= = ship worship & Powr_
A= scribe unto ye
Lord a= scribe unto ye Lord the hon= =or the ho= nor the ho= = = = = = = = = = = = = = =
= nor due ye hon= = = = or due unto his Name bring Presents & come into his Courts come in

to his Courts come in= to his Courts in= to his Courts bring presents & come into his Courts come in
to his Courts come into his Courts come into his Courts
Full.
O wor= = = =
O wor= = ship
O wor= = = = = = = =
O wor= = = = = ship ye
= = = = = = ship ye Lord in the Beau= ty of ho= = liness of holiness of
wor= = = = ship the Lord O wor= = ship O wor= ship ye Lord in ye
= ship worship the Lord O wor= = = ship ye Lord worship the
Lord O wor= ship ye Lord in the Beauty of ho= li= ness of ho= = = = =
ho= = = = = = = = = liness Violins
Beauty of ho= = liness
Lord in the Beauty of holiness Let ye whole earth
liness Let ye

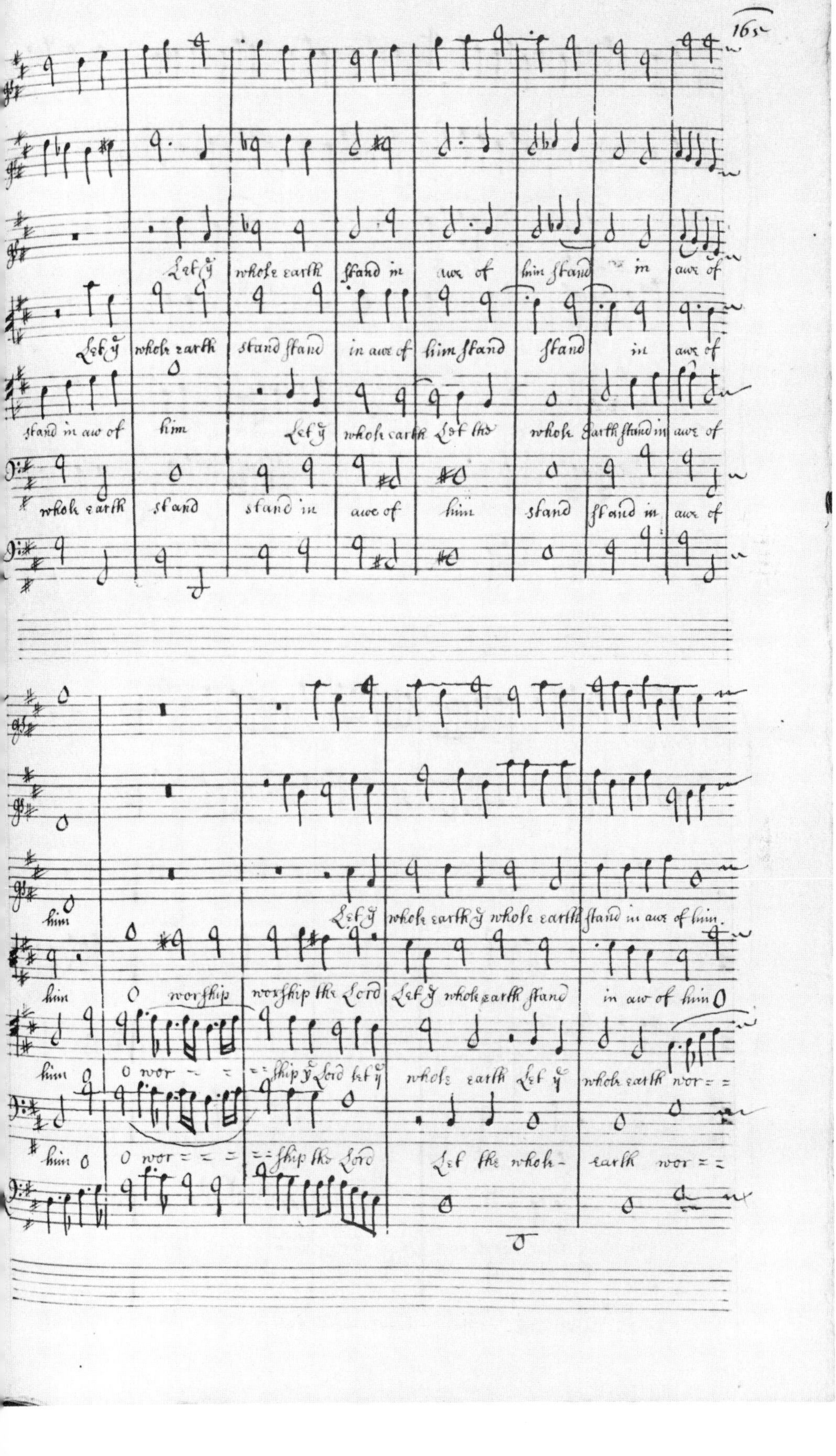
165r
Let y whole earth stand in awe of him stand in awe of
Let y whole earth stand stand in awe of him stand stand in awe of
stand in aw of him Let y whole earth Let the whole earth stand in awe of
whole earth stand stand in awe of him stand stand in awe of
him Let y whole earth y whole earth stand in awe of him.
him O worship worship the Lord Let y whole earth stand in aw of him O
him O wor = = ship y Lord let y whole earth Let y whole earth wor = =
him O wor = = = ship the Lord Let the whole earth wor = =

O wor= ship the Lord O wor= Ship ye Lord let ye whole earth
wor= ship ye Lord let ye whole Earth, worship worship ye Lord Let ye
ship worship ye Lord O wor= Ship ye Lord Let ye
ship the Lord O wor= Ship ye Lord let ye whole earth Let ye
Let ye whole Earth Stand Stand in aw in aw of him.
whole Earth Let ye whole earth Stand Stand in aw of him Allelia allelu:
Let ye whole earth Allelu=
whole earth Let ye whole earth Stand Stand in aw of him
whole earth let ye whole earth Stand Stand in aw of him
let ye whole earth let ye whole earth Stand in aw of him

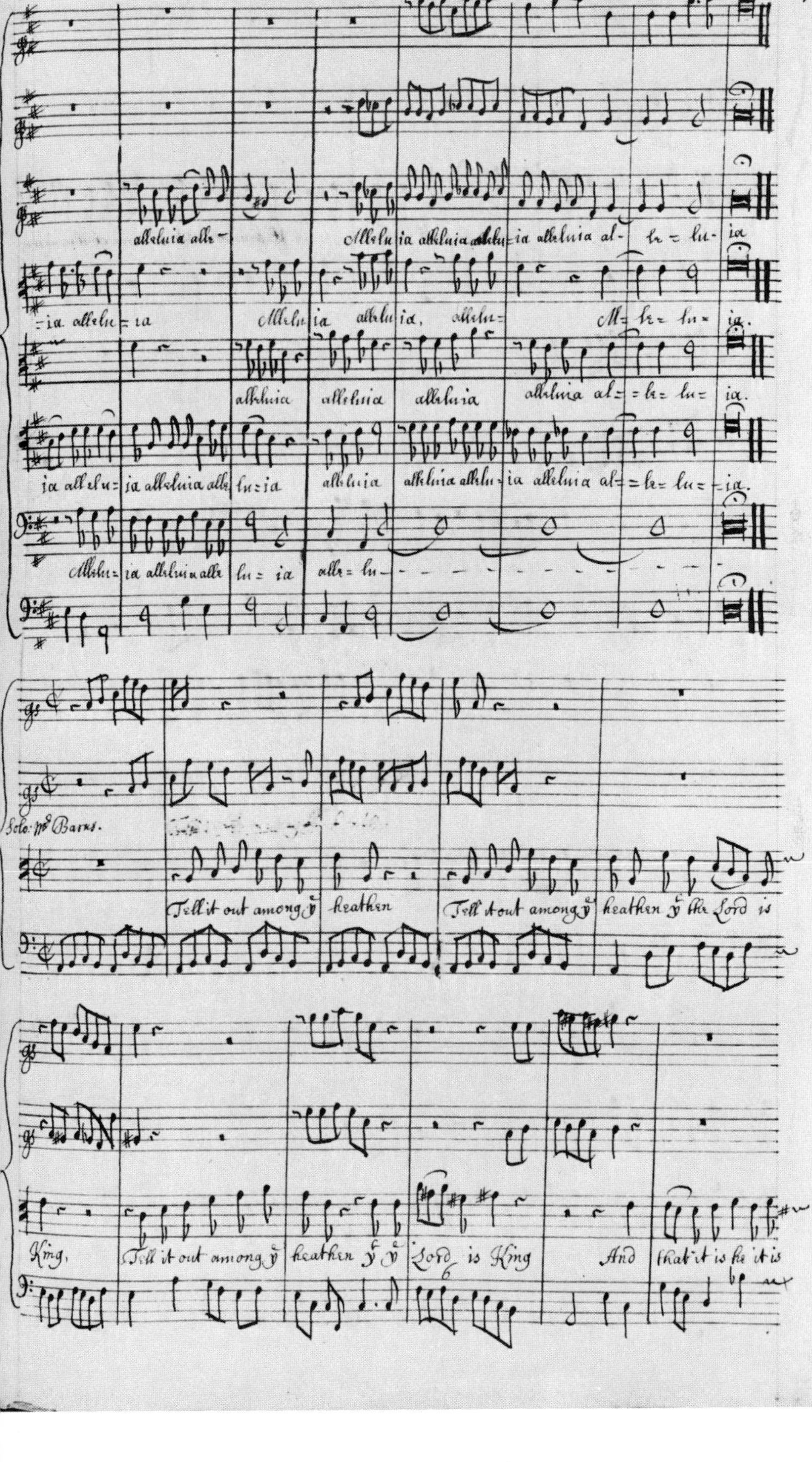
alleluia alle- Allelu ia alleluia allelu ia alleluia al- le- lu- ia
-ia allelu- ia Allelu ia allelu ia, allelu- Al- le- lu- ia.
alleluia alleluia alleluia alleluia al- le- lu- ia.
ia allelu- ia alleluia alle lu- ia alleluia alleluia allelu- ia alleluia al- le- lu- ia.
Allelu- ia alleluia alle lu- ia alle- lu-
Solo: Mr Barns.
Tell it out among ye heathen Tell it out among ye heathen ye the Lord is
King, Tell it out among ye heathen ye ye Lord is King And that it is he it is

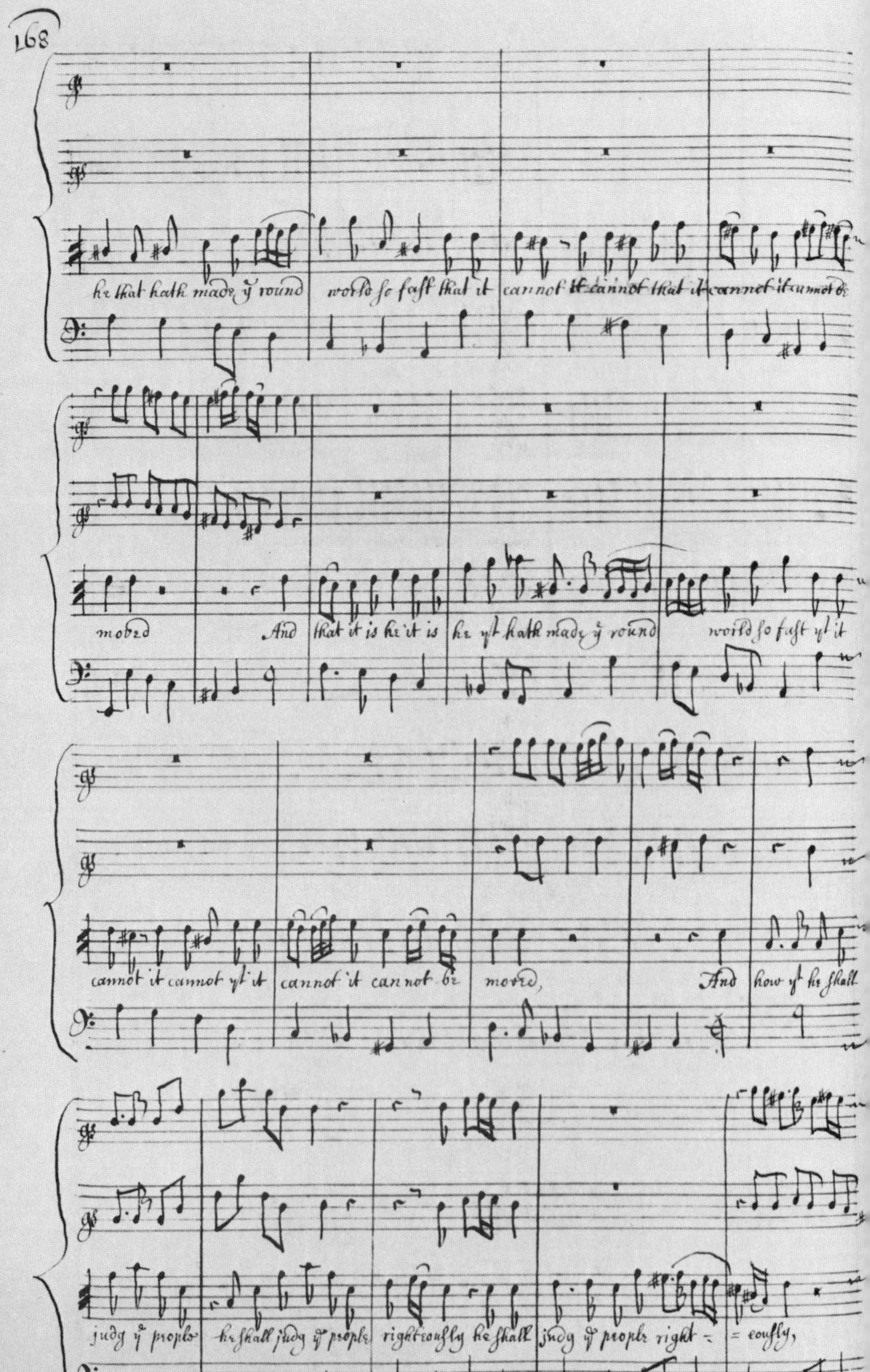
168
he that hath made ye round
world so fast that it
cannot it cannot that it
cannot it cannot be
moved
And
that it is he it is
he yt hath made ye round
world so fast yt it
cannot it cannot yt it
cannot it cannot be
moved,
And
how yt he shall
judg ye people
he shall judg ye people
righteously he shall
judg ye people right =
= eously,

and how yt he shall judg & he shall judg ye people righteously.
Let the heav'ns rejoice Let ye heavns re= joice Re= joice, & let ye earth be
Let ye heavns rejoice re= joice Let ye heavns re = = joyce & let ye earth be-
Let ye heavns re= joyce rejoyce. Re= joice rejoyce. & let ye earth be
Let ye heavns rejoyce - Let ye heavns rejoice rejoice & let ye earth be
Let ye heavns re= joice Let ye heavns rejoice Let ye heavns re= joice & let ye earth be
Let ye heavns re= rejoice Let ye heavns rejoice & let ye earth be

glad Let ye Sea make a noise make a noise and all that therein is let ye
glad Let ye Sea make a noise Let ye Sea make a noise & all yt therein is
glad let ye Sea make a noise let the Sea make a noise and all that therein is let ye
glad let the Sea make a noise let ye Sea make a noise & all yt therein is let ye
glad Let ye Sea make a noise and all yt therein is
glad let ye Sea make a noise Let ye Sea make a noise & all yt therein is
Sea make a noise let ye Sea make a noise and all ye therein is.
Let ye Sea make a noise let ye Sea make a noise and all yt therein is.
Sea make a noise let ye Sea make a noise and all ye therein is let the
Sea make a noise let ye Sea make a noise and all that therein is let the
Let ye Sea make a noise all that therein is let the
Let ye Sea make a noise Let ye Sea make a noise & all yt therein is.

Be joyfull be joyfull
Be joyfull be Let ye Feild be joy = full && all that is in it.
Feild ye Feild be joyfull be joyfull let ye Feild be joy full && all that is in it.
Feild ye Feild be joyfull be joyfull
Feild be joyfull be joyfull let ye Feild be joy full & all that is in it
be joyfull be joyfull
Then shall all the Trees of the wood rejoyce re = joyce then shall all all the
Then shall all all the Trees of ye wood rejoyce re = joyce then shall all all the
Then shall all all the Trees of ye wood rejoice rejoice then shall all all the
Then shall all all the Trees of ye wood rejoyce rejoice then shall all all the
Then shall all all the Trees all rejoyce rejoice then shall all all the
Then shall all all the Trees of ye wood rejoice re = joice then shall all all the

172
Trees of the wood rejoice rejoice before ye Lord
Trees of the wood rejoice rejoice before the Lord.
Trees of the wood rejoice rejoice rejoice before the Lord.
Trees of the wood rejoice rejoice rejoice re joice before ye Lord. Mr Ethrick.
Trees of the wood rejoice rejoice before the Lord For he cometh he
Trees of the wood rejoice rejoice rejoice before the Lord.
cometh, for he cometh he cometh to judg the Earth, And with Righteou
=ness to judg the world wth Righteousness to judg the world and the people the

173
people with his Truth, For he cometh he cometh, For he cometh he cometh to judg ye
Earth, & wth Righteousness to judg the world & ye people with his Truth ye People with his
Truth.
End with ye Chorus
O worship ye Lord
as before:
Page 164
Dr Blow.
musical meeting .

Tenor Solo.

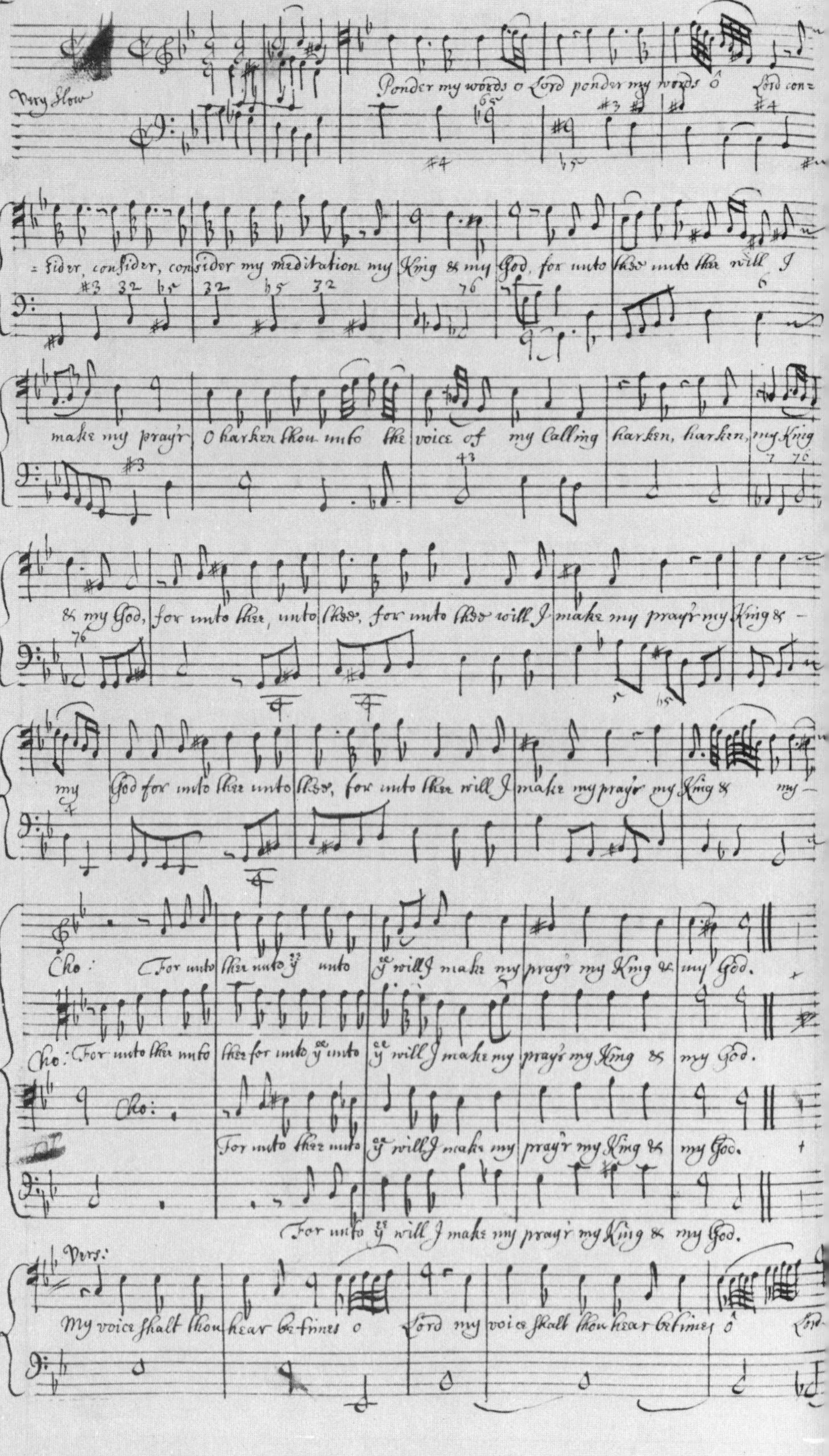
Very Slow
Ponder my words o Lord ponder my words o Lord con=
=sider, consider, consider my meditation my King & my God, for unto thee unto thee will I
make my pray'r O harken thou unto the voice of my Calling harken, harken, my King
& my God, for unto thee, unto thee, for unto thee will I make my pray'r my King & -
my God for unto thee unto thee, for unto thee will I make my pray'r my King & my-
Cho: For unto thee unto ye unto ye will I make my pray'r my King & my God.
Cho: For unto thee unto thee for unto ye unto ye will I make my pray'r my King & my God.
Cho:
For unto thee unto ye will I make my pray'r my King & my God.
For unto ye will I make my pray'r my King & my God.
Vers:
My voice shalt thou hear betimes o Lord my voice shalt thou hear betimes o Lord

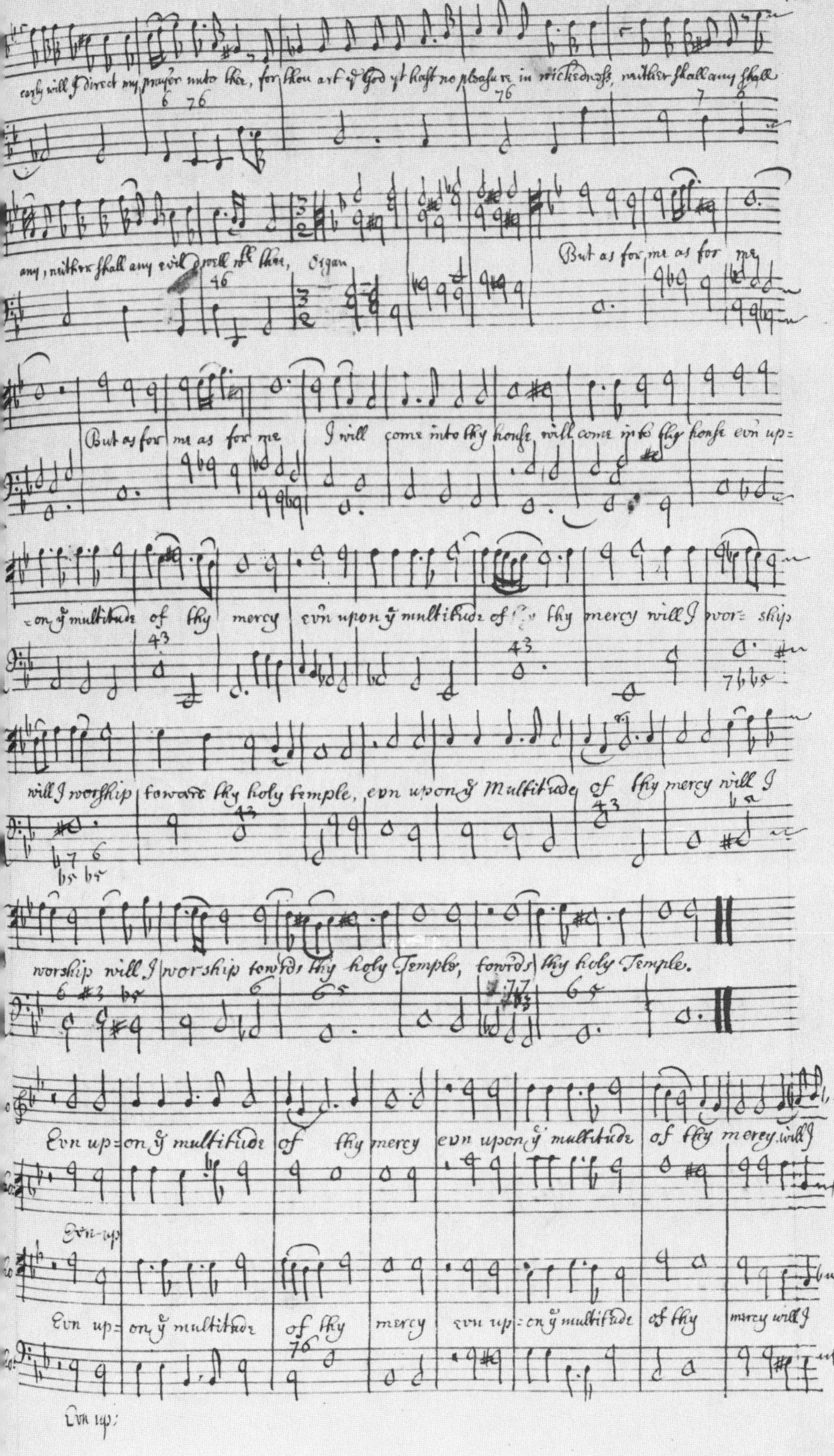
early will I direct my prayer unto thee, for thou art y^e God y^t hast no pleasure in wickedness, neither shall any evil
any, neither shall any evil dwell with thee, Organ
But as for me as for me
But as for me as for me I will come into thy house, will come into thy house even up=
=on y^e multitude of thy mercy even upon y^e multitude of thy mercy will I wor= ship
will I worship toward thy holy temple, even upon y^e Multitude of thy mercy will I
worship will I worship towrds thy holy Temple, towrds thy holy Temple.
Even up=on y^e multitude of thy mercy even upon y^e multitude of thy mercy will I
Even up
Even up=on y^e multitude of thy mercy even up=on y^e multitude of thy mercy will I
Even up;

worship will I worship thee towards thy holy temple.
worship will I worship thee towards thy holy Temple.
Organ
Lead me o Lord in thy righteousness. in thy Righteousness. Lead me o Lord in thy
Righteousness, be- cause of all mine Enemies make thy way plain be- fore thy face
Lead me o Lord in thy righteousness. make thy way plain be fore thy Face & let all them-
let all them that put their trust in thee rejoice
They shall be ever ev-
ever shall be ever giving thanks because thou defendest them. they that love thy name shall be joy - - full in
thee shall be joyfull, shall be joy- full shall be joy full in thee.
Cho:

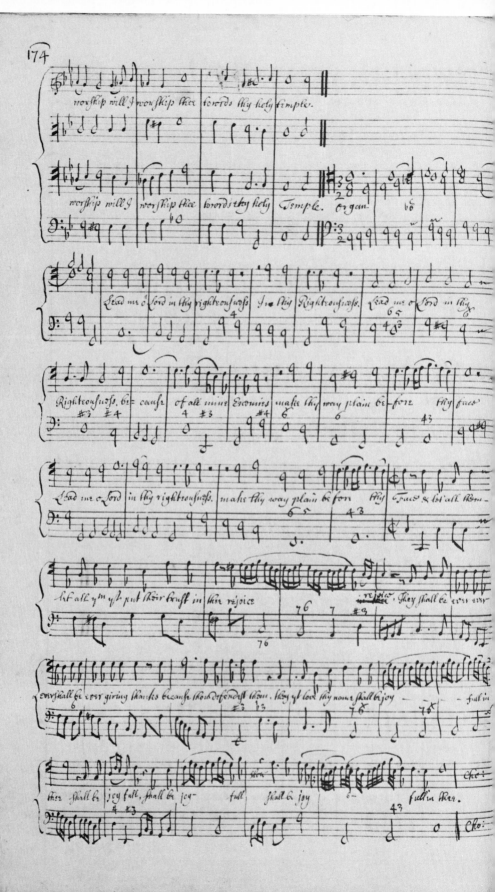

They yt love thy name shall be joy - full in - Thee they yt love thy name shall be
They yt love thy name shall be joyfull be joy - full in Thee shall be Joy -
They that love thy name shall be Joy - full shall be
They yt love thy Name shall be
full in Thee they yt love thy name shall be joy - full shall be joy - - full in thee shall be
full in Thee They yt love thy name, shall be Joy
full in Thee they yt love thy Name shall be Joyfull be joy -
Joy - full in Thee They that love thy name shall be joy -
Joyfull in Thee.
Dr Blow:
full in - Thee
full in Thee
Thee.

176
Be mercifull &c
Dr Blow
Be mercifull be mercifull unto me O God O
Be mer-cifull be mercifull unto me O God be mercifull be mercifull
Be mercifull be mercifull unto me O God be mercifull
God be mercifull, unto me be mercifull be mercifull unto me be mercifull unto me
unto me O God be mercifull be mercifull unto me be mercifull unto me
be mercifull unto me be mercifull unto me For my
Soul my Soul trusteth in thee & under ye shadow of thy wings shall be my Refuge shall be my
For my Soul my Soul trusteth in thee & under ye shadow under the shadow of thy wings shall be my
For my Soul my Soul trusteth in thee & under ye shadow under ye shadow of thy wings shall be my
Refuge

Refuge shall be my Refuge, untill this Tyranny be
Refuge shall be my Refuge untill this Tyranny this Tyranny be
O God be mer = cifull be mer = cifull un = to me
Over past. O God be mer = cifull be mer = ci = full unto me.
Over past, O God be mer = cifull be mer = cifull unto me.
Untill this Tyranny this Tyranny be over = past untill this
Untill this Tyranny this Tyranny be over = past. O
Untill this Tyranny this Tyranny be over = = past, O God
Tyranny this Tyranny be o = ver past untill this Tyranny this Tyranny be over past
God be mer = = cifull be mer = ci = full un = to me.
be mer = ci = full be mer = cifull un = to me.
be mercy = full be mercifull un = = to = me.

178
Vers: 2 voc
I will call will call up= on ye most high God, will call upon ye most high God
I will call will
I will call will call I will call up= on ye most high
call up= on ye most high God I will call will call I will call upon ye most high
God even un= to the God that shall per= form ye Cause yt shall per= form ye
God even un= to the God that shall per= form ye Cause
Cause wch I have in hand that shall per= form ye Cause wch I have in hand that shall
that shall per= form ye Cause shall per= form ye Cause wch I have in hand yt shall per= form shall
form shall per form, ye cause wch I have in hand. I will call will call up= on ye most high God
form shall per form ye Cause wch I have in hand I will call

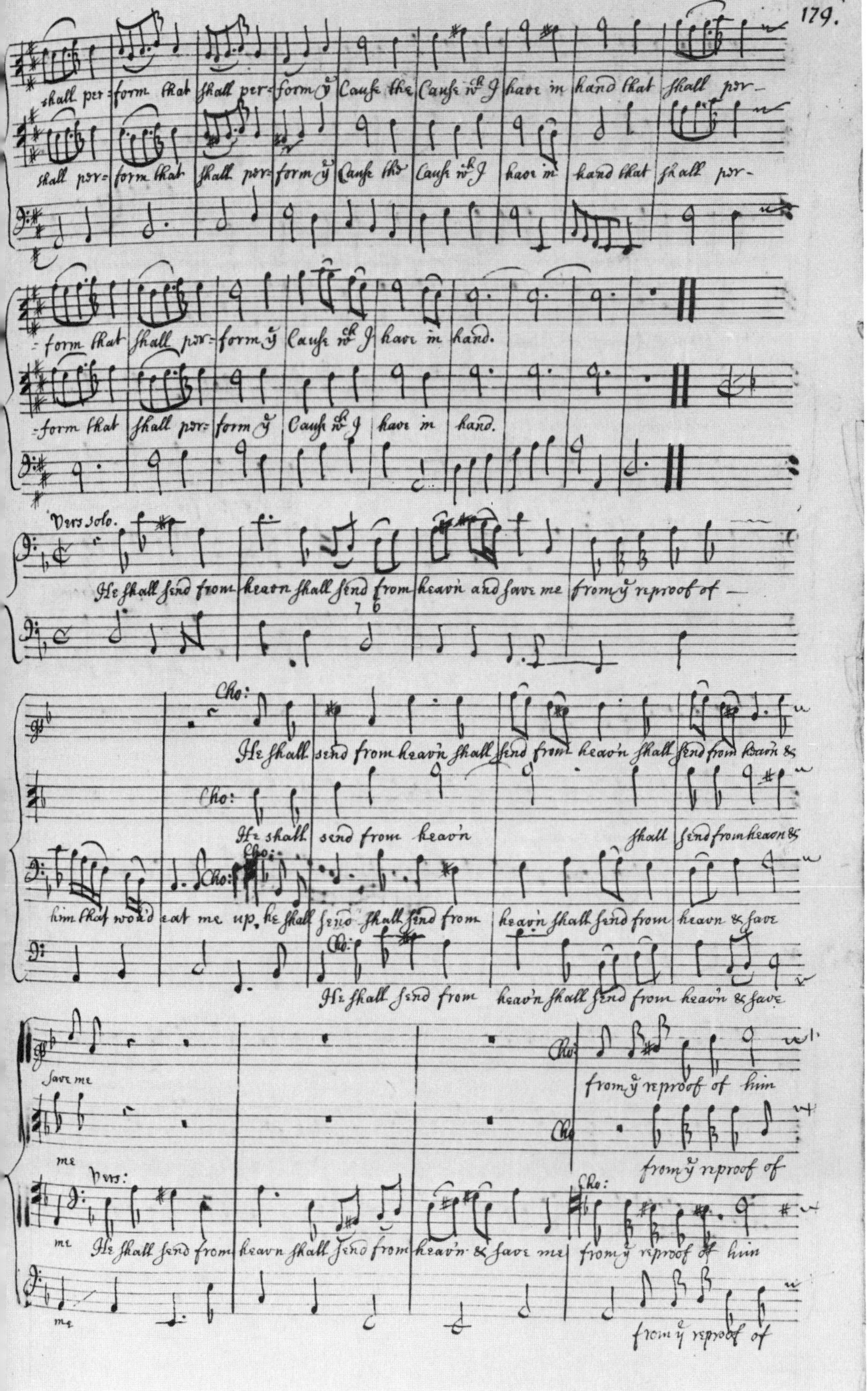
shall per- form that shall per- form ye Cause the Cause wch I have in hand that shall per-
shall per- form that shall per- form ye Cause the Cause wch I have in hand that shall per-
- form that shall per- form ye Cause wch I have in hand.
- form that shall per- form ye Cause wch I have in hand.
Vers solo.
He shall send from heav'n shall send from heav'n and save me from ye reproof of -
Cho:
He shall send from heav'n shall send from heav'n shall send from heav'n &
Cho:
He shall send from heav'n shall send from heav'n &
Cho:
him that would eat me up, he shall send shall send from heav'n shall send from heav'n & save
He shall send from heav'n shall send from heav'n & save
save me
Cho:
from ye reproof of him
me
Cho
from ye reproof of
Vers:
me He shall send from heavn shall send from heav'n & save me from ye reproof of him
me
from ye reproof of

from ye Reproof of him, from ye Reproof of him yt would eat me up.
him from ye Reproof of him him that would eat me up.
from ye Reproof of him from ye Reproof of him that would eat me up - God shall send forth his
him from ye Reproof of him of him that would Eat me up
Cho
He shall send from heavn shall
Cho:
He shall send from heavn shall
mercy his mer = cy & truth my Soul is among Lions
Cho:
He shall send shall send from
Cho:
He shall send from
send from heavn and save me
send from heavn and save me
heavn from heavn and save me God shall send forth his mercy & truth shall
heavn from heavn and save me
Cho:
My soul is among Lions
Cho:
my soul is among Lions
Cho:
send forth his mercy & truth my soul is among Lions
My soul is among Lions
Cho:
My soul is among Lions

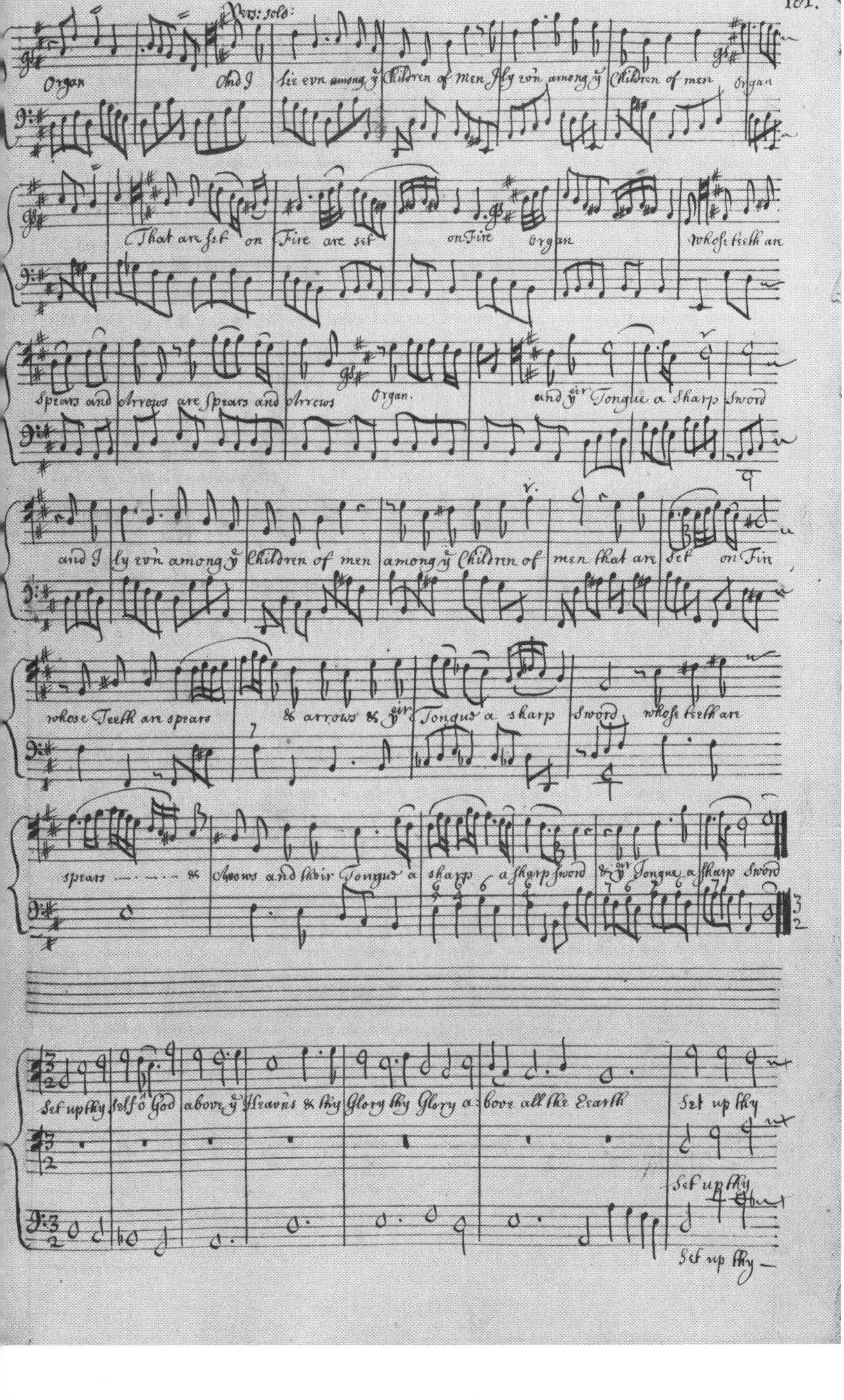
Vers: solo:
Organ
And I
lie even among ye Children of men I ly even among ye Children of men
Organ
That are set on Fire are set on Fire
Organ
whose teeth are
Spears and Arrows are Spears and Arrows
Organ.
and yeir Tongue a sharp Sword
and I ly even among ye Children of men among ye Children of men that are set on Fire
whose Teeth are spears & arrows & yeir Tongue a sharp Sword, whose teeth are
spears — & Arrows and their Tongue a sharp a sharp sword & yeir Tongue a sharp Sword
Set up thy self O God above ye Heavens & thy Glory thy Glory a-bove all the Earth
Set up thy
Set up thy
Set up thy —

Self o God above the heavns & thy Glory thy Glory above all ye Earth. Set up thy Self O God
Self o God above the heavns & thy Glory thy Glory above all ye Earth.
Self o God above the heavns & thy Glory thy Glory a=bove all the Earth
above ye heavns & thy Glory thy Glory a= bove all the Earth Set up thy Self o God above the
Set up thy Self o God above the
Set up thy Self o God above the
heavns & thy Glory thy Glory a= bove all the Earth above all the Earth. Cho: Glory be to ye
heavns & thy Glory thy Glory a- bove all the Earth above all the Earth Cho:
heavns & thy Glory thy Glory a= bove all the Earth above all the Earth Glory be to ye father &
Glory be to the Father & to ye Son & to the holy Ghost & to the holy Ghost. as it was in the begining is
Father & to the Son and to the Son and to ye Son and to the holy Ghost as it was as it was in the begining is
Glory be to ye father & to ye Son and to ye Son and to the holy Ghost as it was in the be- gining is
to the Son Glory be to ye father & to the Son & to the holy Ghost as it was in the be= gining is
now and ever shall be and ever shall be and e= ver ever shall be world without End A= men A= men
now and ever shall be and ever shall be and ever ever shall be world without End A men A= = men
now is now is now and ever shall be and ever and ever shall be world without End A= men A= men
now is now is now & Ever shall be and ever and ever shall be world without End A- men A= men

Thy hands have made me & fashioned me, Thy hands have made me and fashioned me
Thy hands have made me & fashioned me, Thy hands have made me and fashioned me
Thy hands have made me & fashioned me Thy hands have made me and fashioned me o give me under=
Thy hands have made me & fashioned me Thy hands have made me and fashioned me, O give me,
O give me understanding that I may learn may learn thy Com= mandments,
give me under= standing yt I may learn yt I may learn thy Com= mandments O give me
standing yt I may learn that I may learn may learn thy Com= mandments O give me Understanding yt
Understanding O Give me under= standing yt I may learn thy Commandments O give me under=
give me under= standing yt I may learn thy Commandments
Understanding that I may learn thy Command- ments They that
I may learn that I may learn thy Com= mandments They that fear thee may be glad may be
=standing yt I may learn that I may learn thy Commandments They that fear thee may be
They that fear thee that fear thee may be glad when they see me they that fear thee, that
fear thee that fear thee that fear thee may be glad when they see me they that fear thee, that
glad when they see me yt fear thee may be glad when they see me they that fear thee
glad when they see me they that fear thee may be glad when they see me they that fear thee.

fear thee may be glad be glad may be glad when they see me, Be= cause I have put my
fear thee may be glad may be glad when they see me, Because I have
That fear thee may be glad when they see me. Be=
They that fear thee may be glad wn they see me be cause I have put my Trust
Trust in thy word Because I have put my Trust in thy word. O let thy
put my Trust in thy word because I have put my Trust in thy word, O let thy
= cause I have put my trust because I have put my Trust in thy word O let thy mer=
In thy word Be= cause I have put my Trust in thy word O let thy
mercifull kindness let thy mercifull kindness be my Comfort ac= cording to thy word unto thy
mercifull kindness let thy mercifull kindness be my Comfort.
= cifull kindness let thy mercifull kindness be my Comfort. according to thy
mercifull kindness let thy mercifull kindness be my Comfort. ac= cording
Servant un, to thy Servant ac= cording to thy word according to thy word unto thy Servant.
Ac= cording to thy word unto thy Servt accord= ding to thy word un= to thy Servant.
word unto thy Servant according to thy word ac= cording to thy word un- to thy Servant.
to thy word according ac= cording to thy word according to thy word un= to thy Servant.

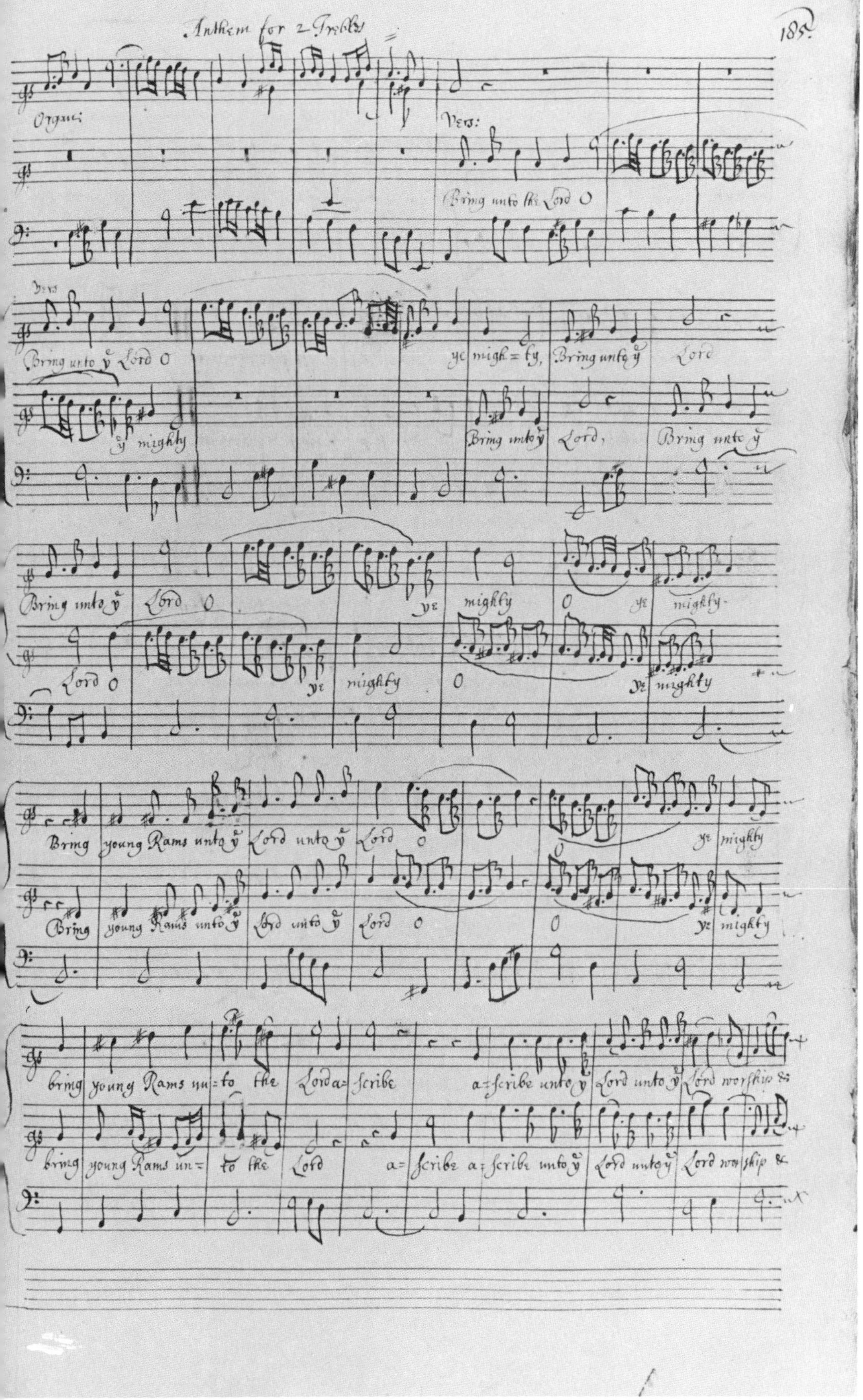
Anthem for 2 Trebles
185
Organ
Vers:
Bring unto the Lord O
Bring unto ye Lord O ye migh=ty, Bring unto ye Lord
ye mighty
Bring unto ye Lord, Bring unto ye
Bring unto ye Lord O ye mighty O ye mighty
Lord O ye mighty O ye mighty
Bring young Rams unto ye Lord unto ye Lord O ye mighty
Bring young Rams unto ye Lord unto ye Lord O O ye mighty
bring young Rams un=to the Lord a=scribe a=scribe unto ye Lord unto ye Lord worship &
bring young Rams un= to the Lord a= scribe a= scribe unto ye Lord unto ye Lord worship &

Strength O ye mighty A= scribe unto ye Lord wor= - ship wor= ship
Strength O ye mighty A= scribe unto ye Lord Un= to ye Lord wor= ship wor= ship
A= scribe unto ye Lord wor- - - - - - ship worship & Strength. Organ.
A= scribe unto ye Lord wor- - - - ship worship & Strength.
Give ye Ld the honour due unto his
Give ye Ld the honor due unto his name
name the honor due the honor the honor due unto his name
Give ye Lord Give the Lord Give the unto his Name Give ye Ld the honor
Give ye Ld the honor due unto his name un= to his name wor= = = = ship wor=
due unto his name. The honor due un- to his name, wor= skip

ship wor - - - - - - - - ship ye Lord wth ho = = ly holy worship with holy ho=
wor - - ship wor= ship ye Lord wth ho = = = ly worship wth ho - ly ho=
ly worship. Cho: Worship ye Lord wth holy worship wor ship, ye Lord with holy ho
ly worship Cho Worship the Lord wth holy worship wor ship ye Lord wth ho=
Cho: Worship the Lord wth holy worship wor ship ye Ld wth ho = = =
Cho: Worship ye Lord wth holy worship wor - ship ye Ld wth holy worship wth
ly holy worship
Vers
ly worship. It is the Lord It is the Lord ye Com=
Organ
ly holy worship. It is the Lord It is the
holy holy worship
=mandeth com = man deth ye waters. It is the Glo = = = = = = = = = = rious
Lord yt Com = mandeth the waters. It is the glo - rious God

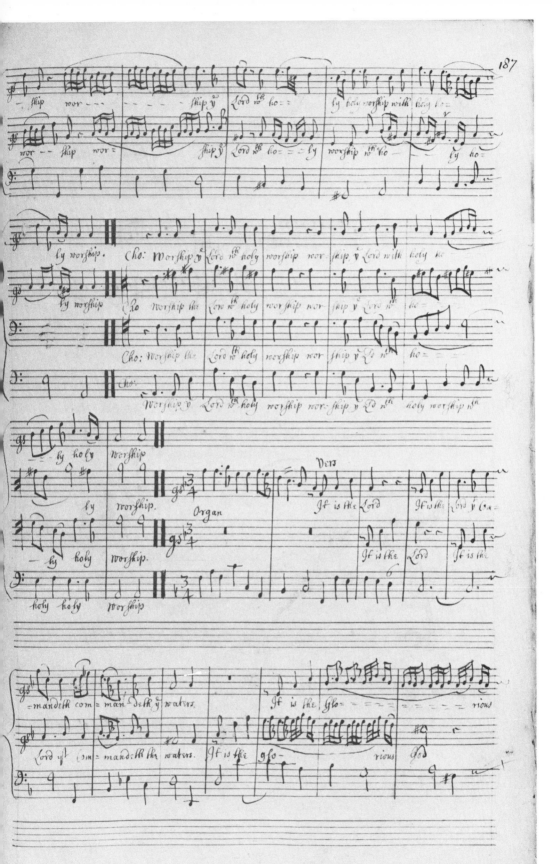

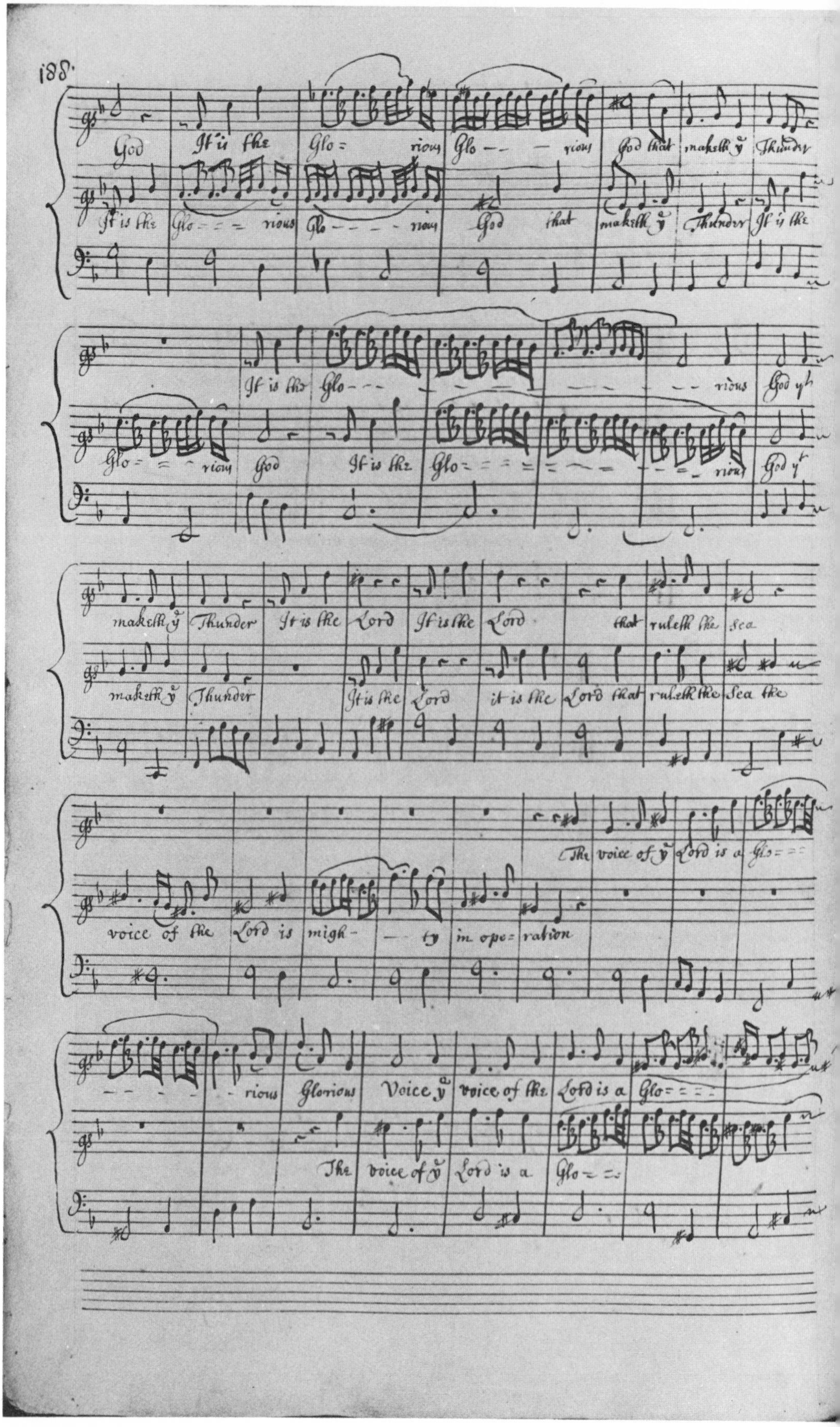
188
God It is the Glo= rious Glo— rious God that maketh ye Thunder
It is the Glo— rious Glo— rious God that maketh ye Thunder It is the
It is the Glo— rious God yt
Glo— rious God It is the Glo— rious God yt
maketh ye Thunder It is the Lord It is the Lord that ruleth the Sea
maketh ye Thunder It is the Lord it is the Lord that ruleth the Sea the
The voice of ye Lord is a Glo=
voice of the Lord is migh— ty in ope=ration
— rious Glorious Voice ye voice of the Lord is a Glo=
The voice of ye Lord is a Glo=

rious Glorious voice a Glo= rious Glorious voice Cho:
rious Glorious voice A Glo= rious Glorious voice Cho:
Cho:
The voice of the Lord is mighty is mighty is mighty in O= pe= ration The voice of ye Lord,
The voice of the Lord is mighty is mighty is mighty in O= pe= ration. The voice of ye Lord is mighty is
The voice of the Lord is mighty is mighty is mighty in O- pe= ration The voice of ye Lord is mighty is
The voice of the Lord is mighty is mighty is mighty in Ope- ration The voice of the Lord is mighty is
is mighty in Operation ye Voice of ye Lord is a
mighty is mighty in Operation The voice of ye Lord is a Glo= rious Glo-
mighty is mighty in Operation The voice of ye Lord is a Glo= rious voice a
mighty is mighty in Operation The voice of ye Lord is a Glo= rious
Glo= rious Glorious voice
rious Glorious voice a Glo= rious Glo= rious voice.
Dr Blow.
Glo: rious voice a Glo rious Glorious voice.
voice a Glo- rious Glorious voice.

140. Vers: 3 voc.
O how amia-ble are thy Dwellings thou Lord thou Lord thou
O how ami-a-ble are thy Dwellings thou Lord thou Lord of Hosts thou Lord thou
Oh how ami-a-ble are thy Dwellings thou
Lord of Hosts thou Ld thou Lord thou Lord of Hosts.
Rit.
Lord of Hosts thou Ld thou Lord thou Lord of Hosts
Lord of Hosts thou Ld thou Lord thou Lord of Hosts.
O how amiable
O how ami-a-ble are thy dwellings thou Lord thou Lord of
O how amiable are thy dwellings are thy dwellings thou Lord thou Lord thou Lord of
are thy dwellings thou Lord of Hosts are thy dwellings thou Lord thou Lord thou Lord of
Hosts, are thy dwellings thou Lord thou Lord of Hosts
Hosts are thy dwellings thou Lord thou Lord thou Lord of Hosts.
Hosts are thy dwellings thou Lord thou Lord thou Lord of Hosts.
Organ:
Vers: solo. My Soul
my Soul

hath a De- sire hath a de- sire hath a de- sire & long- ing
76
7 #6
& long- ing to enter into ye Courts of the Lord my heart & my
Slow
Slow
Flesh re- joyce, my heart & my Flesh re- joice re- joice. re
joyce in ye living God my heart & my Flesh re- joyce, re- joyce re- joyce in ye
li- ving God re- joice in ye liv- ing God.
Ritor.

Vers: 3 voc:

Blessed, blessed are they. blessed blessed are they that dwell in thy house
Blessed blessed are they blessed blessed are they y dwell y dwell in thy house.
Blessed blessed are they blessed blessed are that dwell y dwell in thy house.
They will be all-way They will be all-way prais-ing Thee
They will be all-way they will be all-way prais-ing Thee.
They will be all-way They will be all-way prais-ing Thee.
They will be all-way They will be al-way praising thee. They will be
They will be all-way they will be all-way praising thee. They will be, all-way, be-
They will be all-way, they will be all-way praising thee. They will be al-way,
all-way they will be al-way prais-ing Thee. They will be all-way They will
all-way they will be all-way praising thee. They will be all-way be all-way They will be
They will be all-way be all-way praising Thee. They will be all-way be they will be alway be
Vers:
prais-ing Thee slow. O Lord God O Lord God of Hosts hear o Pray'r Cho: O Lord
prais-ing Thee. slow. O Lord God O Lord God of Hosts hear hear o Pray'r Cho O Lord
Vers:
prais-ing Thee. O Lord God O Lord God of Hosts hear hear o Pray'r Cho: O Lord-
Cho

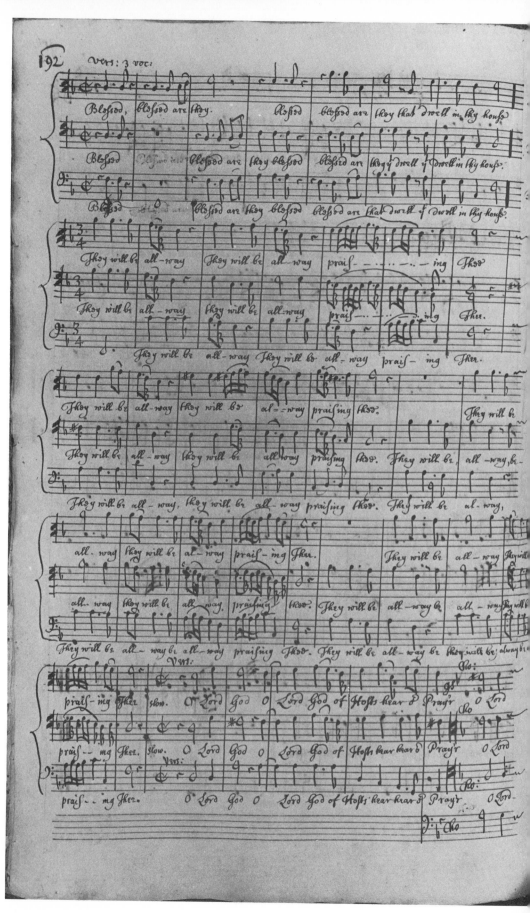

God O Lord God of Hosts hear
God O Lord God of Hosts hear hear
Prayr hearken O God hearken O God O God of Jacob. Cho
God O Lord God of Hosts hear hear
Prayr hearken O God hearken O God O God of Jacob. Cho
God O Lord God of Hosts hear hear
Prayr hearken O God hearken O God O God of Jacob.
Cho:
Hearken O God hearken O God O God O God of Jacob:
Vers: slow
O God of Jacob.
Cho:
Hearken O God hearken O God O God of Jacob.
Vers slow
Hearken O God, O God of Jacob:
Cho:
Hearken O God hearken O God O God of Jacob:
Vers slow
hearken O God O God of Jacob.
Cho:
Hearken O God hearken O God O God of Jacob,
Vers slow
hearken O God O God of Jacob.
Eccho Stop
Vers solus.
Behold O God Be-hold O God Be-
hold O God O God our De-fender
& look upon ye Face upon ye
Face of thine anointed
& look upon ye Face of thine a-

nointed.
Be- hold O God O God our de- fender
look upon ye Face upon ye Face of thine a- nointed & look upon the
Face upon ye Face of thine a- nointed
Rit:
is a Light & de- fence, is a Light a Light and de
is a Light & de- fence, is a Light a Light & de
For ye Lord God For ye Lord God is a Light & de-
:fence is a Light & de fence is a Light, & de fence ye
fince is a Light & de- fence is a Light a Light & de fence ye
fence for ye Lord God is a light a Light fence ye

Lord shall give Grace give Grace & worship ye Lord shall give Grace ye Lord shall give Grace give
slow
Lord shall give Grace give Grace & worship ye Lord shall give Grace ye Lord shall give Grace give Grace give
slow
Lord shall give Grace give Grace & worship ye Lord shall give Grace ye Lord shall give Grace, give
the Lord shall give Grace & worship, & no good thing shall
Grace ye Lord shall give Grace & worship, & no good thing shall he withhold wth
Grace ye Lord shall give Grace & worship, & no good Thing shall he wth hold &
he withhold shall he withold from them yt live a Godly Life shall
hold shall he withhold from them yt live a Godly Life, & no Good thing shall
no good thing shall he withold from them yt live a Godly life & no God thing shall
he withold from them yt live a godly life, & no good thing shall he withold shall he withold from
he withold from them yt live a godly life & no good thing shall he withold shall he withold from
he withold from them yt live a God- ly Life & no good thing shall he withold from

them yt live yt live a Godly Life. slow O how ami a - ble
them yt live yt live a Godly Life. slow Oh how ami a - - ble are thy dwellings thou
them yt live a God - ly Life.
are thy dwellings thou Lord thou Lord thou Lord of Hosts thou Lord thou
Lord thy dwellings thou Lord thou Lord thou Lord of Hosts thou Lord thou
O how ami a ble are thy dwellings thou Lord of Hosts. thou Lord thou
Lord thou Lord of Hosts.
Vers
Lord thou Lord of Hosts.
Vers:
O how amiable
Lord thou Lord of Hosts.
Oh how amiable are thy dwellings thou
Oh how ami a - ble are thy dwellings thou Lord - Thou Lord of Hosts are thy
are thy dwellings are thy dwellings thou Lord thou Lord thou Lord of Hosts are thy
Lord of Hosts. are thy dwellings thou Lord thou Lord thou Lord of Hosts are thy

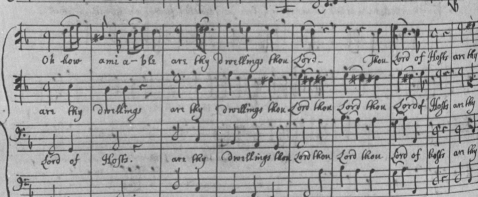

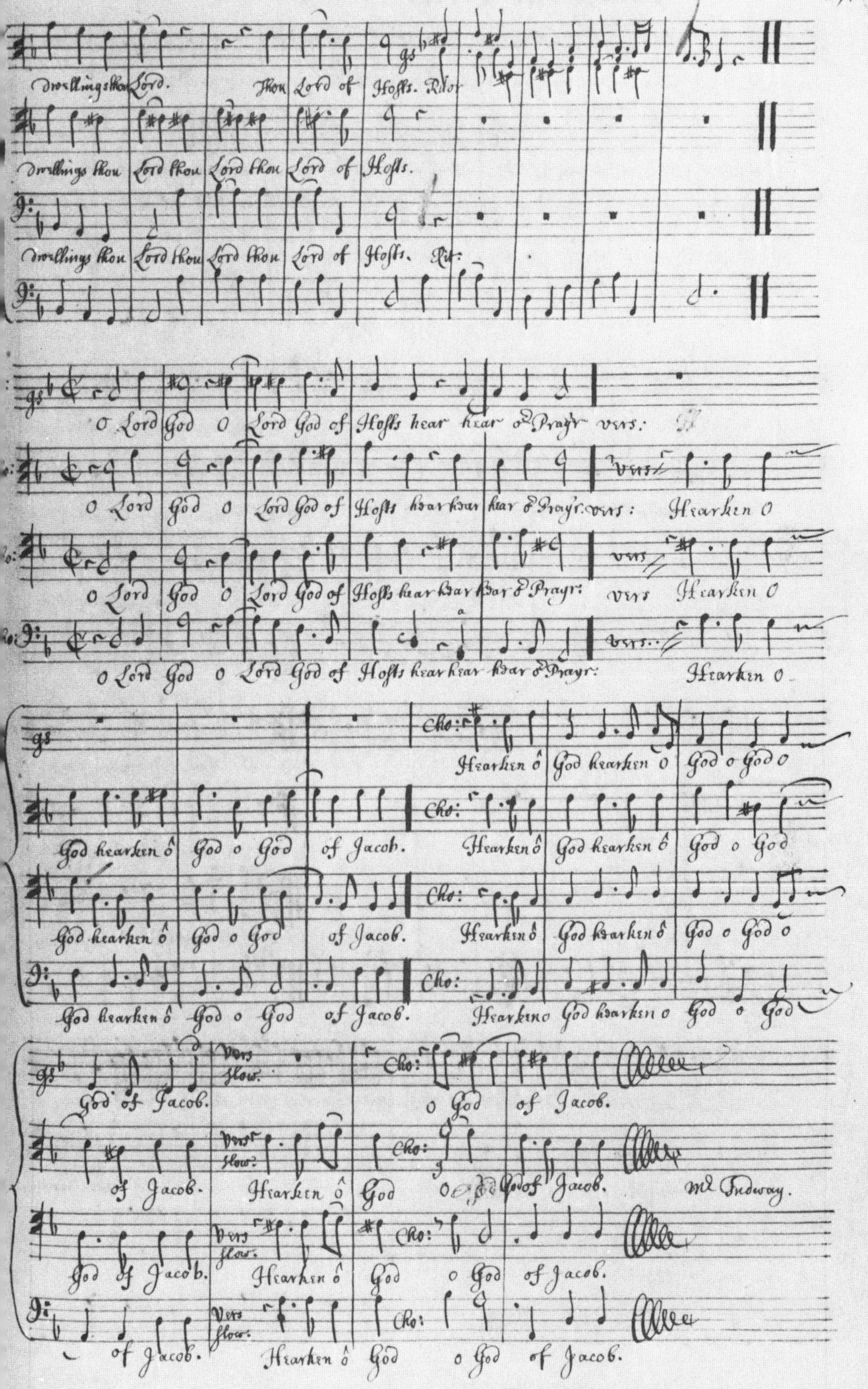
dwellings thou Lord. Thou Lord of Hosts. Rit
dwellings thou Lord thou Lord thou Lord of Hosts.
dwellings thou Lord thou Lord thou Lord of Hosts. Rit:
O Lord God O Lord God of Hosts hear hear o. Prayr vers:
O Lord God O Lord God of Hosts hear hear hear o. Prayr. vers: Hearken O
O Lord God O Lord God of Hosts hear hear hear o. Prayr: vers Hearken O
O Lord God O Lord God of Hosts hear hear hear o. Prayr: vers: Hearken O
Cho: Hearken o God hearken O God o God O
God hearken o God o God of Jacob. Cho: Hearken o God hearken o God o God
God hearken o God o God of Jacob. Cho: Hearkin o God hearken o God o God O
God hearken o God o God of Jacob. Cho: Hearkin o God hearken o God o God
God of Jacob. Vers slow. Cho: O God of Jacob.
of Jacob. Vers slow: Hearken o God Cho: O God of Jacob. Mr Tudway.
God of Jacob. Vers slow. Hearken o God Cho: O God of Jacob.
of Jacob. Vers slow. Hearken o God Cho: O God of Jacob.

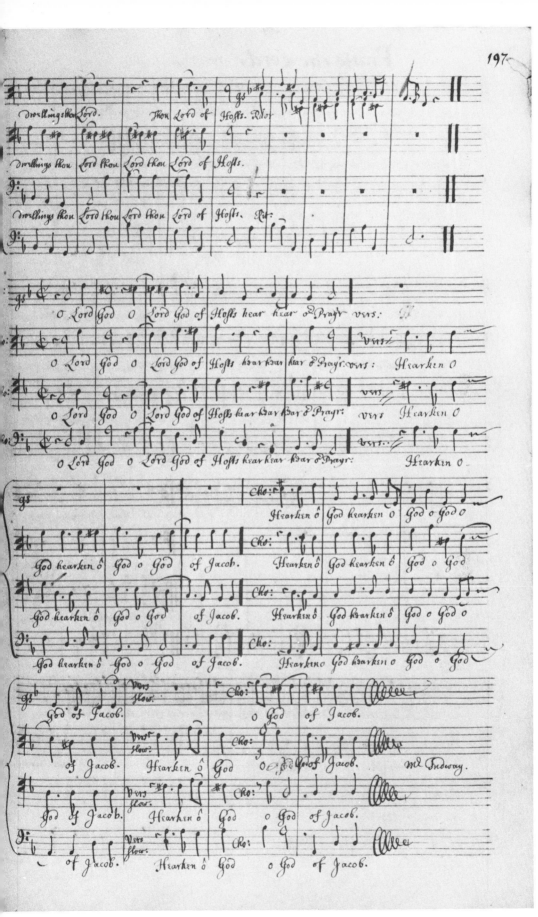

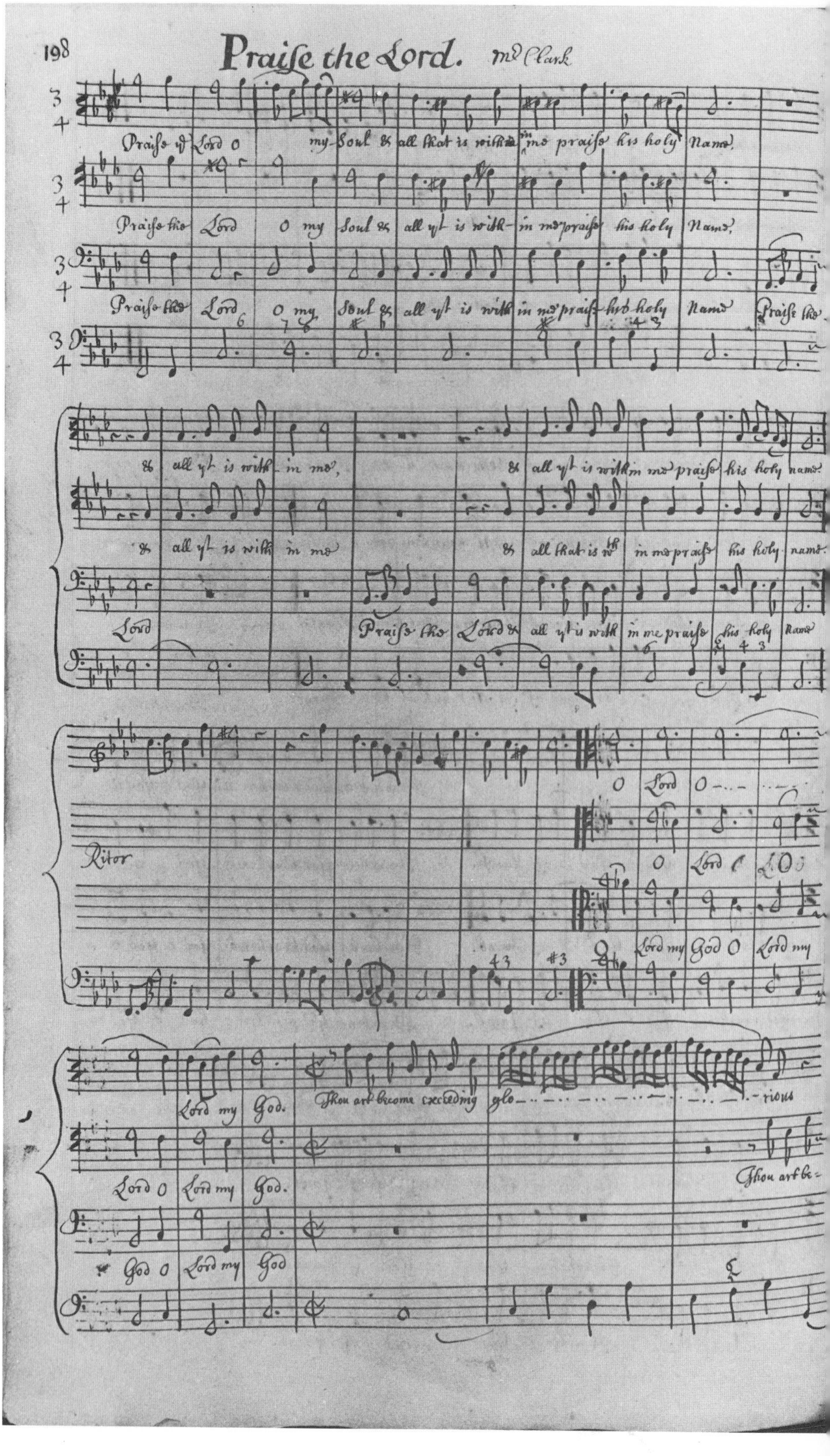
198
Praise the Lord.
Mr Clark
Praise ye Lord O my Soul & all that is within me praise his holy Name.
Praise the Lord O my Soul & all yt is within me praise his holy Name.
Praise the Lord O my Soul & all yt is within me praise his holy Name
Praise the Lord
& all yt is with-in me, & all yt is within me praise his holy name.
& all yt is with in me & all that is wth in me praise his holy name.
Lord Praise the Lord & all yt is with in me praise his holy Name
Ritor
O Lord O
O Lord O Lord
Lord my God O Lord my
Lord my God. Thou art become exceeding glo-rious
Lord O Lord my God. Thou art be-
God O Lord my God

come exceeding glo— — — — — rious
Thou art become exceeding glo— — —
Thou'rt clothd wth Majesty and Honour wth Majesty thou'rt clothd wth Majesty and hono wth Majesty and—
Thou'rt clothd wth Majesty and Honour with Majesty, thou'rt clothd wth Majesty & hono with Majesty and—
–rious Thou'rt clothd wth Majesty & hono and hono— Thou'rt clothd wth Majy & hono and
hono. Organ Trumpet. Thou'rt clothd wth Majesty wth Majesty &
hono. Ritorn. Thou'rt clothd wth Majesty wth Majesty &
hono. Ritor: Thou'rt clothd wth Majesty wth Majesty &
Hono wth Majesty and Hon— — our and hon— — our & hon— —
Hono wth Majesty and Hon— — our and hon— — our & hon— —
Hono Thou'rt clothd wth Majesty and hon— — our and hon— — our &

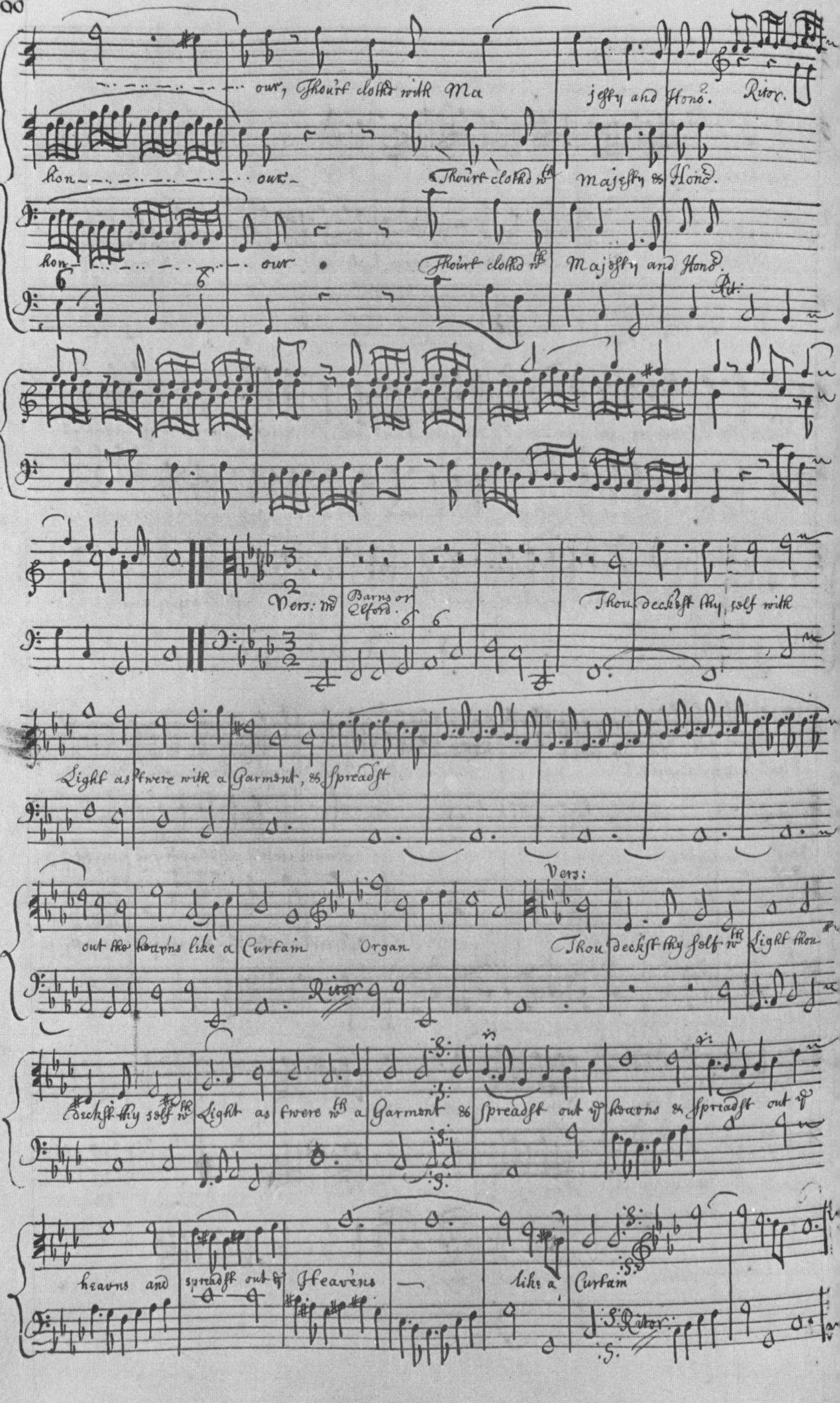
our, Thou'rt cloth'd with Ma jesty and Hono.
Ritor.
hon our Thou'rt cloth'd wth Majesty & Hono.
hon our Thou'rt cloth'd wth Majesty and Hono.
Rit:
Vers: wth Barns or Elford.
Thou deckst thy self with
Light as 'twere with a Garment, & spreadst
out the heavns like a Curtain Organ
Ritor
Vers:
Thou deckst thy self wth Light thou
deckst thy self wth Light as twere wth a Garment & spreadst out ye heavns & spreadst out ye
heavns and spreadst out ye Heavens like a Curtain
S. Ritor.

Vers
Thou hast laid ye foundation of ye Earth yt it never never never yt it never never never ne - ver should be mov'd
Ritor
Vers
Thou hast laid the foundation of the Earth yt it never never never never never never ne - ver should be
mov'd yt it never never ne - ver should be moved.
O Lord how manifold are thy works? O Lord how manifold are thy works in
O Lord how manifold are thy works O Lord how manifold are thy works! in
O Lord how manifold are thy works O Lord how manifold are thy works!
O Lord how manifold are thy works O Lord how manifold are thy works!
Turn over

In wisdom in wisdom in wisdom hast thou
wisdom hast thou made them all in wisdom In wisdom hast thou
In wisdom hast thou made them all in wisdom hast thou made them
In wisdom hast thou made them all in wisdom hast thou
made them all O Lord O Lord how manifold are thy works in wisdom in wisdom hast thou made ye
made them all O Lord O Lord how manifold are thy works in wisdom in wisdom hast thou made ye
made them all O Lord O Lord how manifold are thy works in wisdom in wisdom hast thou made ye
made them all O Lord O Lord how manifold are thy works in wisdom in wisdom hast thou made ye
The earth is full is full of thy Riches ye Earth is full is full of thy Riches.
The Earth is full is full of thy Riches the Earth is full is full of thy Riches.
Vers:

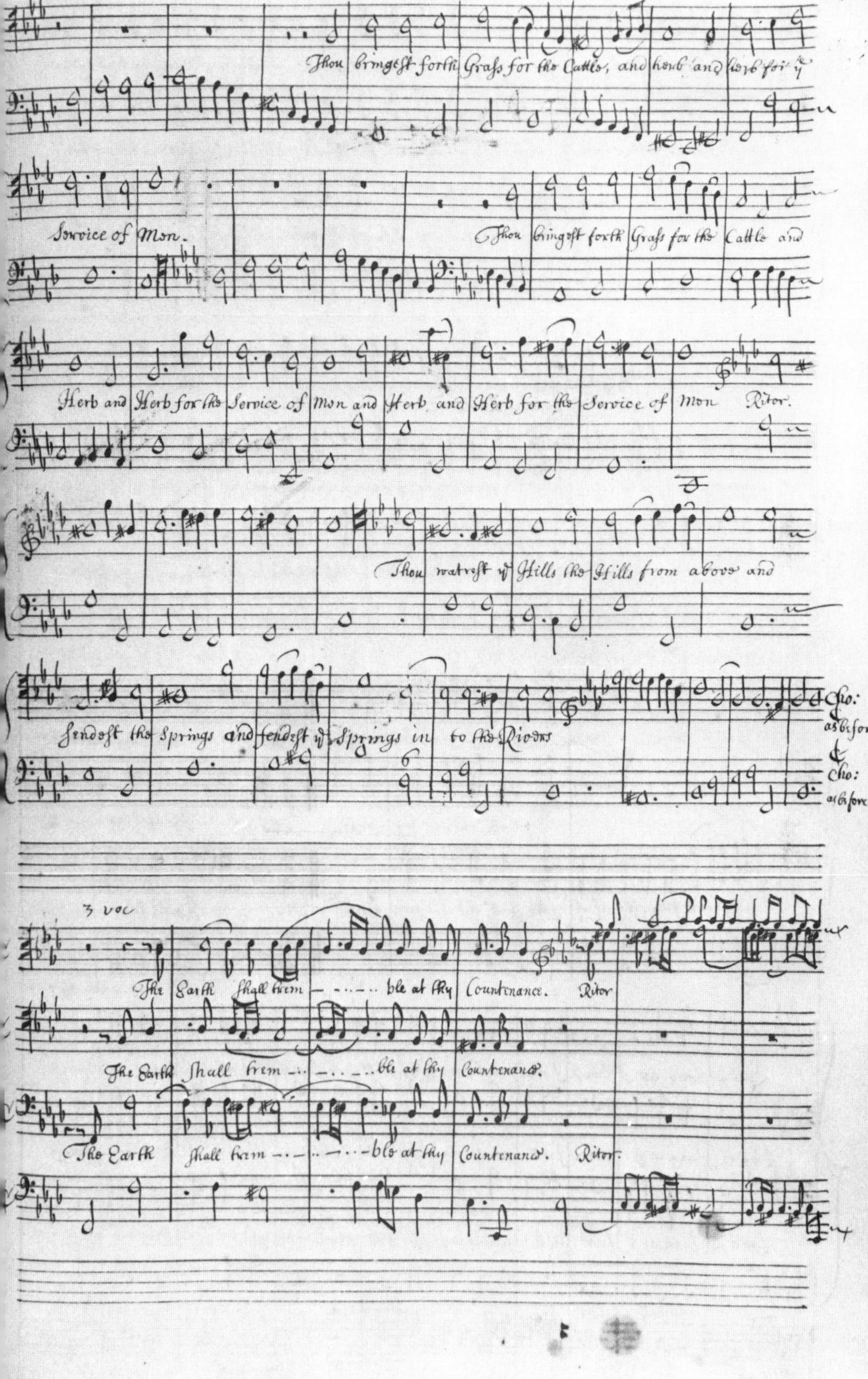
Thou bringest forth Grass for the Cattle, and herb and herb for y
Service of Men.
Thou bringest forth Grass for the Cattle and
Herb and Herb for the Service of Men and Herb and Herb for the Service of Men Ritor.
Thou watrest y Hills the Hills from above and
sendest the Springs and sendest y Springs in to the Rivers
Cho: as before
Cho: as before
3 voc
The Earth shall trem ble at thy Countenance. Ritor
The Earth shall trem ble at thy Countenance.
The Earth shall trem ble at thy Countenance. Ritor.

The hills shall smoak shall smoak ye hills shall smoak shall smoak shall smoak at thy
The hills shall smoak shall smoak ye hills shall smoak shall smoak shall smoak at thy
The hills shall smoak shall smoak ye hills shall smoak shall smoak at thy
presence & ye Glo - - - rious Majesty of ye Ld shall endure for ever shall endure
presence & ye Glo - - - rious Majesty of the Ld shall endure for ever shall endure
presence & ye Glo - - - rious Majesty of the Ld shall endure for ever and ye Glo
shall endure for ever. Cho: I will sing unto the
shall endure for ever. Cho: I will sing unto the
- - - rious Majesty of ye Lord shall endure for ever. Cho: I will sing unto the
Cho: I will sing unto the
Lord as long as I live, I will praise my God will praise my God while I have my Being.
Lord as long as I live I will praise my God will praise my God whilst I have my Being.
Lord as long as I live I will praise my God will praise my God whilst I have my Being.
Lord as long as I live I will praise my God my God whilst I have my Being.

I will Sing unto ye Lord as long as I live I will praise my God while I
I will Sing un- to ye Lord as long as I live I will praise my God while I
I will Sing un- to ye Lord as long as I live I will prayse my God I will prayse my God while I
I will Sing un- to ye Lord as long as I live. I will praise my God my God while I
have my Being will praise my God while I have my Being.
Mr Clark
have my Being will praise my God while I have my Being.
have my Being will praise my God while I have my Being.
Mr J. Clark.
have my Being will praise my God while I have my Being.

Choral Anthems

	Be not wroth very sore ___ Mr Bird & Dr Aldrich	166	
B	Blessed be ye Lord my Strength. Dr Blow. ___	52	June 3d 1688
	Blessed is ye Man. Mr Purcell ___	58	
	Blessed is he yt considereth ye Poor – Mr Purcell ___	147	
	God is ou Hope & Strength. Dr Blow ___	17.	
H.	Hear o' Heavns. Mr Humphreys ___	48.	
	I was Glad Mr Pigott. ___	169	
I.	I will love thee O Lord my strength 1 Mr J. Clark	196	
	I will love thee O Ld my strength – 2d Mr Clark –	203.	
	Is it true. Dr Tudway ___	176	
	Lord how are they increased Dr Blow ___	43.	
L	Lord let me know my End. Mr Lock ___	5.	
	Lord what is Man. Dr Turner ___	73	
	Lord remember David. Dr Blow ___	141	1698
M	My Song shall be alway – Mr Purcell ___	125	
	Man yt is born of a woman Mr John ___	186	
N	Not unto us O Lord Mr Lock	153	
	O God wherefore art thou absent. Dr Blow. ___	13.	
	O Give thanks. Mr Purcell ___	78	1693
	O Lord I have sinned Dr Blow ___	1.	
	O Lord thou hast searched me out. Dr Blow ___	40.	
O	O Lord thou art my God Dr Blow ___	130	Jan: 19, 1688
	O Lord God of my Salvation. Dr Blow ___	181	
P.	Praise ye Lord O Jerusalem Mr Clark	173	
	Save me O God Dr Blow ___	10	
	Save me O God Mr Purcell ___	23	
S	Sing O heavens Dr Tudway ___	190	
	Sing unto God Mr Purcell ___	122	1687
	Sing we merrily Dr Child	130	
	The Lord is King ___	109	
	The Lord even ye most mighty God ___	117	1687
	The Lord is King Mr Purcell ___	135	1688
	The way of God Mr Purcell ___	95	1694
T	Thy Righteousness O God Dr Blow ___	63	1693
	Turn thy face from my sins O Lord Mr Lock ___	26	
	Turn us again Dr Blow ___	86	1694
	Thy Beauty o Israel. Dr Aldrich upon Mr Wise ___	160	
W.	We will rejoyce – Dr Blow ___	102	1696

In all 38.

B

Blessed are y^e people
Blessed be y^e Lord my strength
Behold now praise y^e Lord +

D

Deliver us

G

God is gone up

H

Hear my prayer
Hear my crying
Full) Hear my prayer

I

I will sing
I will always give thanks
I waited patiently
I will magnifie thee
I will lift up mine eyes unto ye hills
I will give thanks
I was glad +
I will magnifie y^ee O God my King +

L

Let my complaint
Lord what love have I

O

Out of the deep
O Sing unto the Lord Thanksgiving Anthem
O Lord God of my salvation
O Praise ye Lord all ye heathen
O Lord God of my salvation (Full)
O Clap your hands
O Praise ye Lord ye that fear him
O Sing unto ye Lord
O come let us sing unto ye Lord
Offer the Sacrifice
O Lord thy word endureth +
O Lord rebuke me not
O Lord grant the King
O Praise ye Lord magnifie him +

Sorrer my [illegible] soul
Praise ye L^d O my soul } for ye sons of ye Clergy +

S

Sing un to the [illegible]

T

The Lord is my strength
The souls of y^e Righteous) for Queen Anns Burial
This is the day
The Earth is y^e Lords
The Lord is my light
The Lord hath appeared for us

U

Unto thee O God do we give thanks

W

We will rejoyce

O Lord I have sinned.

1
O Lord I have sinned. O Lord I have sinned I have sinned, what shall I
O Lord I have sinned I have sinned what
O Lord I have sinned O Lord I have sinned what shall I do what
Doe unto Thee thou preserver of Men? O why hast thou set mee up
shall I do unto Thee thou preserver of Men? why hast thou set me up O-
shall I do unto Thee thou preserver of Men?
as a Mark against Thee? as a Mark against Thee so, so yt I am a-
why hast thou set me up O why hast thou- set me up as a Mark against Thee so yt I am a
why hast Thou set me up O why hast Thou set me up as a Mark against Thee.
Burden to my Self So that I am a Burthen to my Self O pardon my trans=
Burden to my Self So yt I am a Burden to my self. O pardon my trans=
So yt I am a Burthen to my self O pardon my Transgression &
Cho: O pardon my trans=
=gression & take away take away my Sin and take away my Sin. O=
Cho:
=gression, & take away take away my Sin & take away my Sin. O pardon my trans=
take away take away my Sin, and take away, take away my Sin.

2
=gression, & take away my Sin pardon my transgression & take away my Sin and
pardon my transgression &
=gression & take away my Sin & take a=
pardon my Transgression & take away my Sin O pardon my Transgression and take
Vers:
take away my Sin take away my Sin. Mine Age is departed & removed from mee
take away my Sin take a way my Sin. Mine Age is de=
=way my Sin take away my Sin.
away my Sin.
Thou wilt cut me
=parted & removed from me Thou wilt cut me off wth joye
Mine Age is departed & removed from Mee
Mine Age is departed & removed from mee,
off with pining Sickness mine Eyes fail with looking upwards
=ning Sickness wth pi=====ning Sickness mine Eyes
Thou wilt cut mee off wth pi==ning sickness mine
Thou wilt cut me off wth pi===ning Sickness mine

I did mourn as a Dove did mourn as a Dove as a
fail with looking upwards
I did mourn as a
eyes fail wth looking upwards
I did mourn as a Dove
I did mourn as a
eyes fail with looking upwards—
I did mourn as a Dove did mourn as a
Dove O Lord I am oppressed undertake for me o Lord my God
Dove O Lord I am oppressed undertake for me o Lord O Lord my
Dove O Lord I am oppressed undertake for mee, O Lord
Dove O Lord I am oppressed O Lord I am op-pressed, undertake for me O Lord my God
Cho:
Vers:
undertake for me. Undertake for me o Lord my God undertake for mee; O wherefore is
God undertake for me. Undertake for me o Lord my God undertake for me.
my God undertake for me. Undertake for me o Lord my God undertake for me.
undertake for me. Undertake for me o Lord my God undertake for mee.—
light given to him yt is in Misery
wch long for Death but it cometh not wch
Or Life to ye bitter in
Or Life to ye bitter in Soul
wch long for
Or Life to ye bitter in soul wch long for Death but it cometh not wch long for death

long for death but it cometh not; And rejoice exceedingly when they can find ye Grave.
soul long for death but it cometh not; And rejoice exceedingly when they can find ye Grave.
Death but it cometh not: And rejoice exceedingly when they can find the Grave.
but it com=:=eth not And rejoice exceedingly when they can find ye Grave.
& rejoyce exceedingly when they can find ye Grave, For my sighing comes for my sighing
& rejoyce exceedingly when they can find ye Grave; For my sighing comes for my sighing
& rejoyce exceedingly when they can find ye Grave: For my sighing comes for my sighing
& rejoyce exceedingly when they can find ye Grave; For my sighing comes for my sighing
comes before I eat, & my roa= = = rings are poured out are pou==red out
comes before I eat, & my roa = rings are poured out like water & my roa = = = = rings are poured
comes before I eat, & my roa= = = = = rings are poured out
comes before I eat & my roa= = = rings are poured out my roa = = = = = rings are poured out
like water, Cho: For my sighing &c. as before,
out like water; Cho: For my sighing &c, as before
Dr Blow.
like water, Cho: For my sighing &c, as before,
like water; Cho: For my sighing &c as before

Lord let me know my end.

Lord let me know my end & ye number of my dayes yt I may be certifi'd how long I have to
live, how long I have to live
Behold thou hast made my dayes as it were a Span long as it were a
Behold Thou hast made my dayes as it were a Span long as it
Span long, & mine Age is ev'n as nothing in respect of Thee & mine Age is even as
& mine Age is even as nothing in respect of Thee & mine Age is ev'n as nothing as
were a span long & mine Age is ev'n as nothing in respect of Thee & mine Age is ev'n as nothing as
nothing in respect of Thee & verily ev'ry Man living every Man living is altogether vanity alto=
nothing in respect of Thee & verily ev'ry Man living ev'ry Man living is altogether alto=
nothing in respect of Thee & verily ev'ry Man living ev'ry Man living is alto=
=gether Vanity Cho: And verily ev'ry Man living ev'ry Man living is altogether vanity altoge=
Cho: And verily ev'ry Man living ev'ry Man living is altogether
=gether Vanity Cho: And veri-ly ev'ry Man living ev'ry Man living is altogether Vanity alto=
=gether Vanity Cho: And veri-ly ev'ry Man living ev'ry Man living is altogether

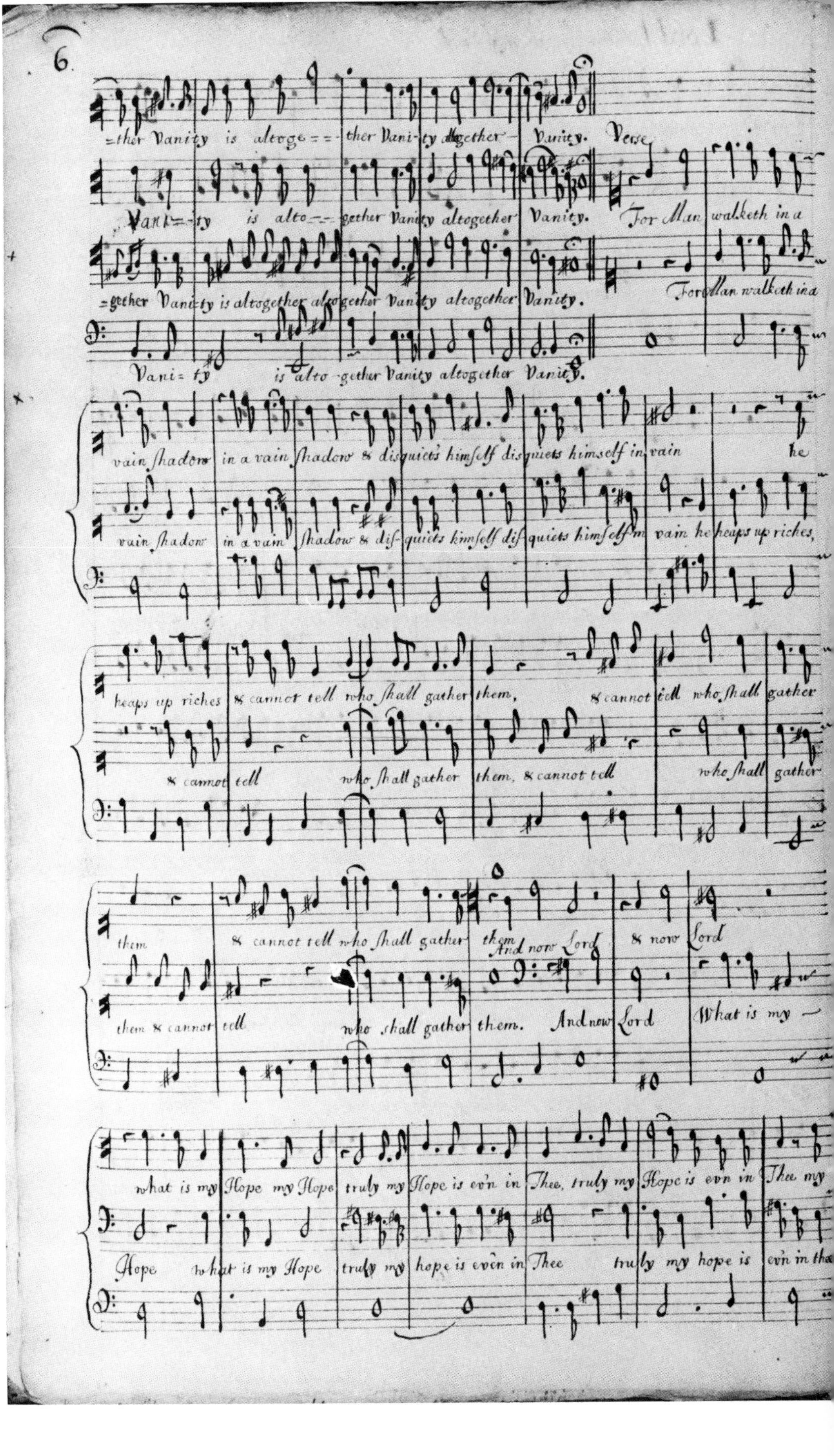
6.
=ther Vanity is altoge= = ther Vani-ty altogether - Vanity. Verse
Vani=ty is alto- - gether Vanity altogether Vanity. For Man walketh in a
=gether Vanity is altogether altogether Vanity altogether Vanity. For Man walketh in a
Vani=ty is alto-gether Vanity altogether Vanity.
vain shadow in a vain shadow & disquiets himself disquiets himself in vain he
vain shadow in a vain shadow & dis- quiets himself dis quiets himself in vain he heaps up riches,
heaps up riches & cannot tell who shall gather them, & cannot tell who shall gather
& cannot tell who shall gather them, & cannot tell who shall gather
them & cannot tell who shall gather them And now Lord & now Lord
them & cannot tell who shall gather them. And now Lord What is my -
what is my Hope my Hope truly my Hope is ev'n in Thee, truly my Hope is ev'n in Thee my
Hope what is my Hope truly my hope is even in Thee truly my hope is ev'n in thee

7.
hope is ev'n in Thee truly my hope is ev'n is ev'n in Thee my hope is ev'n in Thee, is ev'n in Thee
my hope is ev'n in Thee truly my hope is ev'n is ev'n in Thee my hope is ev'n in Thee in Thee
Cho
Truly my hope is ev'n in Thee truly my
my hope is ev'n in Thee. Truly my hope is ev'n in Thee truly my hope is ev'n in
Cho
my hope is ev'n in Thee. Truly my hope is ev'n in Thee truly my hope is ev'n in
Cho:
Truly my hope is ev'n in Thee truly my
hope truly my hope is ev'n in Thee.
Thee truly my hope is ev'n in Thee
Vers.
Thee truly my hope is ev'n in Thee. When Thou with Rebukes dost chasten Man for
Hope is ev'n in Thee.
When Thou with Rebukes dost chasten Man for Sin Thou makst his
Sin Thou makst his Beauty to consume a-

8
beauty to consume away like as it were a Moth fretting fretting a Garment like as it were a
way to consume away like as it were a Moth fretting fretting a Gar=ment like as it were a moth
moth fretting fretting a Garment fretting fretting a Garment. Evry man therefore is but Vani
fretting fretting a Garment fretting fretting a Garment. Evry man therefore is but Vani=
Cho
Evry man therefore is but Vani=
=ty is but Va==nity. Vers. a 5 Voc: Hear my prayer my prayer O Lord
=ty is but Vanity. Hear my pray'r my pray'r O Lord
=ty is but Vanity Hear my Prayer my prayer O Lord O Lord & wth thine
-ty is but Vanity. Hear my Prayer my pray'r O Lord & wth thine ears con=
-ty is but Vanity.
& with thine ears con=sider consider my calling, hold not thy peace at my Tears.
& with thine ears consider my calling hold not thy peace at my tears my Tears.
ears consider my calling hold not thy Peace at my tears at my Tears
=sider my calling hold not thy peace at my tears at my Tears for I am

For I am a Stranger a Stranger wth Thee and a Sojour=
For I am a stranger wth Thee and a Sojour= ner as all my Fathers
For I am a Stranger wth Thee. And a Sojourner as all my Fathers were.
Stranger wth Thee. And a Sojourner as all my fathers were
=ner as all my Fathers were. that I may recover my strength
were as all my Fathers were. that I may recover my strength
as all my Fathers were. O spare mee a little,
as all my Fathers were. O spare mee a little
O spare me a little —
yt I may re=
O spare mee a little, before I go hence
O spare mee a little yt I may recover my Strength, before I go
yt I may recover my strength my strength before before I go
yt I may recover my strength yt I may recover my strength before I go hence I go
=cover my strength yt I may recover my strength before I go-

10
& be no more no more seen
& be no more no more seen & be no more
hence. & be no more seen
& be no more
hence. & be no more no more seen & be no more seen,
hence. & be no more no more seen & be no more be no more
hence, & be no more seen and be no more be no more
seen no more seen.
seen no more seen.
& be no more seen
Mr Lock. extr
seen no more seen.
seen no more seen.
Save me o God.
Save me o God for ye Waters are come in ev'n unto my Soul ye Waters are come
Save me O God for ye waters are come in ev'n unto my Soul ye Waters are come
Save me O God for ye Waters are come in ev'n unto my Soul ye Waters are come
Save me O God for ye Waters are come in ev'n unto my Soul ye Waters are come

in evėn unto my Soul. Vers.
in ev'n unto my Soul. I am weary of crying am weary of crying my Throat is dry
in ev'n unto my Soul. I am weary of crying am weary of crying my Throat is dry,
in ev'n unto my Soul. I am weary of crying am weary of crying my Throat is dry,
My sight faileth me for waiting so long so long upon my God for waiting so long so long upon my God Cho.
My sight faileth me for waiting so long so long upon my God for waiting so long so long upon my God Cho.
My sight faileth me for waiting so long so long upon my God for waiting so long so long upon my God Cho.
And why for thy sake have I suffred Reproofe, and why for thy sake have I suffred re=
And why for thy sake have I suffred Reproof, have I suffred Reproofe & why for thy sake have I suff=
And why for thy sake have I suffred reproofe, & why for thy sake have I suffred re=
And why for thy sake have I suf=fred Reproofe & why for thy sake have I suffred re=
=proof. shame hath covred my Face. Vers. I wept & chastned my soul with Fasting
=red re proof shame hath covered my Face. Verse I wept & chastned my soul wth Fasting I
=proof Shame hath covered my Face. Vers. I wept & chastned my soul wth Fasting
=proof shame hath covred my Face Vers I wept & chastned my

12
I wept and chastned my Soul with Fasting, & that was turned was turned to my Reproof.
wept & chastned my Soul my Soul with Fasting & that was turned to my Reproof.
I wept & chastned my Soul with Fasting & that was turned to my Reproof.
Soul with Fasting & chastned my Soul wth Fasting, & that was turned was turned to my Reproof.
Cho:
But Lord I make my Prayer unto Thee in an acceptable Time hear me o God in ye multitude
But Lord I make my prayer unto thee in an accep= table time hear mee o God O God in ye
But Lord I make my prayer unto thee in an acceptable time hear me o God in ye multitude
But Lord I make my prayer unto Thee in an acceptable Time hear me o God in ye
of thy Mercy hear mee hear me o God in ye multitude of thy Mercy, evn in ye truth of
multitude of thy mercy hear me o God in ye multitude of thy Mercy evn in ye truth of
in ye multitude of thy Mercy hear me o God in ye multitude of thy Mercy evn in ye truth of
multitude of thy Mercy hear mee o God in ye multitude of thy Mercy evn in ye truth of
thy Salvation.
thy Salvation
thy Salvation.
thy Salvation.
Dr Blow.

O God wherefore art thou absent, &c

5 Voc:

O God
O God wherefore art thou absent from us so
O God wherefore art thou absent from us from us so long art thou absent from us so
O God wherefore art thou absent from us so long? art thou absent from us so
wherefore art thou absent from us so long? art thou absent from us so long?
long? O God wherefore art y^u absent from us from us so long?
long? O God wherefore art thou absent from
long wherefore art thou absent from us so long? so long? O God where=
O God wherefore art thou absent from us so long so long
O God wherefore art thou absent from us from us so
O God
us from us so long wherefore art thou absent from us so long?
=fore art y^u absent from us so long O God wherefore art thou absent from us
O God wherefore art thou absent from us so long

14
Verse
long art thou absent from us so long? Why is thy wrath so hot against the sheep of thy pas=
Wherefore art yͧ absent from us so long? Why is thy wrath so hot against the sheep of thy pas=
Wherefore art thou absent from us so long? Why is thy wrath so hot against yͤ sheep yͤ sheep of thy pas=
art thou absent from us so long, long?
art yͧ absent from us so long?
Full
=ture? O think upon thy congregati=
=ture? O think upon thy Congregati=
=ture? Why is thy wrath so hot against yͤ sheep yͤ sheep of thy Pas-ture O think upon thy Congregati=
Why is thy wrath so hot against yͤ sheep the sheep of thy Pas-ture O think upon thy Congregati=
Why is thy wrath so hot against yͤ sheep yͤ sheep of thy Pas-ture O think upon thy Congregati=
=on Whom thou hast purchased and re= deemed of old
=on Whom thou hast purchased & redeemed redeemed of
=on whom thou hast purchased and re= = deemed of old re= deemed of old,
=on Whom thou hast purchased and re= = deemed and re deemed of old & re=
=on Whom thou hast purchased and redeemed of old redeemed of old

151
& re- deemed, and re- deemed of old
old & redeemed of old – & redeemed of old. Verse.
Whom thou hast purchased and redeemed redeemed of old. Think upon ye Tribe of thine in-
= deemed of old, & redeemed re- deemed of old. Think upon ye Tribe of thine in-
& re- deemed of old & redeemed re deemed of old. Think upon ye Tribe of thine in-
Cho
& mount Syon
Cho:
and mount Syon wherein thou hast dwelt
Cho:
-heritance upon ye Tribe of thine Inheritance & mount Syon wherein wherein
Cho:
-heritance upon ye Tribe of thine Inhe- - ri- - tance & mount Syon wherein –
Cho
-heritance upon ye Tribe of thine In- heri- - tance & mount Syon wherein
wherein Thou hast dwelt & mount Sion wherein Thou hast dwelt.
& mount Sion & mount Sion wherein thou hast dwelt.
thou hast dwelt O God Wherefore art thou
thou hast dwelt & mount Sion wherein Thou hast dwelt. O God
Thou hast dwelt & mount Sion wherein thou hast dwelt.

O God where-fore art thou absent from us from us
absent from us from us so-long wherefore art thou absent from us so
Wherefore art thou absent from us so long? O God Wherefore art y
O God Wherefore art y absent from
O God Wherefore art thou absent from us so long?
so long? art thou ab-sent from us so long?
long? Wherefore art thou absent from us so long
absent from us wherefore art thou absent from? us so long?
us so long? art thou absent from us so long? ext r.
Dr Blow's

God is oᵉ hope & strength.

8 voc:

God is our hope & strength a very present help in Trouble. God
God is oᵉ hope and Strength a very present
God is our hope & strength a
God is our hope and strength a very present help in Trouble
God is our
is oᵉ hope and strength God is our hope & strength &
help in Trouble a very present help in Trouble God is our hope and
very present help in Trouble a very present help in Trouble
God is our hope & strength a very present help in Trouble God
a very present help in Trouble God is oᵉ hope and strength a very present
God is our hope and strength a very pᵉsent help in Trouble God
God is oᵉ hope & strength a very present help in Trouble.
hope & strength a very present help in Trouble in Trouble.

Strength. God is our hope & Strength. a very pre- - sent help in
Strength a very present help in Trou=ble a very present help in
God is our hope & Strength a very present help in Trou- ble in Trou=
is our hope and Strength a very present help in Trouble a very present help in trouble in
help in Trouble God is our hope and Strength a very present help in
is our hope and Strength a very present help in Trou=ble, a very present help in
God is our hope & strength a very present help a very present help in Trou=
God is our hope & strength a very present help in
Vers: trouble Therefore will we not fear tho' ye Earth be moved Tho-
Vers: trouble Therefore will we not fear tho' ye Earth be moved
Vers. =ble Therefore will we not fear tho' ye Earth be moved
trouble And tho' ye Hills be carried into ye midst of ye
trouble & tho' ye hills be carried into ye midst of ye
trouble
=ble And tho' ye hills be carried into the midst of ye
Trouble.

ye waters thereof rage and swell rage & swell
Tho
Tho ye waters thereof rage & swell
Tho ye waters thereof rage rage & swell
Sea
Tho ye waters thereof rage rage and
Sea.
Tho ye waters thereof rage rage and
Sea
Tho ye waters thereof rage rage and
ye waters thereof rage rage and swell
Cho:
& tho ye Mountains shake at ye tempest of ye same
Tho ye waters thereof rage and swell
& tho ye mountains shake at ye
Tho ye waters thereof rage rage & swell
And tho ye Mountains shake at ye tempest, &
swell.
And tho ye Mountains shake at the tempest of ye
swell.
& tho ye Mountains shake at ye tempest
And tho ye mountains shake at ye tem=
And tho ye Mountains shake at ye tempest
swell,
And tho ye Mountains shake at ye Tempest of ye same,

20
at yͤ Tempest of the same at the Tem=pest of the Same.
Tempest of yͤ same and tho the mountains shake at yͤ Tempest of yͤ same.
tho yͤ mountains shake at the Tempest of the same at the Tempest of yͤ same, God
same, and thô yͤ Mountains shake at the Tempest of yͤ same, God
yͤ same and thô yͤ mountains shake at the Tem==pest of the same.
=pest of the same & thô yͤ mountains shake at yͤ Tempest of the same.
of the same And tho yͤ mountains shake at yͤ Tempest of yͤ same God is in yͤ
at yͤ Tempest of the same at the Tempest of yͤ same
God is in yͤ midst of her God is in yͤ midst God is in yͤ midst of her God is in yͤ midst
God is in yͤ midst of her God is in yͤ midst of her
is in yͤ midst of her God is in yͤ midst of her God is in yͤ midst of
is in yͤ midst is in yͤ midst of her God is in yͤ midst of her God is
God is in yͤ midst of her God is in yͤ midst of her is in yͤ midst of
God is in yͤ midst of her God is in yͤ midst of her God is in yͤ midst of her is in yͤ midst
midst of her God is in yͤ midst of her is in the midst God is in
God is in yͤ midst of her. God is in yͤ midst of her in yͤ midst of her.

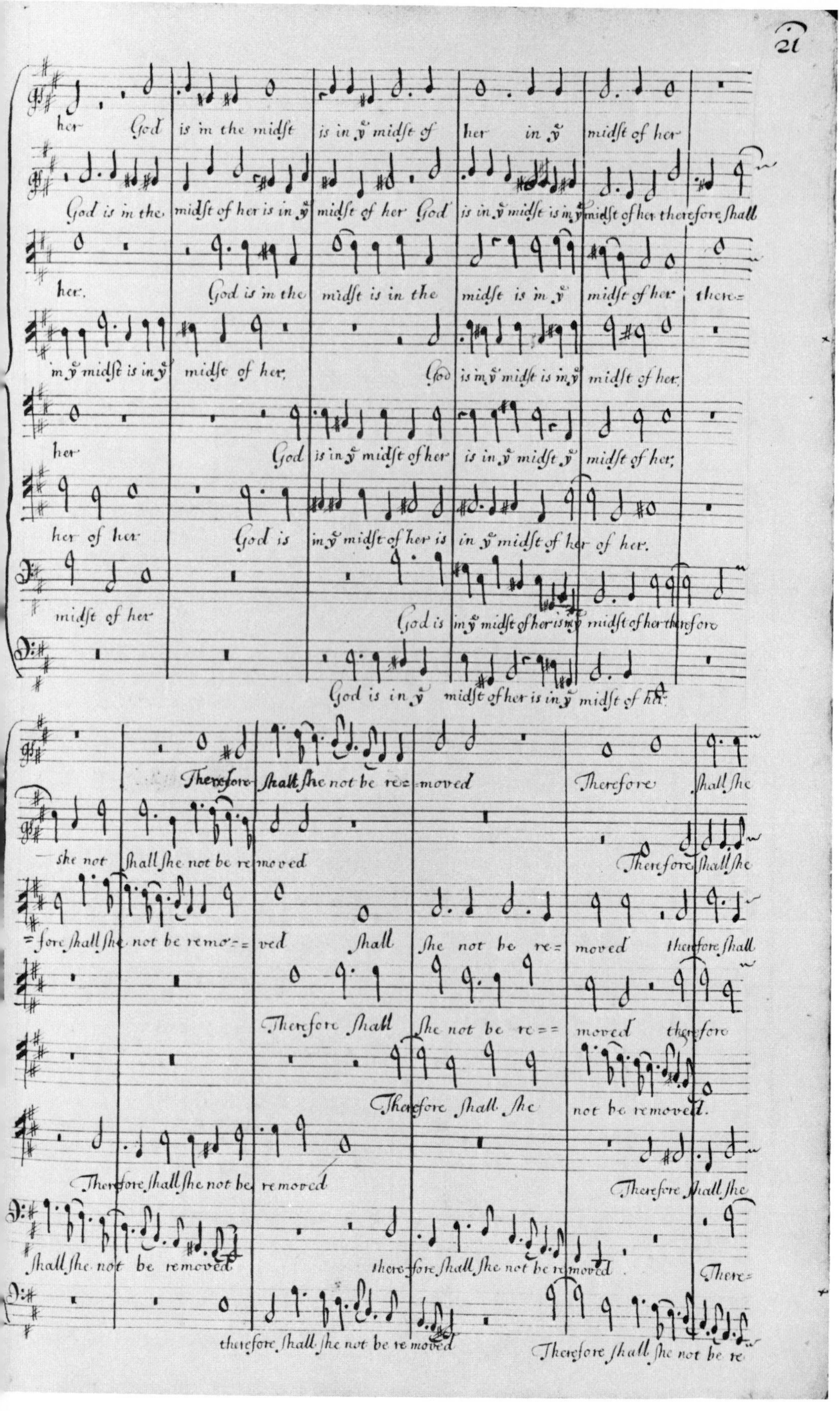
21
her God is in the midst is in y midst of her in y midst of her
God is in the midst of her is in y midst of her God is in y midst is in y midst of her therefore shall
her. God is in the midst is in the midst is in y midst of her there=
in y midst is in y midst of her, God is in y midst is in y midst of her,
her God is in y midst of her is in y midst y midst of her,
her of her God is in y midst of her is in y midst of her of her.
midst of her God is in y midst of her is in y midst of her therefore
God is in y midst of her is in y midst of her.
Therefore shall she not be re=moved Therefore shall she
she not shall she not be removed Therefore shall she
=fore shall she not be remo= =ved shall she not be re= moved therefore shall
Therefore shall she not be re== moved therefore
Therefore shall she not be removed.
Therefore shall she not be removed Therefore shall she
shall she not be removed therefore shall she not be removed There=
therefore shall she not be removed Therefore shall she not be re

22.
not be removed shall she not be removed God shall help her,
not be removed shall she not be removed God shall help her;
she not be re=mo=ved shall she not be removed. Therefore shall she not be
shall she not be removed God shall help her God shall
Therefore shall she not be remo==ved Therefore shall she not be
not be removed shall she not be removed Therefore shall she not
==fore shall she not be re=moved Therefore shall she not be-
moved Therefore shall she not be removed
God shall help her therefore shall she not be remo==ved re==moved.
God shall help her therefore shall she Therefore shall she not be re=moved re=moved
remo=ved God shall help her Therefore shall she not be removed shall she not be re=moved.
help her Therefore shall she Therefore shall she not be re=moved re moved
re== moved Therefore shall she not be removed shall she not be re moved
be re= moved Therefore shall she not be removed therefore shall she not be removed
re mo= ved Therefore shall she not be re mo==ved shall she not be re moved.
Therefore shall she not be re==mo==ved remo==ved.

5 voc

Save me ô God.

Save me ô God for thy names sake and a=
Save me ô God for thy names sake for thy names sake
Save me ô God for thy names sake for thy names sake
Save me ô God for thy names sake save me o God for thy names sake
Save me ô God for thy names sake for thy names sake & avenge
=venge me in thy strength & avenge me in thy strength in thy Strength.
& avenge me in thy strength & avenge me in thy Strength.
& avenge me in thy Strength avenge me in thy strength. Hear hear my
Vers
and avenge me in thy strength in thy Strength Hear hear
me in thy Strength, & avenge me in thy strength avenge me in thy strength Hear - hear
prayer o God hear hear my prayer O God o God, For strangers are risen up
my prayer O God hear my pray'r o God o God For strangers are risen up - for
my pray'r o God hear my prayer ô God For strangers are risen up — for strangers are -
for strangers are risen up are risen up against me. And Tyrants wch have not God before y^eir
strangers are risen up are risen up against me. And Tyrants wch have not God before y^eir
risen up are risen up against me & Tyrants wch have not God before their Eis

24
Cho
Behold God is my helper
The Lord is with
Cho:
Behold God is my helper:
The
eyes seek seek after my soul seek seek after my Soul
Chorus Tenor Decani
Behold God is my helper
eyes seek after my soul seek after my Soul
Behold God is my helper
Tenor Cantoris
Cho:
seek seek after my soul seek after my soul,
Behold God
them yt uphold my Soul
The Lord is with ym yt uphold my soul yt uphold my Soul
Lord is with ym, The Lord is with ym is with ym yt uphold my soul yt uphold my soul yt uphold my Soul
The Lord is with ym is with them the Lord is with them with ym yt uphold my Soul yt uphold my Soul
The Lord is with them is with them yt uphold my soul, ye Lord is with them yt uphold my
is my helper, behold God is my helper ye Lord is with ym yt uphold my Soul yt uphold my Soul
Vers
An Offring of a free heart will I give Thee & praise thy name o Lord because it is so comfort=
An Offring of a free heart will I give thee & praise thy name o Lord because it is so comfort=
An Offring of a free heart will I give thee & praise thy name o Lord because it is so comfort=

25
=able & praise thy name praise thy name ó Lord because it is so comfortable because it is so comfortable
=able & praise thy name praise thy name o Lord because it is so comfortable because it is so comfortable
=able & praise thy name praise thy name ó Lord because it is so comfortable because it is so comfortable,
For he hath delivred me out of all my Trouble out of all my Trouble & mine eyes have seen yeir desire
For he hath delivred me out of all my Trouble out of all my Trouble. & mine eies have seen
For he hath delivred me out of all my trouble out of all my Trouble. & mine
For he hath delivred me out of all my trouble out of all my Trouble. & mine eies have seen yeir de=
For he hath delivred me out of all my trouble out of all my Trouble & mine eies have
upon mine Enemies have seen yeir deire upon upon mine Enemies.
their desire upon mine enemies have seen yeir desire upon mine Enemies.
eies have seen yeir desire upon mine enemies upon mine E==nemies.
=sire upon mine Enemies have seen yeir desire upon upon mine enemies
seen their desire upon mine enemies have seen yeir desire upon mine Enemies
Hen. Purcell.
cxtr

26

Turn thy Face from my sins o Lord.

5 Voc.
Turn thy Face from my Sins o Lord Turn thy Face from my
Turn thy Face from my Sins
Turn thy Face from my Sins o Lord turn thy Face from my sins from my
Turn thy Face from my Sins O Lord turn thy Face from my Sins from my Sins ô
Turn thy Face from my Sins ô Lord from my
Sins O Lord O Lord and put out all my misdeeds my mis=deeds,
Lord & put out all my misdeeds put out all my mis=deeds put out all put out all my mis=deeds
Sins o Lord o Lord & put out all my misdeeds & put, put out all my mis=deeds create
Lord & put out all my misdeeds O Lord put out all my mis= deeds create
Sins o Lord and put out all my misdeeds O Lord put out all my mis=deeds create
& renew a right spirit within mee & renew a right Spirit within
& renew a right Spirit within mee, & renew a right Spirit within
a clean heart in mee O God, & renew a right Spirit a right Spirit within
a clean heart in mee ô God, and renew a right Spirit within mee & renew a right
a clean heart in mee O God, & renew a right Spirit within mee

mee
and renew a right
Spirit a right
Spirit within mee
mee
and renew a right
Spirit within mee
Vers.
mee and renew
& renew a right
Spirit within mee
within mee.
Spirit & renew a right
Spirit within mee
& renew a right
Spirit within mee.
Cast me not away from thy
and renew a right
Spirit within
mee
with- in
mee
Cast
me not away from thy
Presence
& take not thy holy
Spirit thy ho=
Presence
and take not thy holy
Spirit from mee,
& take not thy holy
==ly Spirit
from mee
O give mee the
comfort of thy helpa=
Spirit thy holy Spirit
from mee
O give mee the
Comfort of thy help a=
O give mee the
Comfort of thy help a=gain
=gain
O
give me ye comfort of thy
help again
& stablish mee with
thy free spirit stablish
=gain
O
give me ye comfort of thy
help again
and stablish mee with
thy free spirit stablish
& stablish mee wth
thy free Spirit
O
give me the comfort of thy
help & stablish

Then shall I teach thy waies unto ye wicked and Sin=
Then shall I teach thy wayes unto ye wicked
mee wth thy free Spirit Then shall I teach thy wayes un=
mee wth thy free Spirit Then shall I teach thy wayes unto the
mee wth thy free Spirit
=ners shall bee converted, & Sinners shall bee converted unto Thee & Sinners shall be converted con=
& Sinners shall be converted, unto Thee & Sinners shall be converted Then shall I teach thy wayes
=to the wicked, & Sin=ners shall be converted and Sin=
wicked, & Sinners shall be converted unto Thee Then shall I teach &c: =to ye wicked,
and Sin=ners shall be converted unto Thee Then shall I teach thy wayes unto ye wicked un=
=verted converted unto Thee and Sinners shall be converted unto Thee.
=to the wicked, and Sin=ners shall be con=verted, shall be con=verted unto Thee.
=ners shall be converted unto Thee & Sinners shall be converted unto Thee.
& Sinners shall be converted converted unto Thee conver=ted unto Thee.
to ye wicked & Sinners shall bee con= vert=ted unto Thee.

Glory be to yͤ Father & to the Son & to the holy Ghost, as it was in yͤ Begining is
Glory be to the Father & to the Son & to the holy Ghost as it was in yͤ begining is
Glory be to the Father & to the Son & to the holy Ghost as it was in yͤ begining is
Glory be to the Father & to the Son & to the holy Ghost as it was in yͤ begining is
Glory be to the Father & to the Son & to the holy Ghost as it was in yͤ begining is
now & ever shall bee and ever shall bee is now and ever shall bee world without
now & ever shall be is now & ever shall bee is now world without end is now
now & ever shall be & ever shall bee is now and ever shall be & ever shall be world
now & ever shall be is now & ever shall be & ever shall be is now and ever shall be world wᵗʰout end
now & ever shall bee and ever shall bee world wᵗʰout end and ever shall be is now, &
end and ever shall be world without End Amen.
and ever shall bee world without end A=== men.
without — end & ever shall be world without End Amen.
world without end world without End Amen.
ever shall bee world with-out End Amen.
Mʳ Lock.

30
Sing we merrily unto God our Strength unto god ô Strength
Sing wee merrily unto God our Strength unto God ô Strength
Sing wee merrily unto God ô Strength sing we merrily unto God ô
Sing we merrily unto God ô Strength sing we merrily unto God our Strength unto God ô Strength
Sing wee merrily unto God ô
Sing wee
Sing wee merrily unto God ô Str: unto
wee merrily unto God ô Strength unto God ô Strength make a
Sing wee merrily unto God our Strength unto God ô Strength
Strength sing we merrily unto God our Strength unto God ô Strength unto God our
Sing wee merrily unto God ô Strength unto God ô Strength make
Strength unto God ô Strength Sing wee merrily unto God ô Streng
merrily unto God ô Strength Sing we merrily unto God our Strength,
God our Strength, Sing wee merrily unto God ô Strength make

cheerfull noise make a cheerfull noise make a cheerfull noise
make a cheerfull cheerfull noise make a cheerfull noise make a
Strength make a cheerfull noise make a cheerfull noise make a cheerfull noise make a
cheerfull noise make a cheerfull noise make a cheerfull noise make a cheerfull noise make a
make a cheerfull noise make a cheerfull noise make a cheerfull noise make a cheer=
make a cheerfull noise make a cheerfull noise make a cheerfull noise make a
cheerfull noise make a cheerfull noise make a
unto the God of Ja=== cob unto yͤ God of Jacob
cheerfull noise un=to yͤ God of Jacob un=to yͤ God of Ja==== cob, unto yͤ
cheerfull noise un=to yͤ God of Jacob. unto the God of Ja= cob. un=to yͤ God of
cheerfull noise un=to yͤ God of Ja=== cob, un=to yͤ God of Jacob un=
full noise make a cheer=full noise un= to yͤ God unto yͤ God of Ja==== cob un=
cheerfull noise unto yͤ God of Jacob unto yͤ God of Ja=cob un=
cheerfull noise un=to yͤ God of Ja==== cob un=to yͤ God of Ja== cob unto the

32
unto ye God of Ja=cob, take ye Psalm Take ye Psalm bring hither ye Tabret bring hither ye Ta=
God of Jacob of Jacob Take ye Psalm, bring hither ye Ta= =bret.
Jacob of Ja=====cob, Take ye Psalm Take ye Psalm, bring hither the Ta==
=to ye God of Ja====cob Take ye Psalm Take ye Psalm bring hither the Tabret, bring hither ye
=to ye God of Jacob, Take the Psalm ye Psalm take ye Psalm take ye Psalm take ye Psa bring hither ye Ta=
==to ye God of Jacob Take ye Psalm take The -- Psalm bring hither ye Tabret bring hither
God of Ja=====cob. Take ye Psalm ye Psalm. bring hither ye Tabret
=bret The merry merry Harp ye merry merry Harp ye merry merry Harp ye merry merry Harp with ye
bring hither ye Tabret. The merry merry Harp ye merry merry Harp the merry Harp with ye
=bret bring hither ye Tabret. The merry merry harp ye merry merry harp wth the Lute.
Tabret the Tabret the merry merry harp with ye Lute the merry merry Harp with ye
===bret ye merry merry Harp with the --- Lute The merry Harp wth ye
the Ta=====bret ye merry merry harp ye merry merry mer=ry Harp with the
ye merry merry mer=ry Harp with ye Lute ye merry merry harp with ye

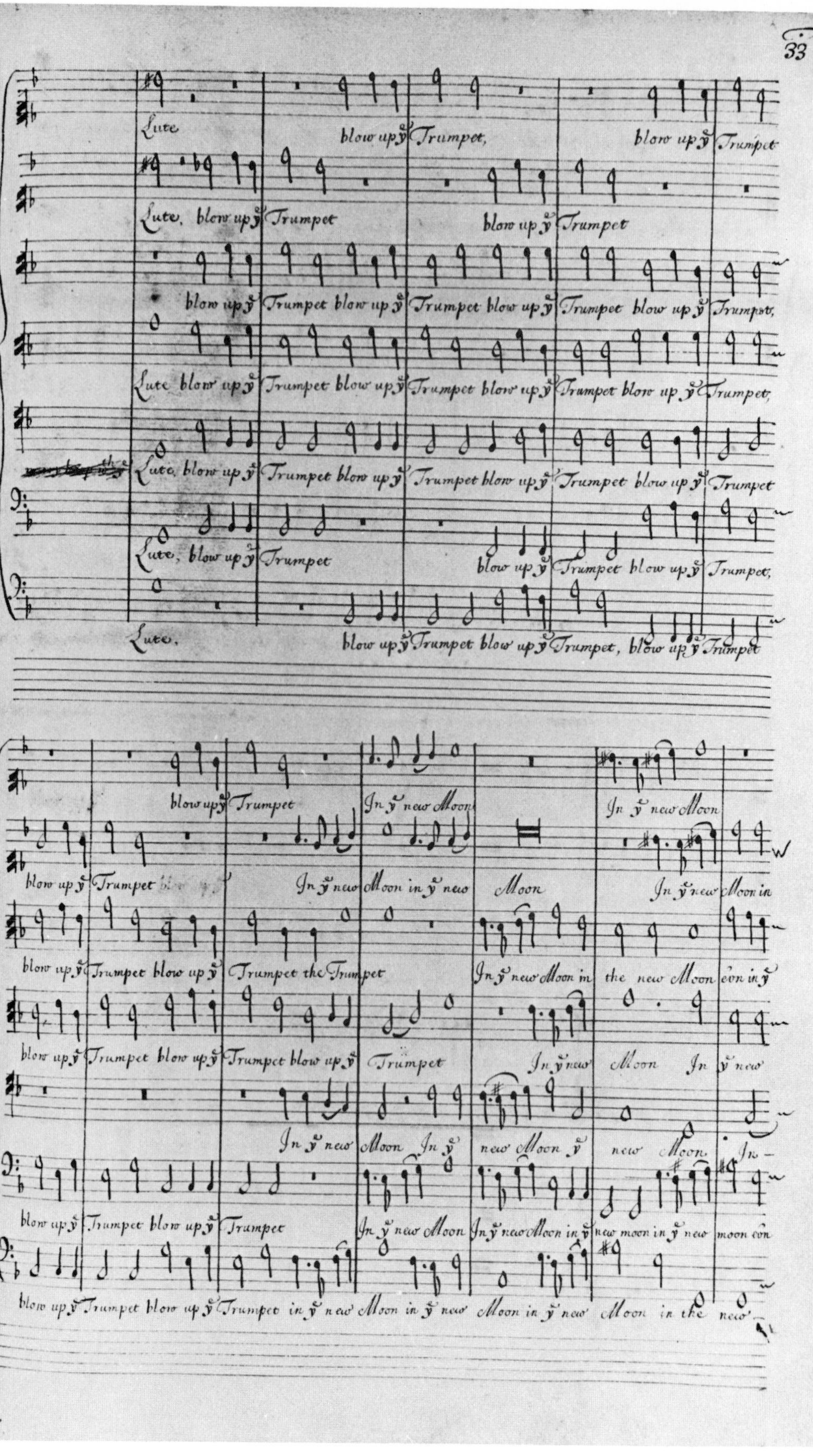
33
Lute blow up ye Trumpet, blow up ye Trumpet
Lute, blow up ye Trumpet blow up ye Trumpet
blow up ye Trumpet blow up ye Trumpet blow up ye Trumpet blow up ye Trumpet,
Lute blow up ye Trumpet blow up ye Trumpet blow up ye Trumpet blow up ye Trumpet,
Lute, blow up ye Trumpet blow up ye Trumpet blow up ye Trumpet blow up ye Trumpet
Lute, blow up ye Trumpet blow up ye Trumpet blow up ye Trumpet,
Lute. blow up ye Trumpet blow up ye Trumpet, blow up ye Trumpet
blow up ye Trumpet In ye new Moon In ye new Moon
blow up ye Trumpet In ye new Moon in ye new Moon In ye new Moon in
blow up ye Trumpet blow up ye Trumpet the Trumpet In ye new Moon in the new Moon even in ye
blow up ye Trumpet blow up ye Trumpet blow up ye Trumpet In ye new Moon In ye new
In ye new Moon In ye new Moon ye new Moon. In
blow up ye Trumpet blow up ye Trumpet In ye new Moon In ye new Moon in ye new moon in ye new moon even
blow up ye Trumpet blow up ye Trumpet in ye new Moon in ye new Moon in ye new Moon in the new

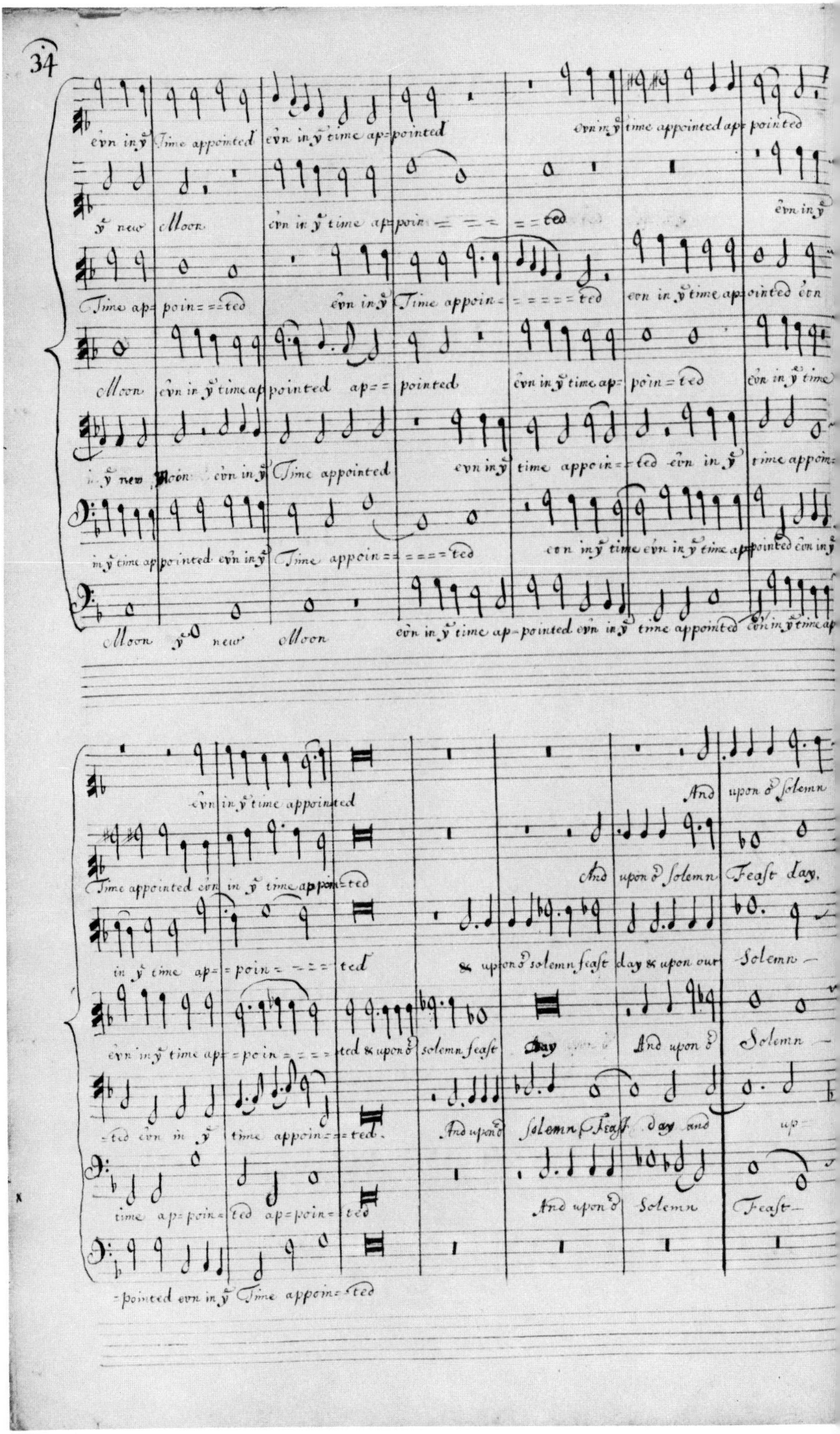
34
ev'n in ye Time appointed ev'n in ye time ap=pointed ev'n in ye time appointed ap=pointed
ye new Moon ev'n in ye time ap=poin= = = = = ted ev'n in ye
Time ap= poin= = ted ev'n in ye Time appoin= = = = = = ted ev'n in ye time appointed ev'n
Moon ev'n in ye time appointed ap= = pointed ev'n in ye time ap= poin= ted ev'n in ye time
in ye new Moon ev'n in ye Time appointed ev'n in ye time appoin= = ted ev'n in ye time appoin=
in ye time appointed ev'n in ye Time appoin= = = = = = ted ev'n in ye time ev'n in ye time appointed ev'n in ye
Moon ye new Moon ev'n in ye time ap-pointed ev'n in ye time appointed ev'n in ye time ap
ev'n in ye time appointed And upon o' Solemn
Time appointed ev'n in ye time appoin=ted And upon o' Solemn Feast day.
in ye time ap= =poin= = = = ted & upon o' solemn feast day & upon our Solemn
ev'n in ye time ap= =poin= = = = ted & upon o' solemn feast Day And upon o' Solemn
=ted ev'n in ye time appoin= = ted. And upon o' solemn Feast day and up=
time ap=poin= ted ap=poin= ted And upon o' Solemn Feast
=pointed ev'n in ye Time appoin= ted

35.
Feast day and upon ye solemn feast day For this was made a Statute for Israel for this
and upon ye solemn Feast day our solemn feast day for this was made a Statute for Israel for this
Feast day and upon ye solemn Feast day for this was made a Statute for Israel for this
Feast day & upon ye solemn Feast day for this
on ye sol= emn Feast day ye solemn feast day for this was made a Statute for Israel for this.
day ye solemn Feast day for this
And upon ye solemn Feast day ye solemn Feast day for this
was made a Statute for Is-- rael & a Law of ye God of Jacob & a law of ye
was made a Statute for Is== rael and a law of ye God of Ja== cob & a law
was made a Statute for Isra== el and a law of ye God of Jacob & a
was made a Statute for Is= ra= el & a law of ye God of Ja= cob & a law of ye
was made a Statute for Isra== el & a Law of ye God of Jacob & a Law of ye God of Jacob.
was made a Statute for Isra== el and a law of ye God of Jacob.
was made a Statute for Isra== el & a law of ye

God of Ja- cob. & a law of yͤ God of Ja- - - - - cob of Ja- cob & a law of yͤ
of yͤ God of Ja cob. and a Law of yͤ God of Jacob of Ja- - - - - cob & a law of yͤ God of Ja-
Law of yͤ God of Jacob & a law of yͤ God of Jacob & a Law of yͤ God of Ja- cob & a Law of yͤ God of
God of Jacob & a law of yͤ God of Jacob & a law of yͤ God of Jacob & a law of yͤ God of Ja- -
& a law of yͤ God of Jacob & a Law of the God of Ja- - cob & a law of yͤ
and a Law of yͤ God of Jacob. & a Law of yͤ God of Ja- cob & a Law of yͤ
God of Ja cob & a law of yͤ God of Jacob & a law of yͤ God of Jacob
God of Ja cob & a law of yͤ God of Jacob Al- le- lu- - - - ia
- cob of Ja cob & a law of yͤ God of Jacob of yͤ God of Jacob al- le lu- - - - - ia. Al- le- lu
Ja- cob & a law of yͤ God of Ja- cob of Ja- - cob Al- le- luia Alle- lu- - ia
- cob yͤ God of Jacob & a law of yͤ God of Ja- - cob of Ja- - cob. Alle- lu- ia Al- le- lu
God of Jacob & a law of yͤ God of Ja- - cob yͤ God of Ja- cob Al- le- lu ia Al- le- lu ia Al-
God of Jacob & a law of yͤ God of Jacob of yͤ God of Jacob Al- le- lu- ia Al- le- lu
& a law of yͤ God of Ja- cob of Ja- - cob Al- le- lu- ia Al- le- lu-

Al=le=lu==ia
Al=ler lu=====ia
Alle=lu===ja
====ja
Al=le=lu=====ia
Al==le==lu==ja
Dr Child
Al=le=lu====ia
alleluia
Al=le=lu===ja
====ia
Alle=lu===ia
Alle=lu===ia
All=le=lu====ia
=le=lu=ja
Al===le=lu=ia
Alle=lu=====ia
Dr Child
====ia
Alle=lu====ia
Al=le=lu=ia
ja Alle=lu===ia
Al=le=lu=========ia

38
O Lord thou hast searched me out &
Lord thou hast searched me out & known me,
thou knowst my down sitting & mine up-ri-sing, thou understandest my thoughts long
long before, Thou art about my Path & about my bed & spiest out all my ways for
lo there is not a word in my Tongue but thou o Lord knowst it altogether thou hast
fashioned me behind & before & laid thine hand upon me, such knowledg is too wonderfull & excel-
-lent for me; too wonderfull & excellent for mee, I cannot attain unto it I cannot, I cannot, cannot
-tain un-to it.
Whither shall I go then from thy Spirit

If I climb up into heav'n thou art there
or whither shall I go then from thy Presence. If I go down to hell thou art
If I climb up into heav'n thou art there If I take y
there also whither shall I go then from thy Spirit
wings of y morning & remain in y uttermost parts of y Sea ev'n there there also shall thy
Ev'n there there there also shall thy
hand lead me & thy right hand shall hold me; If I say peradventure y darkness shall
hand lead me & thy right hand shall hold me
cover me Then shall my night be turned to day
If I say peradventure y darkness shall cover me Then shall my

40
whither shall I go then from thy Spirit
night be turned to Day
or whither shall I go then from thy
O Lord thou hast searched me out & known me,
thou knowst my down
presence
O Lord thou hast searched me out & known me,
sitting & my up rising
Thou understandest my Thoughts under-
Thou knowst my down Sitting & mine up rising
Thou under-standest my thoughts lo
-standest my Thoughts long
before.
Cho: follows
I will
under-standest my Thoughts long before.
next page

I will give Thanks unto Thee o Ld.
for I am fearfully & wonderfully
I will give Thanks unto Thee o Lord, for I am fearfully & wonderfully made
I will give Thanks unto Thee o Lord, for I am fearfully and wonderfully made & wonderfully made
I will give Thanks unto Thee o Lord, for I am fearfully and wonder--fully made
made am fearfully & wonderfully made for I am fearfully & wonderfully made and
for I am fearfully & wonderfully made for I am fearfully & wonderfully made and
for I am fearfully and wonderfully made I am fearful--ly and
For I am fearfully & wonderfully made am fearfully & wonder=
wonderfully made marvelous are thy works & that my soul knoweth right well & that
wonderfully made marvelous are thy Works & that my soul knoweth right well & that my
wonder fully made marvellous are thy works and yt my soul know=
ful==ly made & that my soul knoweth right well marvellous
my soul knoweth right well & that my soul know eth right well mar- velous are thy
soul knoweth right well & that my soul knoweth right well mar= velous are thy
=eth right well & yt my soul knoweth right well mar= velous are thy
are thy works & that my soul knoweth right well knoweth right well mar-velous are thy

works & yt my soul know eth right well knoweth right well
works & yt my soul know eth right well right well & yt my soul know eth right well
works & yt my soul know- eth right well
works are thy works & yt my soul know-eth right well right well and
& yt my soul know eth right well know eth right well.
right well & yt my soul know eth right well know eth right well.
& that my soul knoweth right well knoweth right well
yt my soul knoweth right well knoweth right well

Lord how are they increased &c. Psa: 3.

Lord how are they increased yt trouble me many one there be, yt say of my soul there is no
Lord how are they increased yt trouble me many one there -
help no help for him in his God
ma-ny one there be yt
be yt say of my Soul, there is no help for him in his God no help for him in his God there is no
say of my soul there is no help for him in his God no help for him in his God there is no help
help no help for him in his God, there is no help no help for him in his God. But thou ô
there is no help for him in his God there is no help there is no help for him in his God.
Lord ô Lord art my Defender.
Thou art my
But thou ô Lord ô Lord art my Defender;

worship & ʸᵉ lifter up, ʸᵉ lifter up of my head. Thou art my worship & ʸᵉ Lifter up
Thou art my worship & ʸᵉ lifter up, ʸᵉ lifter up of my head. Thou art my worship & ʸᵉ Lifter up.
& ʸᵉ Lifter up of my head ʸᵉ Lifter up of my head, ʸᵉ Lifter up of my head.
Cho:
& ʸᵉ Lifter up of my head, The Lifter up of my head ʸᵉ Lifter up of my head.
Cho:
But Thou ô Lord o Lord art my Defender, Thou art my worship, & ʸᵉ Lifter up,
Cho:
But thou ô Lord ô Lord art my Defender, thou art my Worship & ʸᵉ Lifter up,
and ʸᵉ Lifter up of my head the Lifter up of my head, ʸᵉ Lifter up of my head.
and ʸᵉ Lifter up of my head ʸᵉ Lifter up of my head ʸᵉ Lifter up of my head.

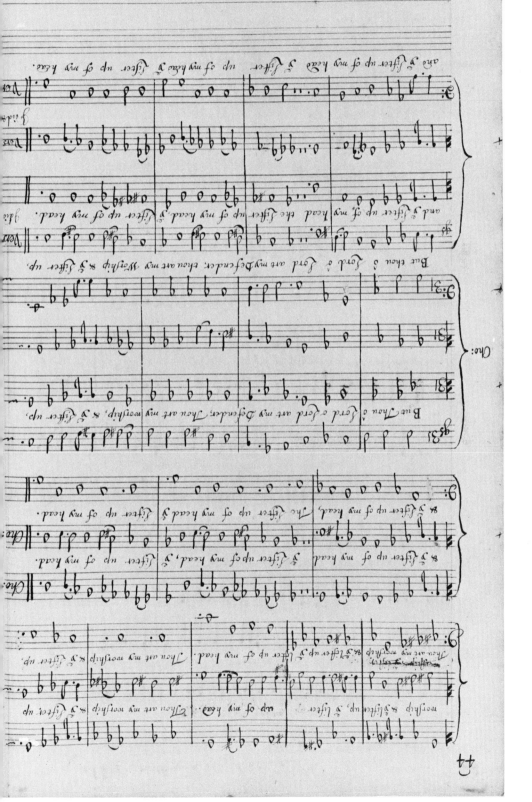

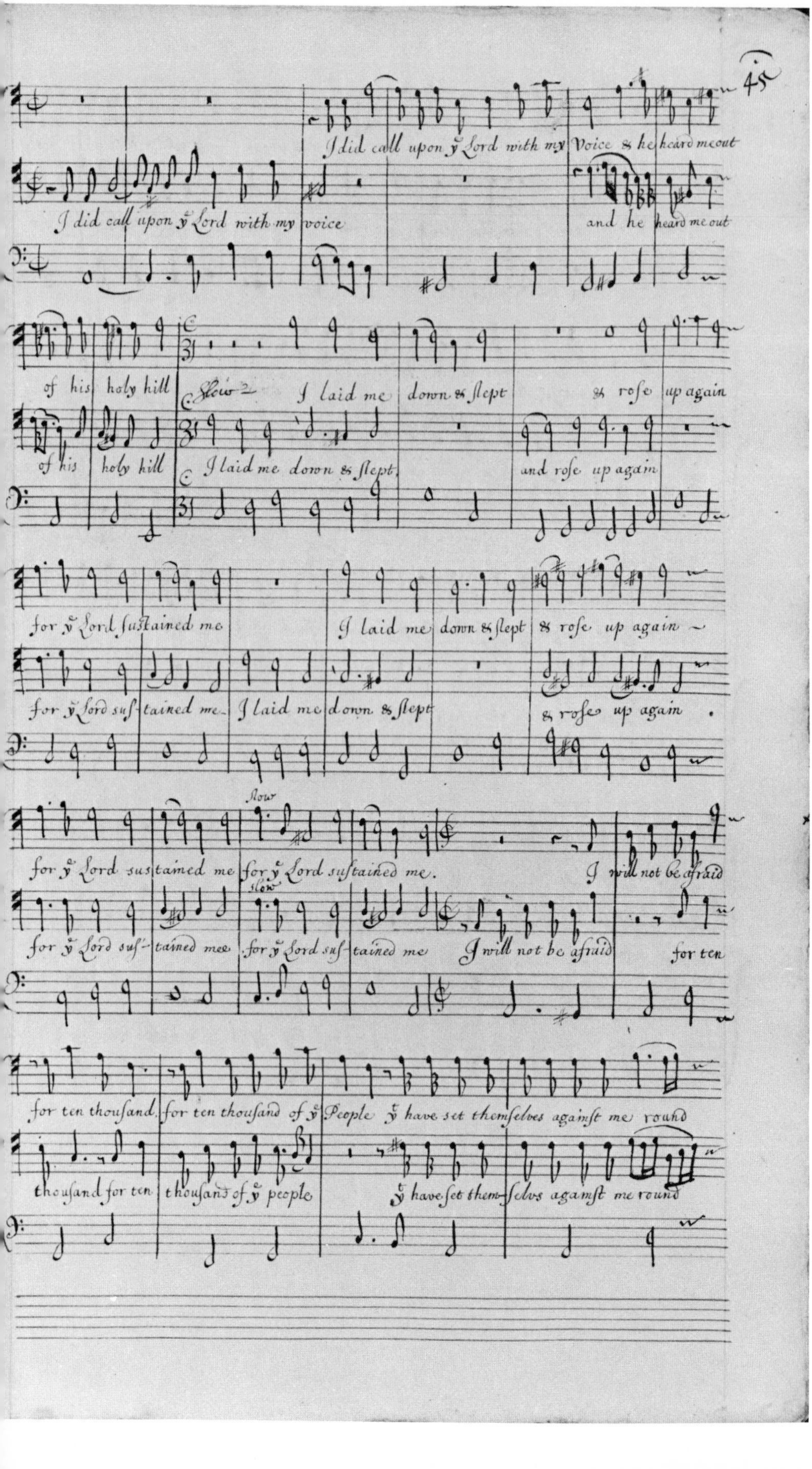
45
I did call upon ye Lord with my Voice & he heard me out
I did call upon ye Lord with my voice and he heard me out
of his holy hill
Slow
I laid me down & slept & rose up again
of his holy hill
I laid me down & slept and rose up again
for ye Lord sustained me I laid me down & slept & rose up again
for ye Lord sus-tained me I laid me down & slept & rose up again
Slow
for ye Lord sus tained me for ye Lord sustained me. I will not be afraid
Slow
for ye Lord sus-tained mee for ye Lord sus-tained me I will not be afraid for ten
for ten thousand for ten thousand of ye People yt have set themselves against me round
thousand for ten thousand of ye people yt have set them-selves against me round

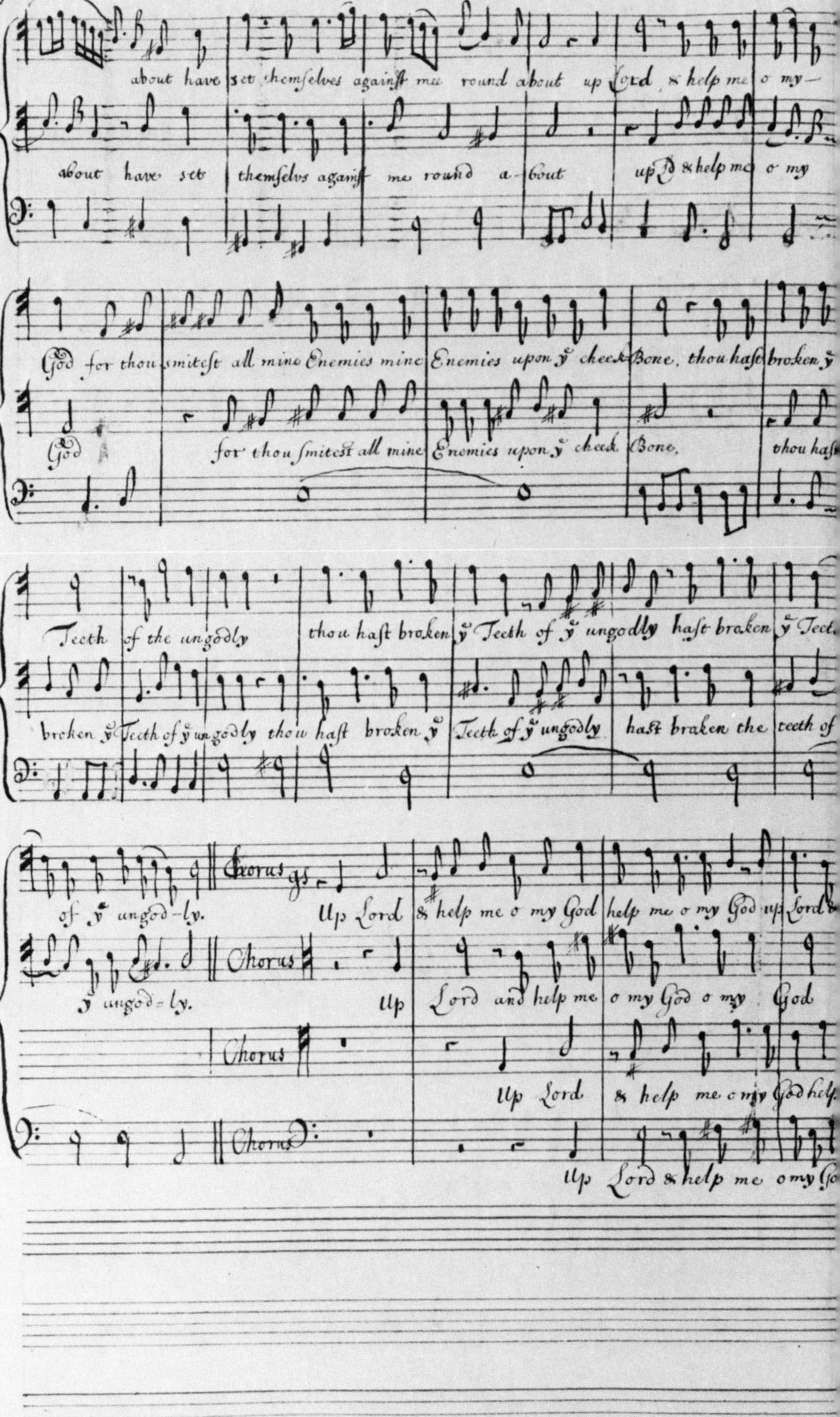
about have set themselves against mee round about up Lord, & help me o my—
about have set themselvs against me round a-bout up Lord & help me o my
God for thou smitest all mine Enemies mine Enemies upon ye cheek Bone, thou hast broken ye
God for thou smitest all mine Enemies upon ye cheek Bone, thou hast
Teeth of the ungodly thou hast broken ye Teeth of ye ungodly hast broken ye Teeth
broken ye Teeth of ye ungodly thou hast broken ye Teeth of ye ungodly hast broken the teeth of
of ye ungod-ly. Chorus Up Lord & help me o my God help me o my God up Lord &
ye ungod-ly. Chorus Up Lord and help me o my God o my God
Chorus Up Lord & help me o my God help
Chorus Up Lord & help me o my God

help me o my God for thou smitest all mine Enemies, upon ye Cheek-bone Thou hast broken ye
o my God For thou smit-est all mine Enemies upon the Cheek bone
me o my God for ye smitest all mine Enemies thou smitest all mine Enemies upon ye Cheek
help me O my God for thou smitest all mine Enemies thou smitest all mine enemies upon ye Cheek
Teeth of the ungod-ly of ye ungodly ye ungodly thou hast bro=ken ye teeth of the
Thou hast broken, the Teeth of ye ungodly ye ungodly ye ungodly Thou hast
bone Thou hast broken ye Teeth hast broken ye Teeth of ye ungodly hast brok=
bone Thou hast broken the Teeth of ye ungodly ye ungodly thou hast
ungodly of ye ungodly ye ungodly hast broken the Teeth of the un-god--
broken ye teeth of ye ungodly ye ungodly hast broken ye Teeth of the un=godly thou hast
- en ye teeth of ye ungodly ye ungodly of the un godly thou hast
broken ye Teeth of ye ungodly ye ungodly of the un- god- ly
=ly
broken ye Teeth, thou hast broken ye Teeth of ye ungod-ly.
Dr Blow
broken ye Teeth thou hast broken the Teeth of ye un-god-ly
thou hast broken ye Teeth of the ungod- ly

48
Hear ô heavns.
Solus.
Hear ô heavns & give Ear ô Earth for yͤ Lord hath spoken I have nourished &
brought up children & they have rebelled against mee
ah sinfull nation
a seed of evil=
=doers children yͭ are Corrupters, they have forsaken yͤ Lord
ah; sinfull nation they
have provoked yͤ holy one of Israel unto anger
ah sinfull nation
ah sinfull sinfull Nation
ah sinfull nation
a seed of
doers children yͭ are Corrupters, they have forsaken yͤ Lord ah sinfull Nation ah sinfull
ah,
ah

Cho:
Nation ah ah sinfull Nation They have provoked ye holy one of Israel unto
sinfull nation ah, ah sinfull Nation They have provoked ye holy one of Israel unto
sinfull natio ah sinfull nation They have provoked ye holy one of Israel unto
They have provoked ye holy one of Israel unto
anger, ah sinfull nation sinfull nation, ah sinfull Na=tion.
Verse
anger, ah sinfull nation sinfull nation ah sinfull nation.
make you clean
anger, ah ah sinfull nation ah sinfull nation.
Wash you
anger ah ah sinfull nation ah sinfull nation
put away ye evil of yor doings from before mine Eyes.
learn to do
cease to do Evil
seek Judgmt.
plead plead
well
Judge ye Fatherlesse
for ye widow, for ye widow
releive ye oppressed
for ye widow for ye widow

plead for ye widow come now let us reason together saith ye Lord,
plead for ye Widow come now let us reason together saith ye Lord
plead for ye Widow come now let us reason together saith ye Lord, thô yo sins be as
they shall be as white as Snow
they shall be as white as Snow
Scarlet thô they be red like Crimson they shall be as Wooll,
they shall be as wooll thô yo
they shall be as wooll,
Sins be as Scarlet,
like Crimson they
they shall be as white as Wooll thô they be red like Crimson, like Crimson
they shall be as white as Wooll, thô they be red like Crimson like Crimson
they shall be as wooll like Crimson they shall be as Wooll.
soft
they shall be as wooll thô they be red like Crimson like Crimson, they shall be as Wooll.
they shall be as wooll thô they be red like Crimson like Crimson they shall be as Wooll.

Cho:
Thô yoʳ Sins be as Scar- -let, they shall be as white as Snow; thô they be-
Thô yoʳ Sins be as Scarlet they shall be as white as white as Snow;
Thô yoʳ Sins be as Scarlet as Scarlet they shall be as white as Snow thô they be red like
Thô yoʳ Sins be as Scarlet they shall be as White as Snow, thô they be red like
red like Crimson thô they be red like Crimson like Crimson, they shall be as Wooll
thô they be red like Crimson thô they be red like Crimson they shall be as Wooll
Crimson thô they be red like Crimson they shall be as Wooll thô they be
Crimson thô they be red like Crimson red like Crimson they shall be as Wooll thô they be
thô they be red like Crimson thô they be red like Crimson like Crimson they shall
thô they be red like Crimson thô they be red like Crimson They
red like Crimson thô they be red like Crimson they shall
red like Crimson thô they be red like Crimson red like Crimson they shall
be as Wooll.
PH
shall be as Wooll.
be as Wooll.
be as Wooll.

Blessed be ye Lord my Strength.

Vers. sol.
Blessed, blessed, blessed be ye Lord my strength who teacheth my hands to war
who teacheth who teacheth my hands to war and my Fingers to fight my hope & my
Fortress my Castle and deliverer my Defender in whom I trust My-
Hope & my Fortress my Castle & deliverer my Defender in whom I trust who sub-
-dueth my People that is under me who subdueth my people yt is under me who
subdueth ye People that is under me.
Cho:
Cho:
Who subduth my people yt is under me who subduth m
who subduth my People that is under me is under me who-
Who subduth ye people yt is under me who sub-duth my people that is
Who subduth my People that is under me who subduth my people yt is

people that is under me ÿ is under me.
subduth my people ÿ is under me.
2d verse.
under me ÿ is under me.
Lord, Lord what is man ÿ
under me ÿ is under me.
Or ÿ Son of man ÿ thou so regardest
Thou thou hast such Respect un-to him
Man
him
Man is like
a thing of nought
his
is like
a thing of nought
Man is like
a
Time passeth a-way like a shadow Man is like
a thing of nought his
thing of nought
his time passeth a-way like a shadow
his Time
Time his Time passeth away like a shadow passeth away like a shadow. Lord
his Time passeth a way like a shadow Lord what is Man ÿ thou hast

what is Man Man is like a thing of nought his time passeth away a
such respect unto him Man is like a thing of nought his time passeth away a
way like a Shadow a way like a Shadow.
way like a shadow a way like a Shadow.
Cho: Man is like a thing of nought Man is like a thing of nought his time passeth a
Man is like a thing of nought Man is like a thing of nought his time passeth a
Cho: Man is like a thing of nought his time passeth away like a Shadow passeth away
Cho: His time passeth a-way like a shadow his time passeth away
way like a shadow passeth away away like a Shadow.
way like a passeth a way away like a Shadow.
Vers:
like a Shadow his Time passeth away a-way like a Shadow. Bow thy heavns o
like a Shadow passeth away a way like a Shadow.
Lord & come down bow thy heavns o Lord & come down come down

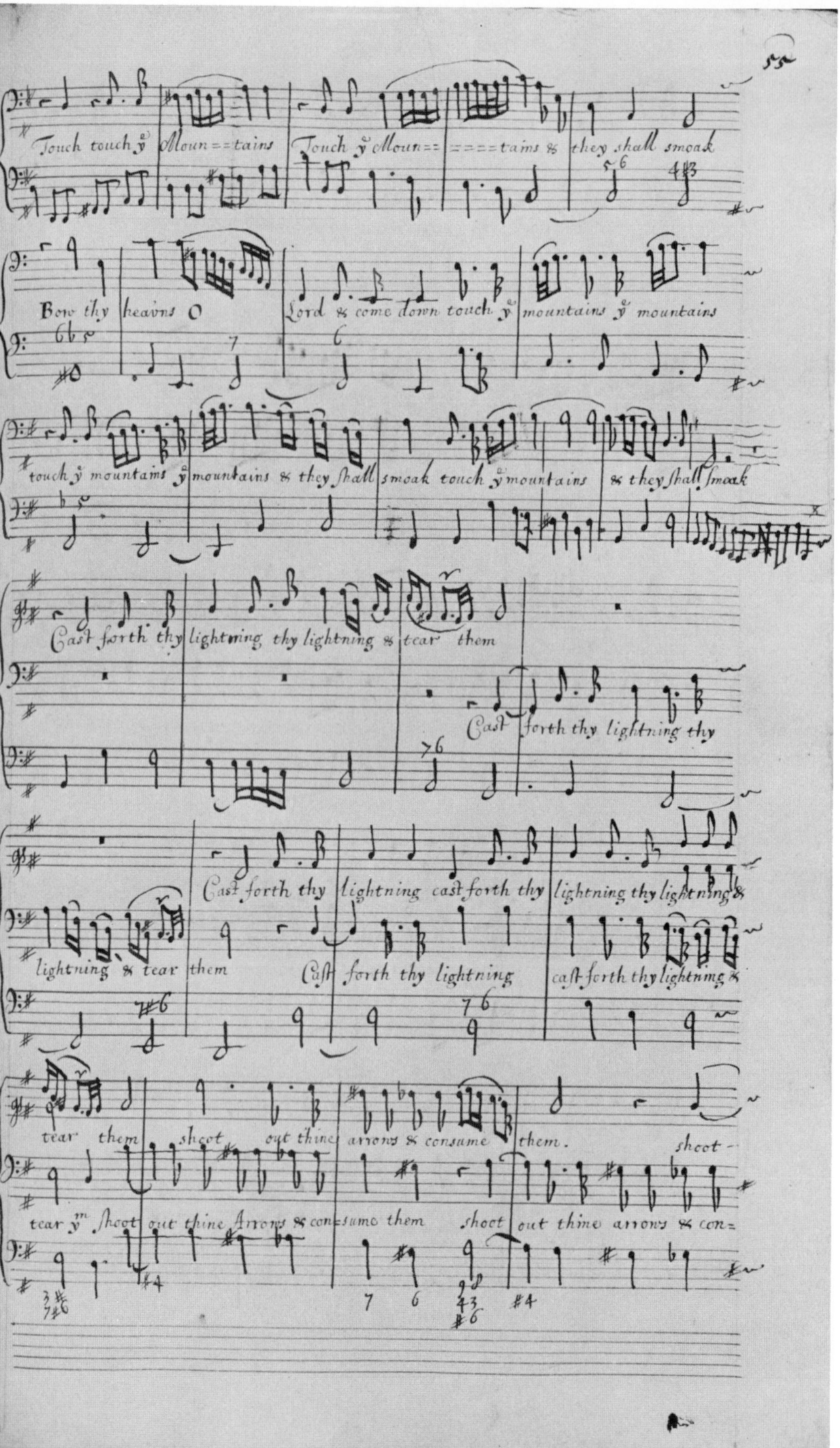

Touch touch y^e Moun==tains Touch y^e Moun== ====tains & they shall smoak
Bow thy heavns O Lord & come down touch y^e mountains y^e mountains
touch y^e mountains y^e mountains & they shall smoak touch y^e mountains & they shall smoak
Cast forth thy lightning thy lightning & tear them
Cast forth thy lightning thy
Cast forth thy lightning cast forth thy lightning thy lightning &
lightning & tear them Cast forth thy lightning cast forth thy lightning &
tear them shoot out thine arrows & consume them. shoot -
tear y^m shoot out thine Arrows & consume them shoot out thine arrows & con=

out thine arrows shoot out thine arrows & con===sume them
==-sume them con- sume them shoot out thine arrows & consume them send down
send down down thine hand from a bove from a bove send down thine hand from
down down thine hand from a bove send down down down thine
=bove from a- bove deli==ver me & take me out take me out of ye great wa-ters from ye
hand from a bove deli==ver me and take me out take me out of ye great waters,
hand of strange children ye hand of strange children take me out out of ye great
From ye hand of strange children ye hand of strange children & take me take me
waters from the hand From ye hand ye hand of Strange Child
out from ye hand of strange children: ye hand of strange children from ye hand of Str: children

Cho:
Whose mouth talketh of Vanity talketh of Vanity & their right hand & their right hand
Cantorii
Idem &c.
right hand is a right hand of Iniquity
is a right hand of In-iquity
i = quity
Composed by Dr Blow
June 30. 1688.

Psalm. Anthem for ye Charter-house sung upon ye Founders day, by Mr Barmclee & Mr Bowman.

Organ
Blessed
Blessed is ye Man that seareth ye Lord.
Blessed Blessed is ye Man that seareth ye Lord.
Blessed is ye Man that seareth ye Lord Blessed is ye Man ye seareth ye Lord he hath
Blessed Blessed is ye Man ye seareth ye Lord ye seareth ye Lord
great delight in his Commandments hath great de-
he hath great de- light in his Commandmts hath great
-light in his Commandments. Blessed Blessed is ye Man ye seareth ye Lord.
delight in his Commandments. Blessed Blessed is ye Man ye seareth ye Ld, he hath

he hath great de=light in his Com=mandments hath great de=
great de=light he hath great de=light hath great de=
=light in his Commandm.ts hath great delight in his Commandm.ts
=light in his Com=mandm.ts hath great de=light in his Com=mandm.ts
Organ
His seed shall be migh=== ty shall be migh====
His seed shall be migh====
==ty u=====pon Earth, the Gene=ration of ye Faithfull shall be bless'd ye
==ty u=======pon Earth the Gene=ration of the Faithfull
Gene=ration of ye Faithfull shall be bless'd ye Gene=ration of ye Faithfull-
shall--- be bless'd ye Gene=ration of ye Faithfull shal be bless'd ye-

shall - - be blessd shall be blessd.
Riches &
Generation of ye Faithfull shall be blessd.
Riches &
Plenteousness shall be in his House & his Righteousness endureth for ever for
Plenteousness shall be in his House & his Righteousness endureth en-du-
ever for ever for ever his Righteousness endureth en-du-
-reth for ever his Righteousness endureth for ever for e-ver for
reth for e-ver en-du- -reth for e-ver Organ.
soft
soft
e-ver for ever for ever for ever for ever for ever.
Unto ye Godly there ari- -seth

Light in ye darkness he is mercifull is mercifull lo==ving & righteous
a good man is
76
6 4
7 5
mercifull
he hath dispersed abroad.
A Good Man
he hath given to ye Poor a
6 76
a good Man
Good man a Good man is mercifull is mercifull his name shall be ex=alted ex=
a good man is mercifull is mercifull
his Name shall be ex=
=alted ex=alted his name shall be ex=alted exalted ex=al= = = = = ted ex=
=alted ex=alted his name shall be ex=alted exalted shall be exal= = =
=al= = = = = = = ted ex al= = = = = = ted ex=alted wth hono wth hono wth hono his
= =alted exal= = = = = = =alted exal= = = = = = = ted wth hono wth hono wth hono his

62
Name shall be exal=ted exal=ted wth hono.
Organ
Name shall be exalted ex= =alted wth honour.
Alleluia alleluia Alleluia alleluia
Alleluia Alleluia Alleluia alleluia
Alleluia al= = = = lelu=ia alle= =luia alle=luia alle=luia al= = = =le=lu=
Alleluia Alle= = = =lu= =ia Alle=luia Alleluia alle=lu= = =ia alle=lu=
=ia al= = = = = = = = = = = = = le=lu= ia Al= = = = = = = = = = = = = = le=lu= =ia.
=ia al= = = = = = = = = = = = = = le= =lu= =ia Al= = = = = = = = = = = = = le= =lu= =ia.
Cho
Cho:
Cho:
ho:

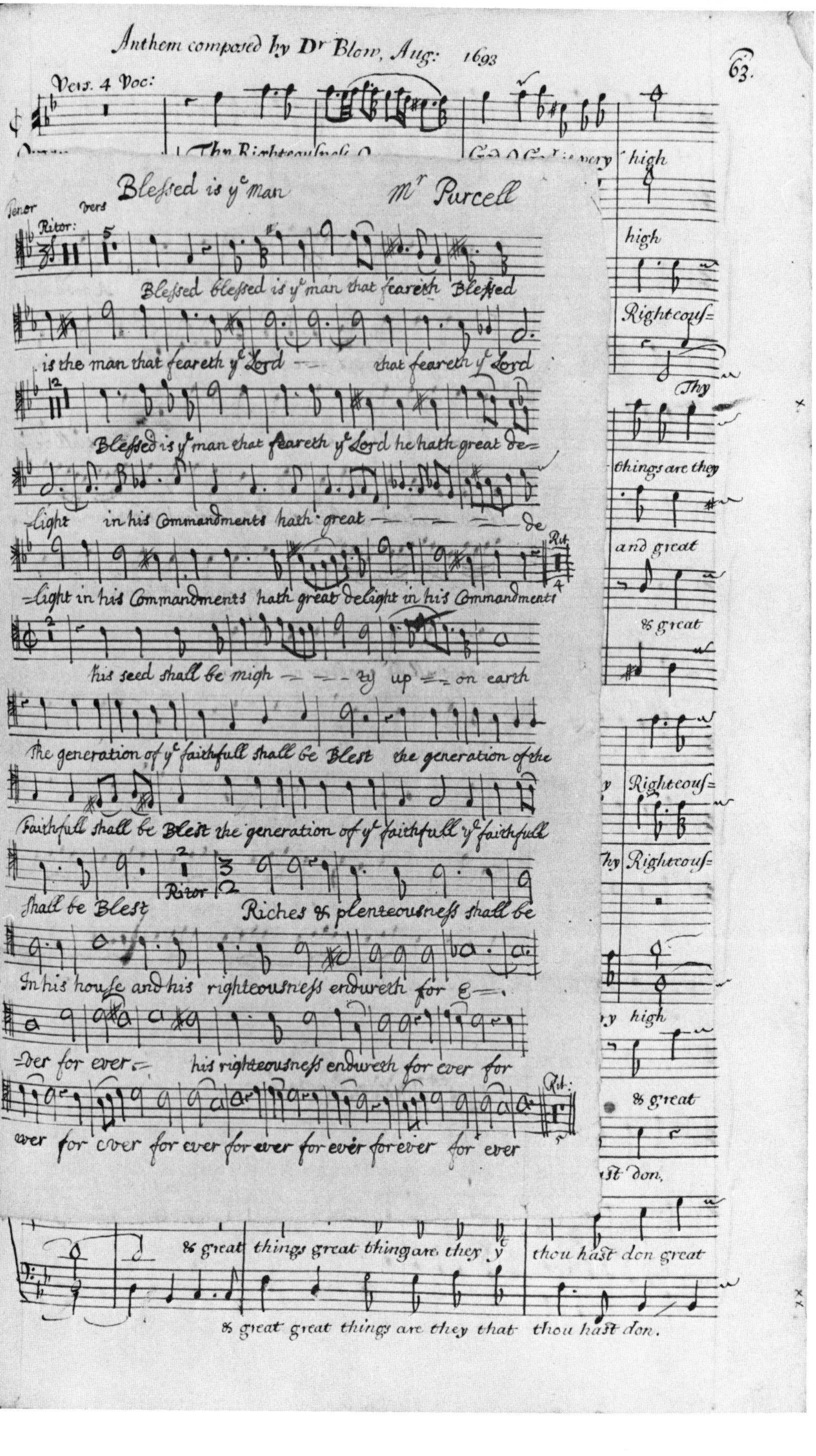
Anthem composed by Dr Blow, Aug: 1693
63.
Vers. 4 Voc:
Blessed is ye Man
Mr Purcell
Tenor
vers
Ritor:
Blessed blessed is ye man that feareth Blessed
is the man that feareth ye Lord that feareth ye Lord
Blessed is ye man that feareth ye Lord he hath great de=
=light in his Commandments hath great de
=light in his Commandments hath great delight in his Commandments
his seed shall be migh ty up on earth
The generation of ye faithfull shall be Blest the generation of the
Faithfull shall be Blest the generation of ye faithfull ye faithfull
Ritor
Shall be Blest Riches & plenteousness shall be
In his house and his righteousness endureth for E
=ver for ever his righteousness endureth for ever for
ever for ever for ever for ever for ever for ever for ever
Rit:
high
high
Righteous=
Thy
things are they
and great
& great
Righteous=
Righteous=
high
& great
& great things great thing are they ye thou hast don great
& great great things are they that thou hast don.

62
Name shall be exal-ted exal-ted wth hon
Name shall be
Alleluia al-
Alleluia
-ia al-
-ia al-
Hallelujah
Halle
Hallelujah
Hall-
vers
he hath dispersed abroad
A good man
A good man is mercifull is mercyfull his name shall
be exalted his name shall be exalted his name shall be e
-alted exalted exalted shall be exalted ex al- ted
al- ted wth honour wth honor wth honor h
name shall be exalted wth honor:
Hallelujah Hall Ha Ha
Hallelujah Ha Ha
Halle lu jah Hal
-le-lu-jah Hal le-lu-jah

Anthem composed by Dr Blow, Aug: 1693

Vers. 4 Voc:
Organ
Thy Righteousness O
God O God is very high
Thy Righteousness O
God is very
high
Thy Righteous=
Thy
is very high very high & great things are they
is very high very high and great
=ness O
God is very high
& great
Righteous-ness O
God is very high
and great things are they ye thou hast don
O God thy Righteous=
things are they that thou hast don O God Thy Righteous=
things are they ye thou hast don O God
Thy Righteous-ness O God is very high
ness O God is very high
& great
ness O God is very high & great things are they ye thou hast don,
& great things great thing are they ye thou hast don great
& great great things are they that thou hast don.

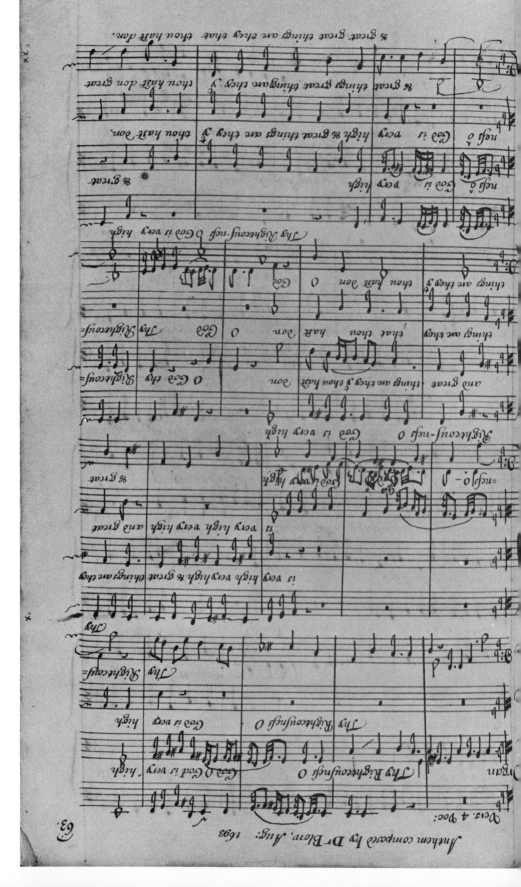

things are they yt thou hast don O God who is like unto thee o God who
O God who is like unto —
things are they yt thou hast don
O God who is like unto thee who who is
who is like unto thee? O God who is like unto thee who
thee un=to thee? O God who is like unto thee who who is like unto thee who
O God who is like unto thee who! O God who is like unto
like un=to thee ô God who is like unto thee who is like unto thee ô God
who is like unto thee? who! who who is like unto thee?
who is like unto thee? who! who who is like unto thee?
thee o God thy Righteousness is very high who who is like
who is like unto thee?
O God who is like unto thee who who is like unto ye?
O God who is like unto thee who who is like unto thee who who is like unto thee?
unto thee O God who is like unto thee who is like unto ye?
who is like unto thee who is like unto thee ô God who is like unto thee?

Slow.
O what great troubles & adversities hast thou
Slow
shewd me.
yet didst thou turn & re=
O wt great troubles & adversities hast thou shewd me!
yet didst thou
fresh, me
yet didst thou turn
& refresh me o what great
turn
yet didst yu turn & re fresh me
troubles & adversities hast thou shewd me!
yet didst thou
O
wt great troubles & adversities hast yu shewd me!
turn didst thou turn yet didst thou turn
& refresh me
yet didst thou turn
yet didst thou turn
& refresh me

yea & broughtest me from ye deep of ye Earth again
yea & broughtest me from ye deep of ye earth again,
yea & broughtest me from ye
O wt great troubles & adversities hast thou shewd me
deep of ye earth again,
yet didst thou turn
yea & broughtest me from ye deep of ye earth again, yea and
& re-fresh me
yea & broughtest me from ye deep of ye earth
broughtest me from ye deep of ye earth a-gain yea & broughtest me from ye deep of ye
-gain & broughtest me from ye deep of ye earth again yea & broughtest me fro ye deep of
Vers: 3 voc.
earth again. Thou hast brought me to great hono
Cho:
Thou hast brought me to great
earth again. Thou hast brought me to great hono,
Thou hast brought me to great
Thou hast brought me to great hono,
Thou hast brought me to great
Thou hast brought me to great

Cho:
hono,
Vers:
And comforted me comforted me on ev'ry side,
hono, And comforted me, And comforted me comforted me on ev'ry side.
hono, And comforted me, And comforted me comforted me on ev'ry side.
Cho:
hono, And comforted me, And comforted me comforted me on e'vry side,
Vers. Comforted me on e=v'ry side.
Vers. 2 voc.
Vers. Comforted me on ev'ry side.
Therefore will I praise thee
Vers: Comforted me on e=v'ry side.
Therefore will I
Comforted me on e=v'ry side
Therefore will I praise thee & thy Faithfull-ness
Therefore will I
praise thee & thy Faithfullness
Therefore will I praise thee
praise Thee & thy faithfullness thy faithfullness O God
& thy faithfull-ness thy faithfull-ness O

playing upon an In==strument of Mu==sick
Therefore will I
God
playing upon an In==stru=ment of Musick
praise thee will I praise thee & thy Faithfullness O God O God,
therefore will I praise thee will I praise thee & thy faithfull – ness O God
playing upon an Instru- ment of Musick, playing upon an In=strument of
playing upon an In=stru-ment of Musick playing upon an In=strument of
Musick Unto thee will I sing upon ye Harp O, O thou holy one of Isra=
Musick.
--el.
unto thee will
Unto thee will I sing upon ye Harp O O thou holy one of Is-rael

sing upon ye Harp O O thou ho=ly one of Is=ra= el. unto thee will I sing
unto thee will I sing upon ye harp upon the
upon ye Harp O O thou holy one of Israel O O thou
Harp O thou holy one of Is=rael O thou holy one of Israel thou
holy one of Israel,
My Lips shall greatly shall greatly re=
holy one of Israel,
=joice when I sing unto Thee shall
My Lips shall greatly shall greatly re-
greatly re- joice when I sing unto thee && so will my soul && so will my
=joyce when I sing unto Thee,

soul whom thou hast re-
Shall greatly re-joice re-
My Lips shall greatly shall greatly rejoice rejoice
joice rejoice rejoice when I sing when I sing unto
My Lips shall greatly re-joice when I sing unto
Thee so will my soul so will my soul whom thou hast redeemed
Thee And so will my
So will my soul whom thou hast whom thou hast redeemed so will my
soul so will my soul whom thou hast whom thou hast re-deemed so will my sou
soul so will my soul whom thou hast redeemed. Organ.
so will my soul so will my soul whom thou hast redeemed.
My tongue also shall talk shall talk of thy Righteousness all y day long

71
Vers: a 3.
For they are confounded for they are confounded they are confound, & brought unto
For they are confoun-ded for they are confounded they are confounded & brought unto
For they are confoun-ded for they are confounded they are confounded & brought unto
shame y seek that seek to do me evil
shame y seek y seek to do me evil, For they are confounded, for they
shame y seek y seek to do me evil, For they are confounded for they
y seek y seek to do me evil For they are confounded for they
My tongue al= so shall
are confounded they are confounded & brought unto shame.
are confounded they are confounded & brought unto shame.
are con: &c
talk shall talk of thy Righteousness all y day long
For thy are confoun:
For they are confoun=
For they are confoun=

for they are confounded they are confounded & brought brought unto shame yt
=ded for they are confoun ded for they are confounded & shame yt
ded for they are confounded for they are confounded & brought brought unto shame yt
ded for they are confounded they are confounded & brought unto shame unto shame
seek that seek to do me evil that seek that seek to do me evil. Glory
seek yt seek to do me evil that seek yt seek to do me evil Glory
seek to do me evil that seek yt seek to do me evil
Cho: Glory be to ye Father & to ye son & to ye holy Ghost as it was in ye beginning is
Cho: Glory be to ye Father & to ye Son & to ye holy Ghost as it was in ye beginning is
Cho: Glory be to ye Father & to ye Son & to ye holy Ghost as it was in ye beginning is
Cho:
now is now & ever shall be world without end Amen world without end A= men Amen
now is now & ever shall be world without end Amen world without end Amen Amen
now is now & ever shall be world wth out end A — men world wth out end A= men Amen
now is now & ever shall be world without end Amen world wth out end without end A=men

For 2 Con: Lord what is Man. Psa: 8. Ver. 4.
& one Bass:

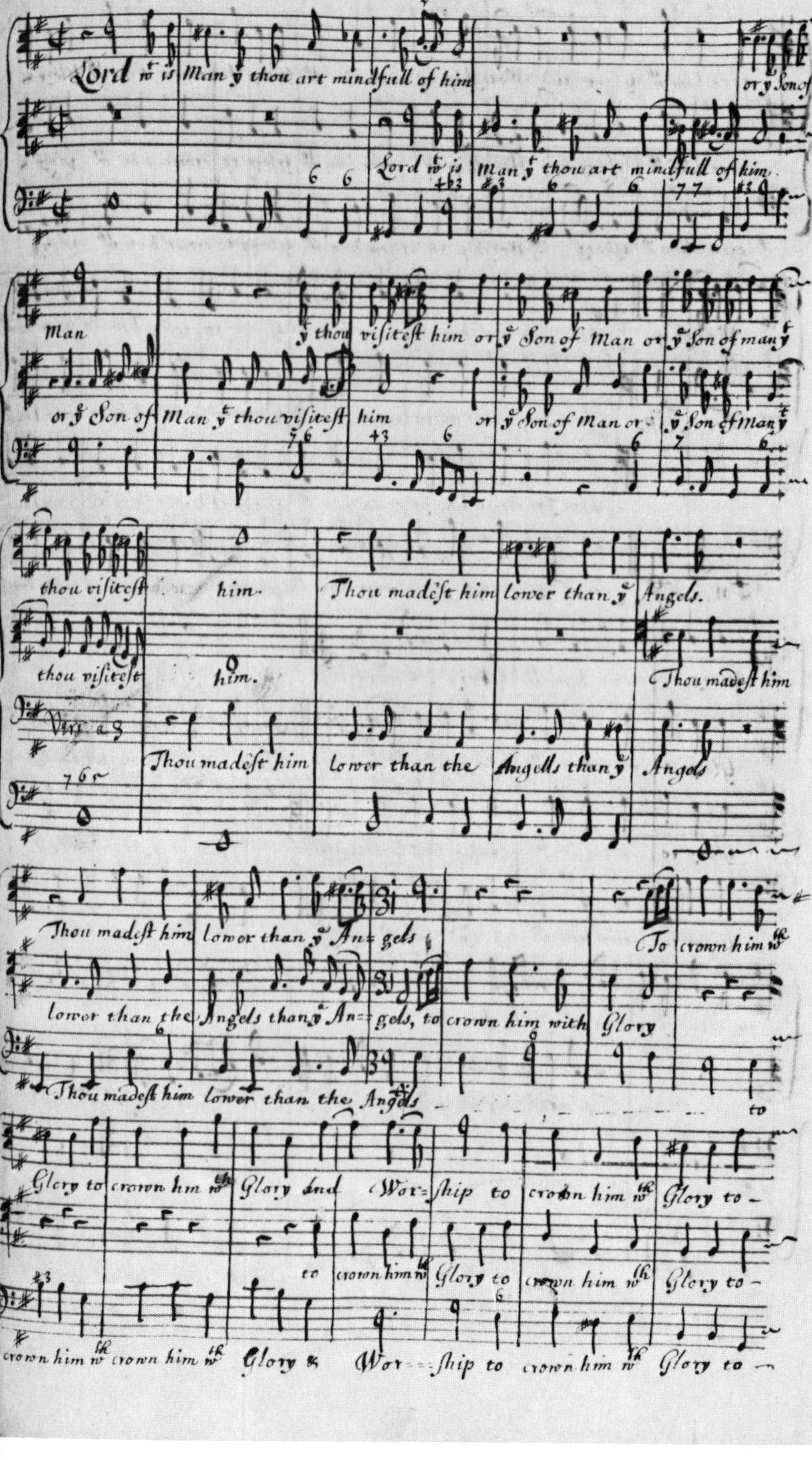
Lord wth is Man yt thou art mindfull of him
or ye Son of
Lord wth is Man yt thou art mindfull of him.
Man
yt thou visitest him or ye Son of Man or ye Son of man yt
or ye Son of Man yt thou visitest him
or ye Son of Man or ye Son of Man yt
thou visitest him.
Thou madest him lower than ye Angels.
thou visitest him.
Thou madest him
Vers a 3
Thou madest him lower than the Angells than ye Angels
Thou madest him lower than ye An= gels
To crown him wth
lower than the Angels than ye An= gels, to crown him with Glory
Thou madest him lower than the Angels
to
Glory to crown him wth Glory and Wor= ship to crown him wth Glory to
to crown him wth Glory to crown him wth Glory to
crown him wth crown him wth Glory & Wor= ship to crown him wth Glory to

74

crown him wth Glory and Worship to crown him wth Glory to crown him wth Glory &
crown him wth Glory and Worship to crown him wth Glory to crown him wth Glory &
crown him wth Glory & Worship to crown him wth Glory to crown him wth Glory
Worship Cho: To crown him to crown him wth Glory to crown him to crown him
Wor- ship Cho: To crown him to crown him wth Glory to crown him to crown him
Cho: To crown him to crown him wth Glory to crown him to crown him
& Worship Cho: To crown him to crown him wth Glory to crown him to crown him
Glory to crown him wth Glory & wor= ship
vers. a 3
Glory to crown him wth Glory & Wor= ship Thou makest him to have Do=
Glory to crown him wth Glory & wor= ship.
Glory to crown him wth Glory & Worship.
minion of ye works of thy hands
Thou makest him to have Dominion of ye works of thy Hands thou

Thou makst him to have Dominion Thou makst him to have dominion of ye
makst him to have Dominion
Thou makst him to have Dominion of ye
Thou makst him to have dominion of ye
Works of thy Hands.
And
Works of thy Hands. And thou hast put all things in subjection un=
Works of thy Hands. & thou hast put all things in Subjec==tion under his
Thou hast put all things in Subjection under his Feet. And thou hast put all
==der his Feet under his Feet & thou hast put all things in Subjec=tion under his
Feet. And thou hast put all things in Sub=jec=tion under his
things in Subjection under his Feet. All sheep & Oxen all Sheep & Oxen
Feet in Subjec==tion under his Feet. All Sheep & Oxen yea and ye
Feet in Subjection under his Feet. All Sheep & Oxen yea & ye Beasts of ye

yea & the Beasts of ye Feild the Fowls of ye Air of Air & ye Fishes
Beasts of ye Feild the Fowles of ye Air & ye Fishes of the Sea and whatsoever
Feild ye Fowles of ye Air & ye Fishes ye Fishes of ye Sea. and
of the Sea and whatsoever walketh & whatsoever walketh thro ye Paths thro
walketh thro ye Paths of the Sea & whatsoever walketh thro ye Paths thro
whatsoever walketh thro ye paths of ye Sea. and whatsoever walketh thro ye
ye Paths of ye Sea. O Lord o Govern-o how excellent
ye Paths of the Sea, O Lord o Gov-ern- o how excellent is thy name
Paths of ye Paths of ye Sea. O Lord o Governour, how
is thy name in all ye world how excellent is thy name in all ye World!
how excellent is thy name is thy name in all ye World!
excellent is thy name how excel-lent is thy name in all ye World!

Chorus.

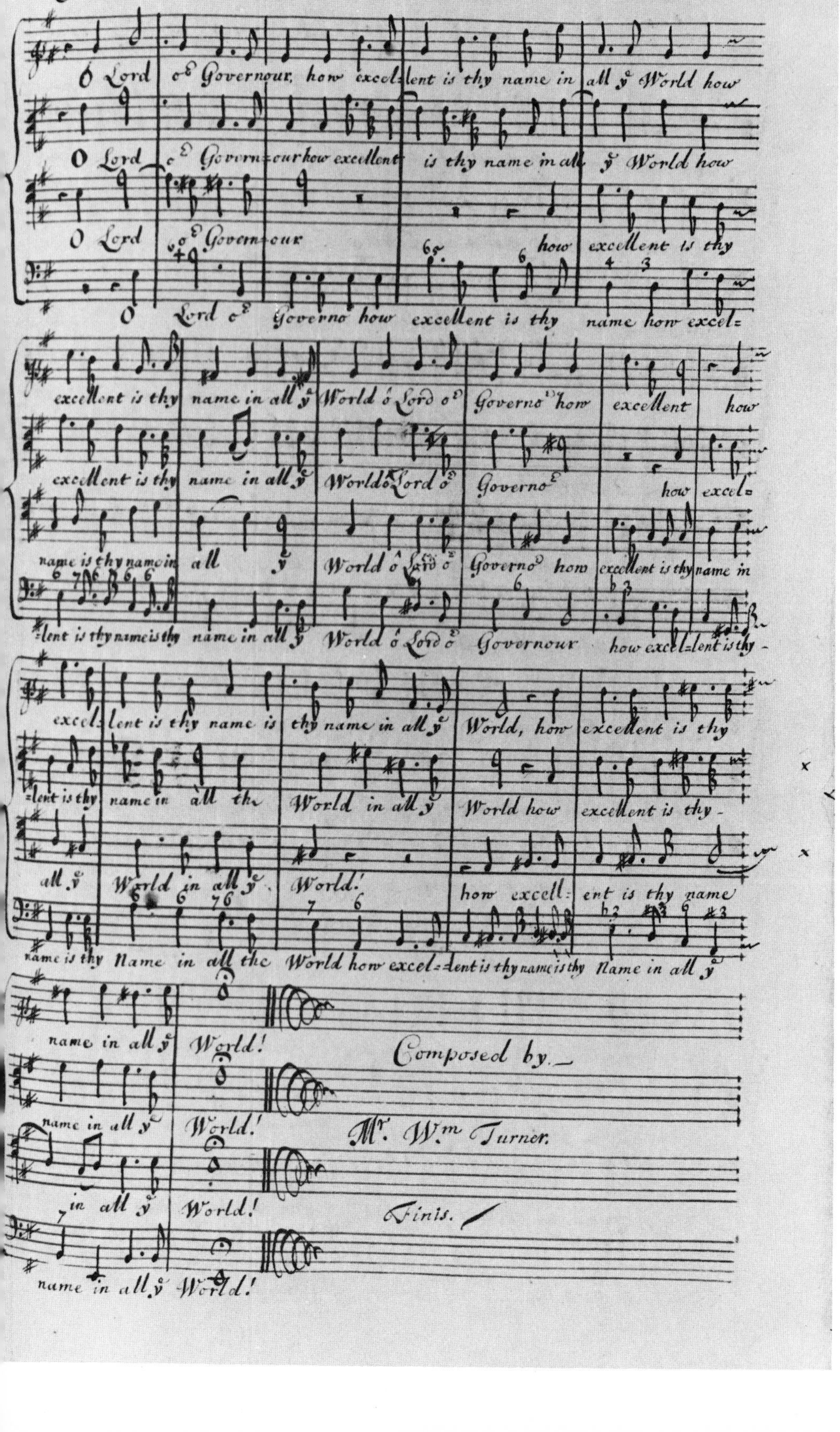
O Lord o Governour, how excel=lent is thy name in all ye World how
O Lord o Govern=our how excellent is thy name in all ye World how
O Lord o Govern=our how excellent is thy
O Lord o Governo how excellent is thy name how excel=
excellent is thy name in all ye World o Lord o Governo how excellent how
excellent is thy name in all ye World o Lord o Governo how excel=
name is thy name in all ye World o Lord o Governo how excellent is thy name in
=lent is thy name is thy name in all ye World o Lord o Governour how excel=lent is thy
excel=lent is thy name is thy name in all ye World, how excellent is thy
=lent is thy name in all the World in all ye World how excellent is thy
all ye World in all ye World! how excell=ent is thy name
name is thy Name in all the World how excel=lent is thy name is thy Name in all ye
name in all ye World!
name in all ye World!
in all ye World!
name in all ye World!
Composed by.
Mr. Wm Turner.
Finis.

Psa: 106. Verses 1. 2. 4. 5. & last. Composed by Mr Purcell. 1693.

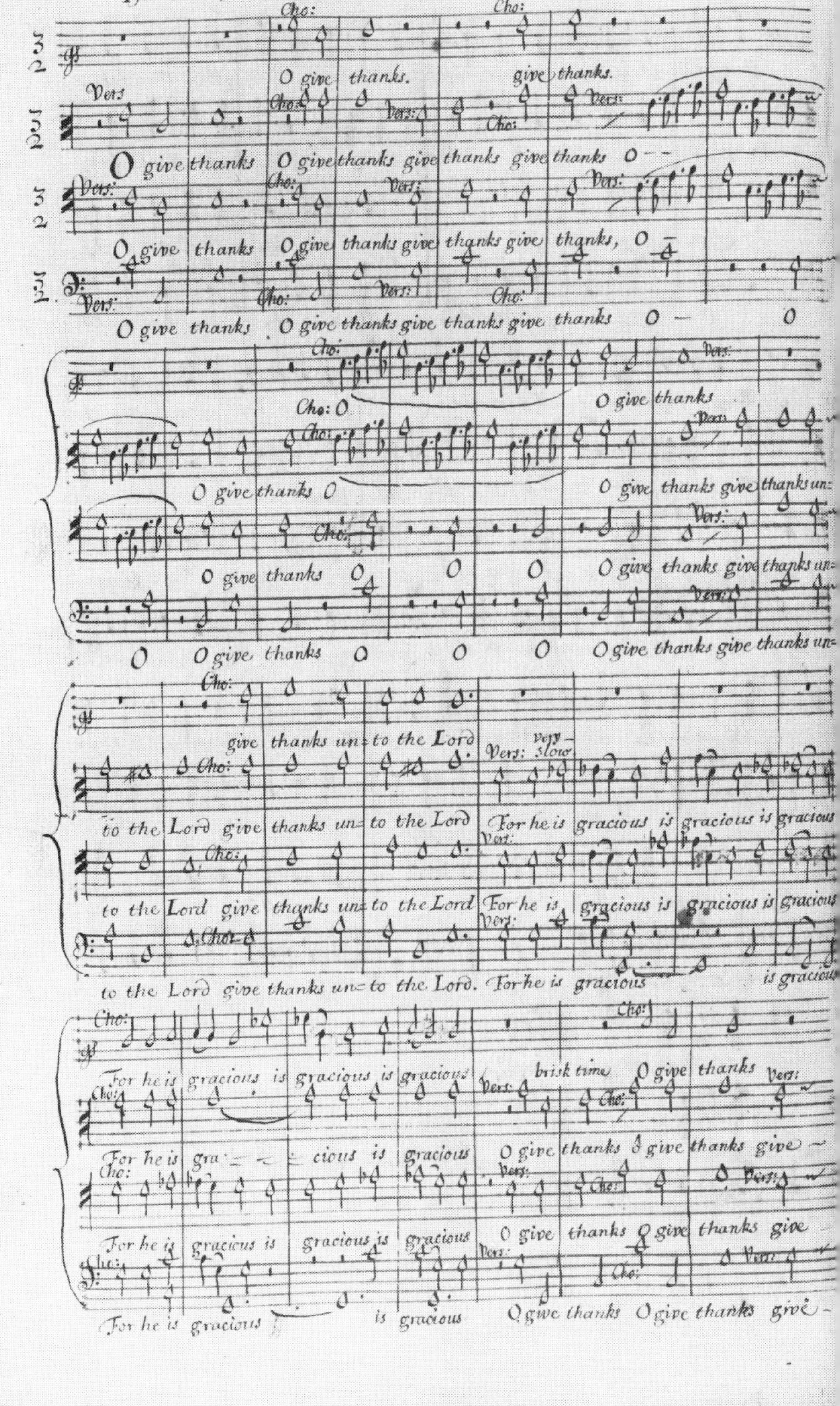
Cho:
O give thanks. give thanks.
Vers
O give thanks O give thanks give thanks give thanks O
O give thanks O give thanks give thanks give thanks, O
O give thanks O give thanks give thanks give thanks O O
Cho: O
O give thanks O O give thanks give thanks un-
O give thanks O O O O give thanks give thanks un-
O O give thanks O O O O give thanks give thanks un-
give thanks un- to the Lord
Vers: very slow
to the Lord give thanks un- to the Lord For he is gracious is gracious is gracious
to the Lord give thanks un- to the Lord For he is gracious is gracious is gracious
to the Lord give thanks un- to the Lord. For he is gracious is gracious
For he is gracious is gracious is gracious
brisk time O give thanks
For he is gra- cious is gracious O give thanks O give thanks give
For he is gracious is gracious is gracious O give thanks O give thanks give
For he is gracious is gracious O give thanks O give thanks give-

Cho:
Cho: give thanks Vers: O give
thanks give thanks give thanks ô O O O give
thanks give thanks give thanks ô O O O give
thanks give thanks give thanks O O O O O give
Very slow.
thanks un to ye Lord Cho: For he is gracious is gracious is
thanks un- to ye Lord give thanks un- to ye Lord. Cho: For he is gracious is gracious is
thanks un- to ye Lord give thanks un- to ye Lord Cho: For he is gra = = = = = = cious is
thanks unto ye Lord give thanks un-to ye Lord. Cho: For he is gracious is
gracious
gracious For he is gracious is gracious is gracious And his
gracious For he is gracious is gracious is gracious And his mercy en=
gracious For he is gracious is gracious And his mercy endureth his
And his mercy en- dureth his mercy en- dureth for e = = = = = ver his
mercy en- dureth for ever his mercy en- dureth for e = = = = = ver for e = = = =
dureth en- dureth for e= ver his mercy en- dureth for ever his
mercy en- dureth for e - - - - ver his mercy en- dureth for ever his

Cho
mercy en=dureth for ever for ever.
for ever
Ver. Cho: Ver:
--ver en=dureth for ever for ever, for ever for ever for ever
Ver: Cho: Ver: Cho:
mercy en=dureth for ever for ever, for ever for ever for ever
Ver: Cho: Ver: Cho: his
mercy en=dureth for ever for ever for ever for ever for ever; his mercy en=
Cho:
his mercy en=dureth his mercy en=dureth for- e - - - -
Cho
his mercy en=dureth for ever his mercy en=dureth for --e - -ver for
mercy en=dureth en=dureth for e=ver. his mercy en=dureth for
-dureth his mercy en=dureth for- e - - - - - ver his mercy en=dureth for
- ver his mercy endureth for ever. Ritornella
e== = ver en=dureth for ever.
ever his mercy en=dureth for ever. Ritornella.
ever his mercy en=dureth for ever.
Vers 2 voc:
Who who can express ye no====
Who who can express ye no:-- --ble Acts of ye
7 6 4 3 7 6

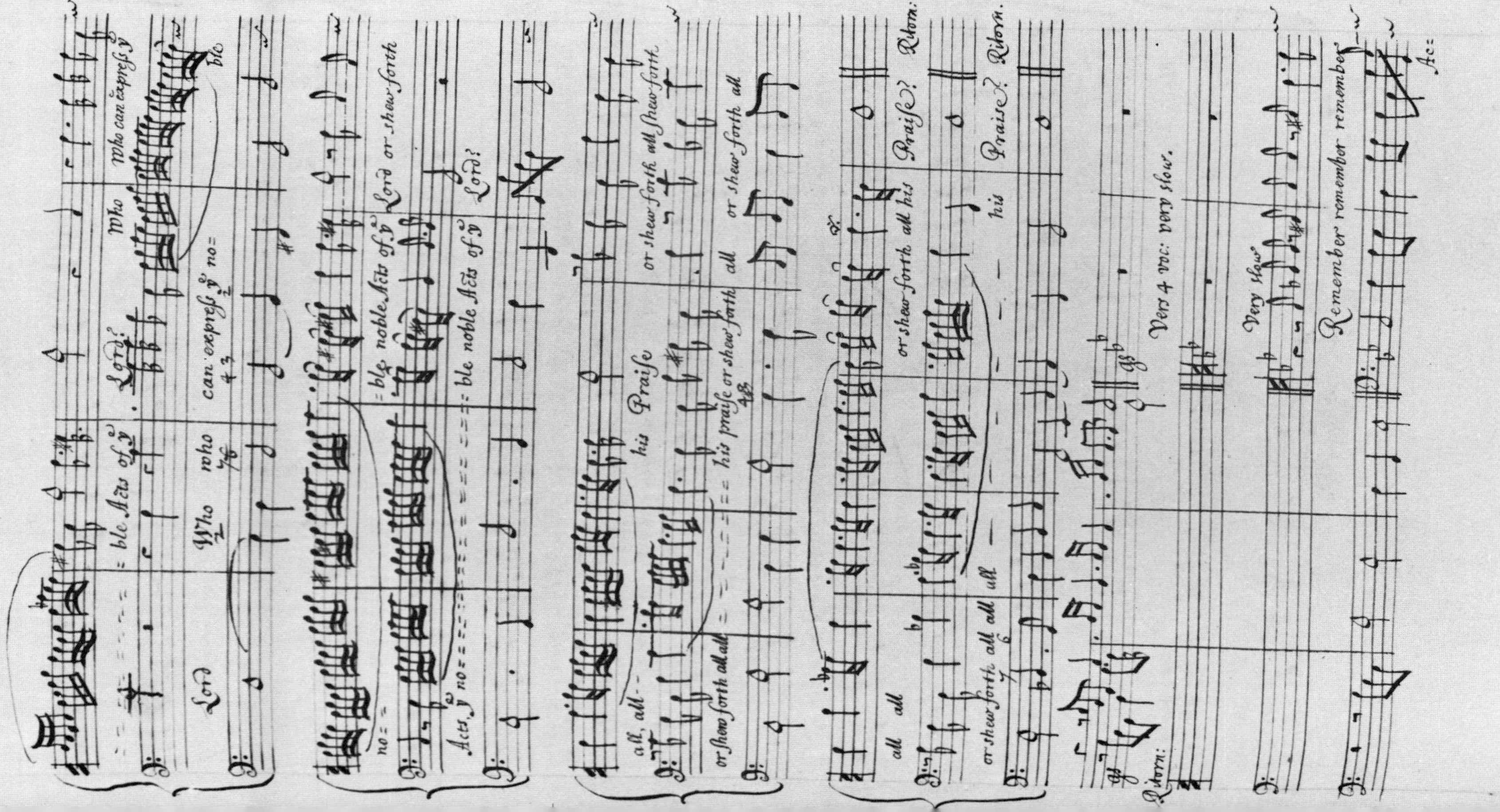
ble Acts of ye Lord? Who can express ye no=
Lord Who who can express ye no=
Who Who can express ye
ble
no= ble noble Acts of ye Lord or shew forth
Acts ye no= ble noble Acts of ye Lord?
all, all his Praise or shew forth all shew forth
or shew forth all all his praise or shew forth all or shew forth all
all all or shew forth all his Praise? Ritorn:
or shew forth all all all his Praise? Ritorn.
Ritorn:
Vers 4 voc: very slow.
Very slow
Remember remember remember
&c:

ac=cording to ye favor ye thou bearst unto thy people remember re=
remember re=member remember me o Lord ac=cording to ye favor ye thou
me o Lord. ac=
=cording to ye favor ye thou bearst unto thy people re=member remember re=
=member remember me o Lord ac=cording to ye favor ye thou bearst unto thy
bearst unto thy people re=member remember re=member me o
=cording to ye favor ye thou bearst unto thy people ac=cording to ye favor ye thou
-member me o Lord according to ye favor ye thou bearst unto thy people
people rememember me o Lord remember remember remember me o Lord, o Visit me o
Lord remember me o Lord according to ye favor ye thou bearst unto thy people o visit me
bearst unto thy people remember re=member me o Lord o visit me
Re=member remember re=member me o Lord o visit me o

visit me ô visit me wth thy Salvation O visit me o visit me O visit me with
O visit me O visit me wth thy salvation, ô visit me o visit me ô visit me wth
O visit me O visit me wth thy salvation. O visit me O visit me O visit me wth
visit me ô visit me with thy salvation ô visit me ô visit me ô visit me wth
thy salvation. Cho: O visit o visit me with thy Sal= vation. Organ
thy salvation. Cho: O visit O visit me with thy sal= vation.
thy salvation. Cho: O visit ô visit me wth thy sal= vation.
thy salvation. Cho: O visit ô visit me with thy sal= vation. Organ.
Vers: alone
That I may see, yt I may see ye Fe=
=li- - - - - - - - - - city of thy chosen & rejoice
wth ye Gladness ye Glad- ness of thy people

84

That I may see yͤ I may see yͤ Feli=city of thy chosen, And re=joice—
with yͤ Gladness yͤ Gladness of thy people and give
thanks & give thanks wth thine Inheritance, & give thanks
& give thanks give thanks wth thine In=
=heritance.
Ritor:
Vers: 4 voc.
Blessed blessed be the
Blessed blessed be the
Ritor.
Vers. Blessed blessed be the
Blessed, blessed be the
Lord God of Israel
blessed blessed be yͤ
Lord God of Israel from ever=las— ting everlasting
blessed blessed be yͤ
Lord God of Israel from ever=las— -ting everlasting
blessed blessed be yͤ
Lord God of Israel.—
blessed blessed be yͤ

Lord God of Israel from ever-las-ting everlasting
Lord God of Israel,
from ever-las-
Lord God of Israel,
from ever-las-
Lord God of Israel, from ever-las-ting everlasting,
from everlas-ting everlasting
and world without
ting
from ever-las-ting
and world without
ting
from ever-las-ting
and
from ever-las-ting e-verlasting. & world without end and
end and world without end & world without end & world without end & world without end.
end & world without end & world without end & world without end without end.
world without end and world without end and world without end world without end.
world without end & world without end & world without end without- end,
And let all ye people say, let all ye people say Amen Amen Amen. let
Cho: Vers:
And let all ye people say, let all ye people say Amen A-men Amen. let
And let all ye people say, let all ye people say Amen A-men Amen let
And let all ye people say, let all ye people say Amen A-men Amen, let

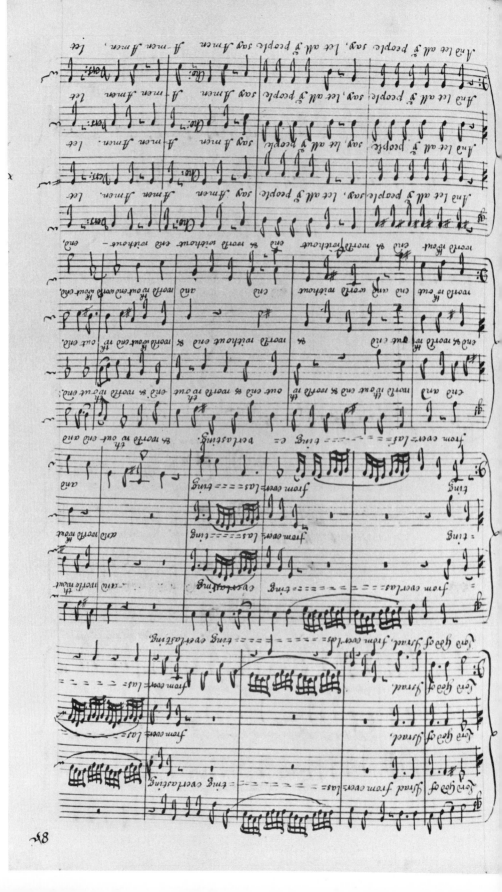

all y^e people say Amen Amen Amen. Let all y^e people say Amen Amen
Cho: Vers: Cho:
all y^e people say A= men Amen A= men. Let all y^e people say Amen A= men
all y^e people say A= men Amen A= men Let all y^e people say Amen Amen
Cho: Vers Cho:
all y^e people say Amen Amen Amen Let all y^e people say Amen Amen
Vers Cho:
Amen A- men.
A= men A= men
Mr Hen: Purcel.
A= men A= men
Amen Amen
Turn us again &c.
Organ
Vers:
Turn us again turn us again O God, shew y^e Light of thy countenance
Verse
Turn us again turn us a gain O God shew y^e Light of thy countenance
Turn us a gain turn us again again O God Turn

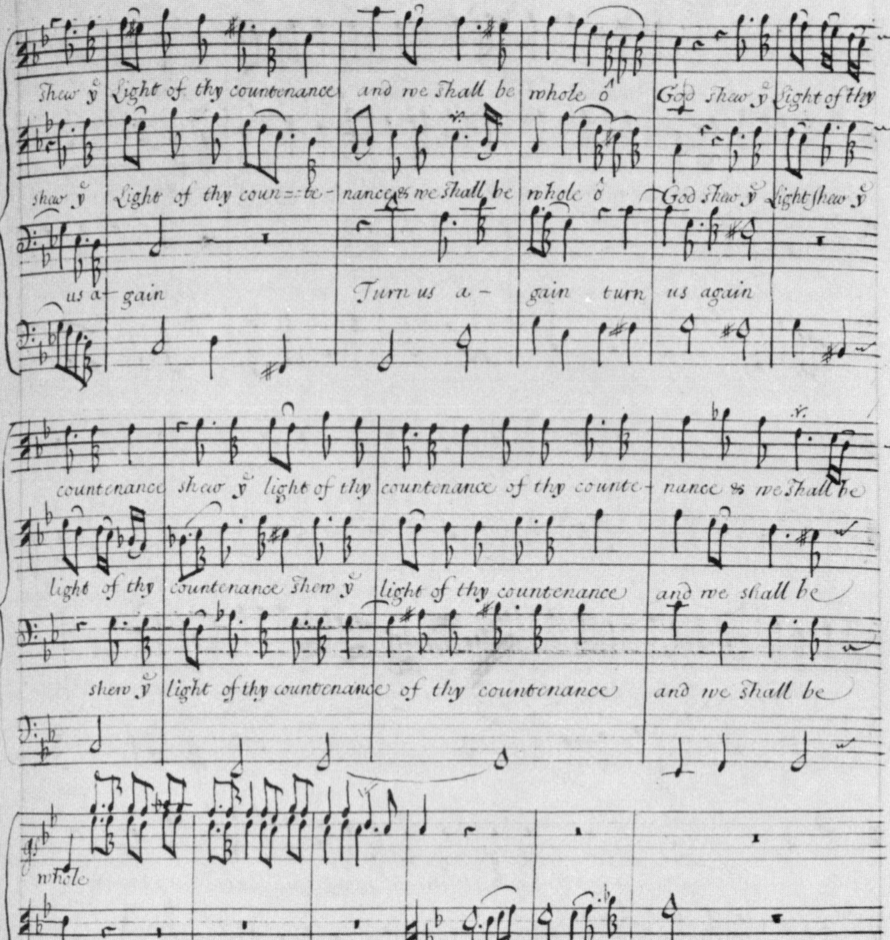
Shew ye Light of thy countenance and we shall be whole o God shew ye Light of thy
shew ye Light of thy coun=te-nance & we shall be whole o God shew ye Light shew ye
us a-gain Turn us a-gain turn us again
countenance shew ye light of thy countenance of thy counte-nance & we shall be
light of thy countenance shew ye light of thy countenance and we shall be
shew ye light of thy countenance of thy countenance and we shall be
whole
whole O Lord God of hosts
whole How long wilt thou be
O- Lord God of hosts how long wilt thou be angry
angry how long wilt thou be angry O

88
how long wilt thou be angry with thy people yt prayeth!
Lord God of hosts, how long wilt thou be angry wth thy people yt prayeth!
Thou feedest them
thou hast
with ye bread of tears, & givst ym plen ------------- teousness of tears to drink. —
thou hast made us a very strife unto or neighbours
made us a very strife unto or neighbors hast made us a very strife unto or neighbours
And or
And or enemies laugh
& or enemies laugh laugh- laugh
enemies laugh us to scorn

Slow
laugh us to scorn. Turn us again Turn us a=gain thou
laugh — us to scorn. Turn us again Turn us again thou
Turn us a=gain, turn us again a=gain thou
God of hosts, shew ye light of thy countenance, shew ye light of thy countenance
God of hosts shew ye light of thy countenance shew ye light of thy coun=te—
God of hosts
Turn us a==gain
and we shall be whole thou God of hosts shew ye Light of thy countenance shew ye
nance & we shall be whole thou God of hosts shew ye Light ye Light of thy counte=
Turn us a- gain thou God of hosts;
Shew ye Light of thy
Light of thy countenance of thy countenance & we shall be whole,
=nance shew ye Light of thy countenance and we shall be whole,
countenance of thy countenance and we shall be whole

Thou hast cast out yͤ heathen & plan----
Thou hast brought a Vine out of Egypt,
---- ted it.
Thou madest room for it, & wⁿ it had taken root it filled yͤ
Why then hast thou broken down her hedg?
Why yⁿ hast yᵘ broken down down why
Land.
Why then hast thou broken down her
Why yⁿ hast yᵘ
broken down down down down her hedg why then hast thou
then hast thou broken down down down her hedg! why then hast thou
hedg! Why then hast yᵘ broken down down why

broken down down her hedg? y^t all they y^t all they that go by pluck off her
broken down down her hedg? y^t all they y^t all they that go by pluck off her
then hast y^u broken down her hedg? y^t all they y^t all they y^t go by pluck off her
grapes y^t all they y^t all they that go by pluck off her grapes? Turn thee again
grapes y^t all they y^t all they that go by pluck off her grapes? Turn thee again
grapes y^t all they y^t all they y^t go by pluck off her grapes, Turn y^ee again turn-
turn thee a-gain thou God of Hosts look down look down
turn thee a-gain thou God of hosts look down look down
thee again a-gain thou God of hosts, look down look down down from heavn
And y^e place of y^e Vineyard y^t thy right hand hath
behold behold behold visit this Vine

92
& ye place of the Vineyard yt thy right hand hath planted, & ye branch yt yu madst so
planted
And ye branch yt thou madst so
strong, so strong so strong for thy self, let thy hand be upon ye man of thy right
strong so strong so strong for thy self.
hand
And upon ye son of man
let thy hand be upon ye Man of thy right hand
And upon ye Son of
that thou madst so strong for thy— self so strong so strong for thine own self
Man yt thou madst so strong for thy self so strong so strong for thine own self
& so will not
O let us
we will not we go back from thee o let us live and we shall call upon thy

93.
O let us live and we shall call upon thy Name o let us live & we shall call up=
live o let us live & we shall call upon thy Name ô let us live & we shall call up=
name & we shall call upon thy Name, o let us live & we shall call shall call up-
=on thy name O let us live & we shall call shall call upon thy
=on thy name ô let us live & we shall call shall call upon thy
=on thy name ô let us live & we shall call- shall call upon thy
name. Turn us again turn us a=gain ô Lord God of hosts Cho: Turn us a=
name. Turn us again turn us a=gain o Lord God of hosts Cho: Turn us a=
name, Turn us a=gain turn us again a=gain ô Lord God of hosts Cho: Cho:
=gain O Ld God of hosts turn us again o Ld God of hosts shew yͤ light of thy
=gain O Ld God of hosts turn us again ô Ld God of hosts shew yͤ light of thy
O Ld God of hosts turn us a=gain O Ld God of hosts.
O Ld God of host turn us a=== gain

countenance and we shall we shall be whole shew y light of thy
countenance and we shall we shall be whole
shew the light of thy countenance & we sh: be whole we sh: be whole shew y light of thy
Shew y light of thy countenance and we shall be
countenance of thy countenance shew y light of thy countenance & we shall be
shew y light of thy countenance shew y light of thy countenance & we shall be
countenance of thy countenance shew y light of thy countenance & we shall be
whole o God shew y light of thy countenance of thy countenance & we shall be
whole shew y light of thy countenance of thy countenance & we shall be whole & we
whole O Ld God of hosts shew y light of thy counte- nance and we shall be whole & we
whole o Ld God of hosts sh: y light of y countenance of thy countenance & we shall be whole & we
whole o Ld God of hosts shew y light y light of thy countenance & we shall be whole & we

Composed by Dr John Blow
Septemb: 1694.
shall be whole
shall be whole
shall be whole
shall be whole
Organ
The way of God: &c
Organ.
Verse
The way of God is an
The way of God is an undefiled way ye word of the
The way of God is an undefiled way
The
undefiled way.
The word of ye Lord
Lord also is try'd in ye Fire
word of ye Lord also is try'd in ye Fire he is the de-
also is try'd also is try'd in ye Fire he is ye Defender of all them yt

he is ye defender of all yem that put their trust in him.
Organ
=fender of all them yt put their trust in him.
put their trust in him of all yem yt put their trust in him.
It is God, It is God yt gird==eth me wth strength of
Who who is God but ye Lord
Who who is God but ye Lord
War & maketh my way perfect.
He teacheth mine
hands to fight to fight to fight, & mine Arms shall
Who hath any strength except or God
Who hath any strength except or God
break evn a Bow of Steel.

Thou hast girded me wth strength unto ye battel
thou shalt throw down down down down down mine Enemies under me thou shalt
throw down down down down down mine enemies under me. I will smite them
yt they shall not be able to stand will smite ym yt they shall not be able to stand but
fall but fall under my feet but fall but fall under my feet.
For this Cause will I give thanks
For this Cause will I give thanks for this Cause will I give thanks
unto thee o Lord and sing praises sing prais-
unto thee O Lord and sing praises sing prais--

Cho:
Alle=luia- Alle=luia Alle-
--ses un=to thy name Alle= lu=ia Alle- luia, Alle- luia
ses un=-to thy name Alle- luia, Alle- luia Alle- luia
Cho:
Alle- luia. Alle- luia Alle
Cho:
Alle= luia. Alle- luia, Alle-
Cho:
Alle= luia Alle- luia. Alle luia, Alle-
Cho:
Cho:
luia Al= le=lu=-ia Al= lelu- ia
Cho: Ver: Cho:
Al=-le-lu-ia Al= lelu- ia All-elu- ia.
Cho: Vers: Cho:
Cho:
-luia Al= le-lu- ia. Al= le-lu- ia.
Cho:
=luia Al= le lu- ia Al lelu- ia.
Ver: Cho:
luia Al- le= lu- ia Al= lelu= ia Al= le-lu- ia. Thou hast made min
Cho:
vers.
Enemies also to turn their backs upon me & I shall destroy ym

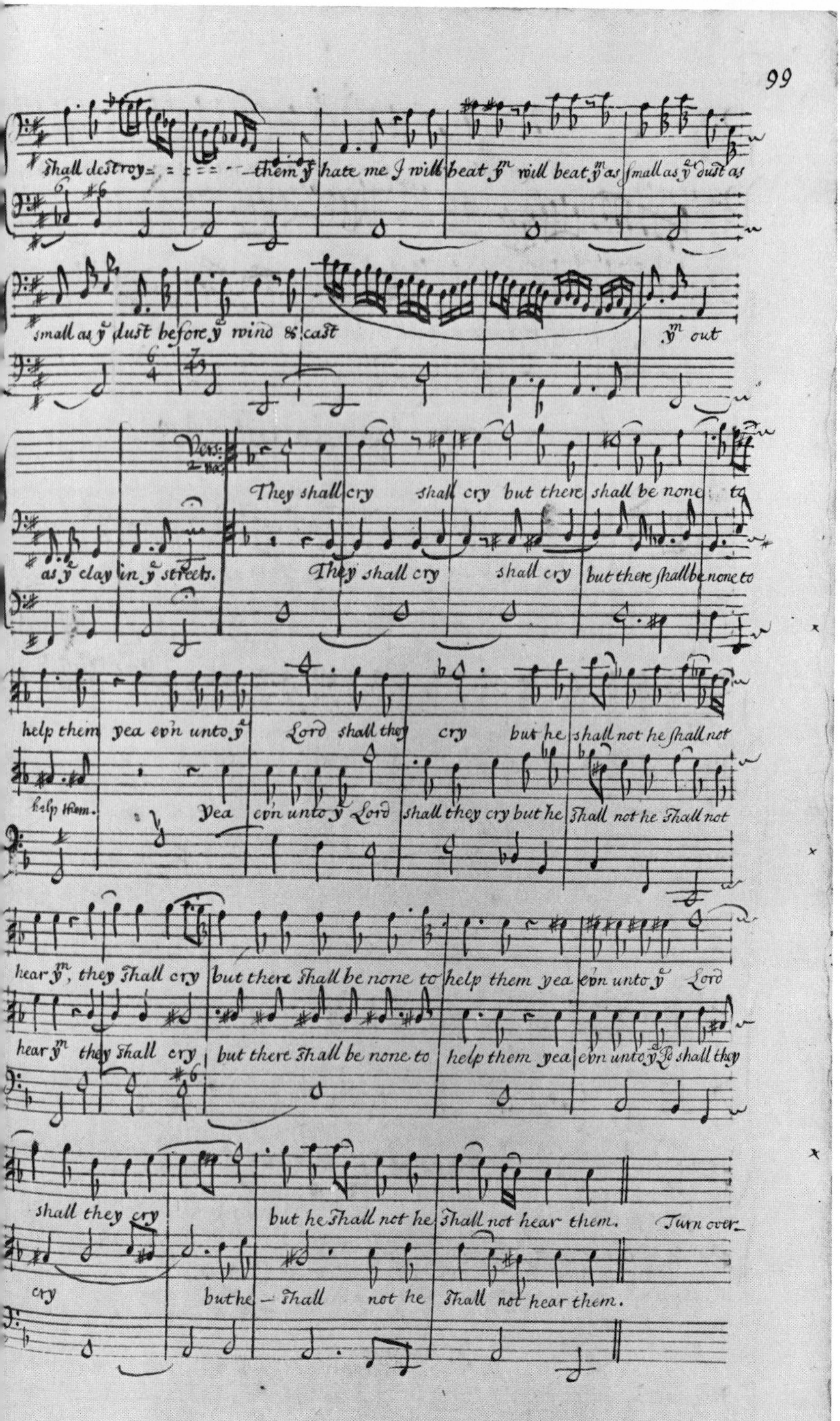
99
Shall destroy = = = = = them ye hate me I will beat ym will beat ym as small as ye dust as
small as ye dust before ye wind & cast ym out
Vers: 2 vo:
They shall cry shall cry but there shall be none to
as ye clay in ye streets. They shall cry shall cry but there shall be none to
help them yea evn unto ye Lord shall they cry but he shall not he shall not
help them. Yea evn unto ye Lord shall they cry but he shall not he shall not
hear ym, they shall cry but there shall be none to help them yea evn unto ye Lord
hear ym they shall cry but there shall be none to help them yea evn unto ye Lo shall they
shall they cry but he shall not he shall not hear them. Turn over
cry but he - shall not he shall not hear them.

The Lord liveth. ye Lord liveth & blessed & blessed be my strong
helper, and praised be ye God & prais - - - sed
Great great prosperity giveth he unto his King
be ye God of my Salvation Great great prosperity giveth he unto his King
It is
he that hath deliverd me from my cruel enemies & set me up above mine
great
Great great pros
adversaries thou shalt rid me shalt rid me from ye wicked man
great pros per=ity giveth he unto his King. great pros- perity giveth he
=perity giveth he giveth he unto his King Great great pros pe=rity
Great great pros perity giveth he unto his King great pr

giveth he un= to his King
giveth he giveth he unto his King. and sheweth lo=
=perity giveth he unto his King, & sheweth lo= =ving loving kindness lo=
& sheweth lo= =ving loving kindness unto David his anoint=
=ving loving kindness & sheweth lo= =ving loving kindness unto David his anoint=
=ving loving kindness & sheweth loving kindness unto David his anoint=
=ed & un= to his seed for e= = =ver more for e= = = = = = = ver more
=ed & un= to his seed for ev= =er more for e= = = = = = = ver more
=ed & un= to his seed for ever more for e= = =
for e= = = = = = = = = = ver more. Alle-
e= = = = = = = = ver more Alle
= = ver more for ever more Alle Lu ia.

Cho: Alle-luia, Alle-luja, Alle-luia, Allelu-ia
Alleluia, Alleluia, Al-le-lu-ia Al-lelu-ia Al lelu-ia.
Alleluia, Alleluia, Al-lelu-ia, Al-lelu-ia Allelu-ia
Alleluia, Alle luia, Alleluia Al-lelu-ia Al-lelu-ia.
Mr Purcell: November ye 11th 1694
King william then returnd from Flanders.
We will rejoice in thy Salvation
1696
Anthem made upon ye discovery of ye plot against King william
Sung April 16: 1696. the Thanksgiving Day.
We will rejoice in thy salvation
We will re-joyce in thy salvation re-
We will rejoyce in thy sal-vation
We will re-joice will re-

joyce – in thy sal vation and triumph trizzumph & triumph in ye
joice – in thy sal= vation and triumph trizzumph & triumph in ye
we will re- joice in thy sal= vation & triump tri= umph & tri = = = = = = umph in ye
name of ye Lord o[e] God & triumphtrizzumph tri= umph and triumph tri= = umph in ye
slow.
name of ye Lord o[e] God & triumph trizzumph tri= = umph and triumph tri= = umph in ye
slow.
name of ye Lord o[e] God and tri= = = = = = = umph and triumph in ye
slow
name of ye Lord our God in ye name ye name of the Lord o[e] God of ye Lord o[e] God.
Cho:
name of ye Lord o[e] God in ye name in ye name of ye Lord o[e] God of ye Lord o[e] God.
Cho:
name of ye Lord our God in ye name ye name of ye Lord o[e] God of ye Lord o[e] God.
Cho:
Cho
We will rejoyce re= joyce in thy sal= vation, will rejoyce in thy salvation. And
Vers:
We will rejoyce re= joyce rejoyce in thy salvation
Vers
We will rejoyce re= joyce in thy Sal= vation will rejoyce in thy salvation
Vers
We will rejoyce in thy sal= vation We will rejoyce in thy salvation.
Vers:

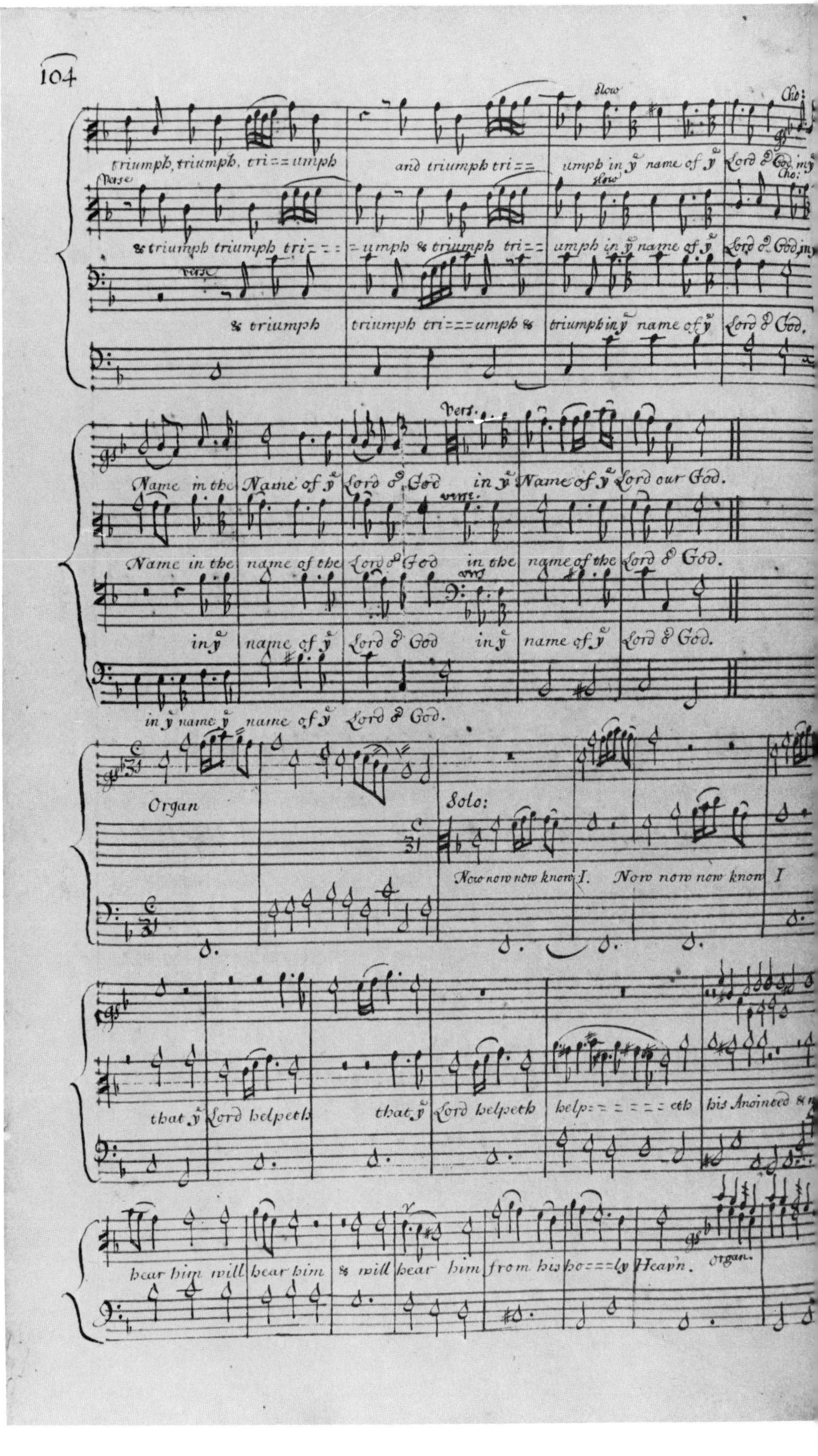
104
Verse
Slow
Cho:
triumph, triumph, tri==umph and triumph tri== umph in ye name of ye Lord & God, my
& triumph triumph tri=== =umph & triumph tri== umph in ye name of ye Lord & God, in
Verse
& triumph triumph tri===umph & triumph in ye name of ye Lord & God.
Vers.
Name in the Name of ye Lord & God in ye Name of ye Lord our God.
Name in the name of the Lord & God in the name of the Lord & God.
in ye name of ye Lord & God in ye name of ye Lord & God.
in ye name ye name of ye Lord & God.
Organ
Solo:
Now now now know I. Now now now know I
that ye Lord helpeth that ye Lord helpeth help======eth his Anointed &
hear him will hear him & will hear him from his ho===ly Heavn. organ.

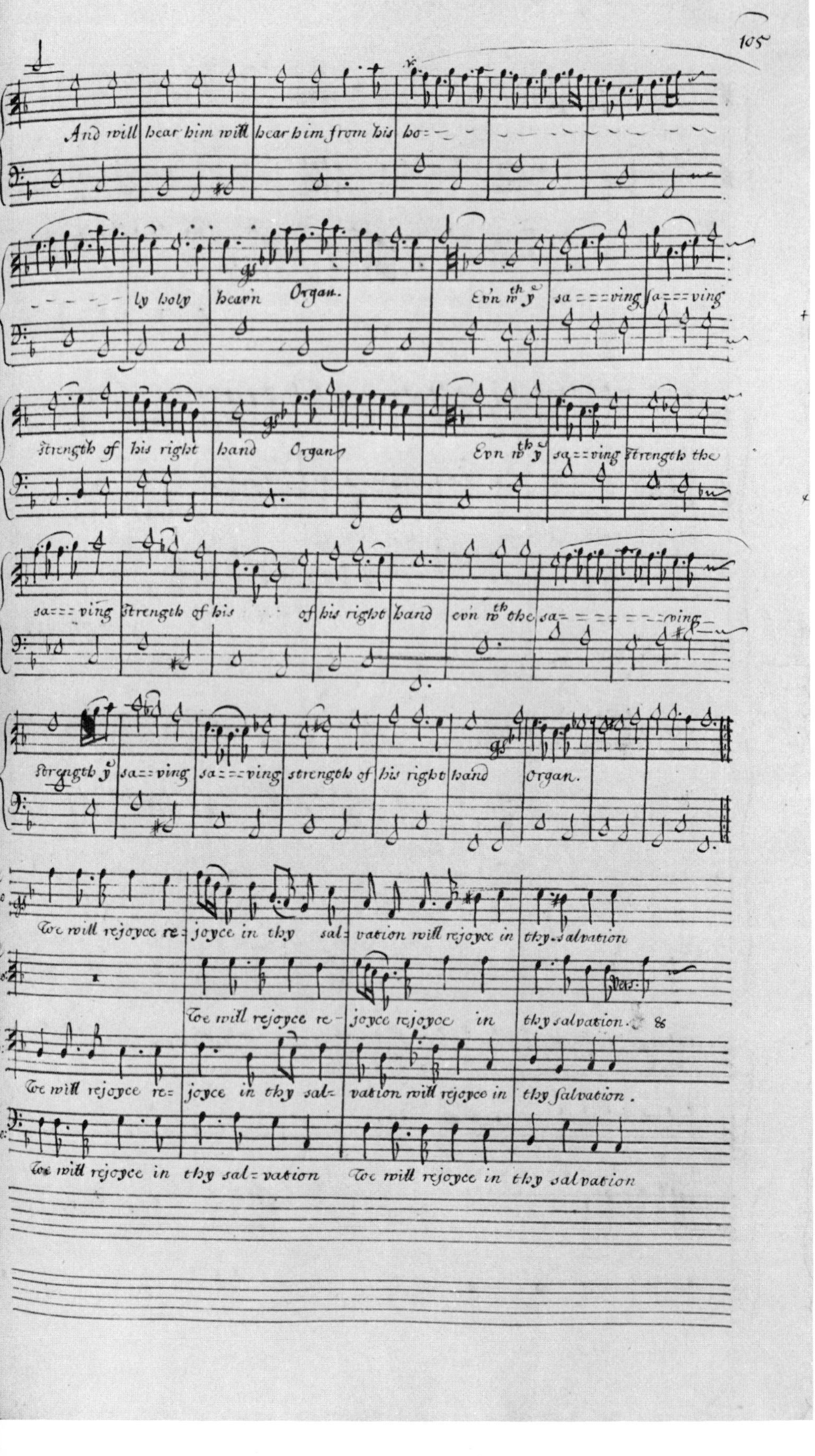

105
And will hear him will hear him from his ho-
ly holy heavn Organ. Evn wth ye sa-ving sa-ving
strength of his right hand Organ Evn wth ye sa-ving strength the
sa-ving strength of his of his right hand evn wth the sa-ving
strength ye sa-ving sa-ving strength of his right hand Organ.
We will rejoyce re-joyce in thy sal-vation will rejoyce in thy salvation
We will rejoyce re-joyce rejoyce in thy salvation
We will rejoyce re-joyce in thy sal-vation will rejoyce in thy salvation.
We will rejoyce in thy sal-vation We will rejoyce in thy salvation

106.

Vers. triumph triumph trizzzumph and triumph trizz=umph in ye name of ye Lord ye
Slow
Verse & triumph triumph trizz=umph & triumph trizz=umph in ye name of ye Lord ye
& triumph triumph trizzumph & triumph in ye name of ye Lord ye
Verse
God in ye name ye name of the Lord ye God of ye Lord ye God. Organ
God in ye name ye name of the Lord ye God of ye Lord ye God.
God in ye name ye name of the Lord ye God of ye Lord ye God.
Some put their trust in Chariots and
Some put their trust in Chariots, & some in horses and
Some put their
Some in Horses but we we will re-member remember we will re-member ye name of ye
Some in Horses but we we will re-member remember we will re-member some put their
trust in Chariots some put their trust in Chariots & Some and

Lord of God but we
but we we will remember
some put their trust in
Chariots and some in
trust in Chariots and
some in Horses but
we we will remember re-
member we will remember ye
some in horses but
we we will remember re-
member remember ye
name of ye Lord of
Horses some put their
trust in Chariots and
Some in horses but
we we will remember re
name of ye Lord of
God but we will remember we will remember remember but
we we will re-
God but we we will re-
member remember re-
member remember but
we we will rememb re-
member ye name of ye
Lord of God.
But we are risen we are
risen & stand up-
member ye name of ye
Lord of God.
But we are risen we are
risen & stand up-
member ye name of ye
Lord of God they
are brought down &
falln.
They are brought
right. They
are brought down and
falln.
But we are
risen we are risen we are
right. They
are brought down and
falln.
But we are
risen we are risen but
down and falln
They are brought
down & falln
but we are

Cho: slow.
risen and stand upright and stand upright.
Save Lord & hear us o King of heavn
Cho: slow.
we are risen we are risen and stand upright.
Cho: slow
Save Lord & hear us ô King of heavn
risen we are risen we are risen & stand upright.
Save Lord & hear us ô King of heavn
Cho: slow.
Save Lord and hear us o King of heavn
Verse quicker.
when we call when we call up= on Thee.
We will rejoyce in thy salvation
Verse.
when we call when we call up= on Thee.
We will rejoyce in
Verse
when we call we call up= on Thee.
Vers:
when we call we call up= on Thee.
And triumph triumph tri=umph & triumph tri=
thy salvation
And triumph triumph tri= umph & triumph tri=
We will rejoyce in thy salvation.
And triumph triumph tri=umph and
slow
=umph in ye name of ye Lord our God.
Cho:
Save Lord & hear us o King of heavn to we
slow
=umph in ye name of ye Lord our God.
Cho:
Save Lord & hear us ô King of heavn-
slow.
triumph in ye name of ye Lord & God.
Cho:
Save Lord & hear us ô King of heavn-
Cho:
Save Lord and hear us ô King of heavn.

call upon Thee when we call upon Thee when we call upon Thee when we call upon
when we call upon thee when we call upon thee when we call up = = on thee when we call upon
when we call upon thee when we call upon y^e when we call upon thee upon
when we call upon
Thee Amen.
Composed by Dr Blow. Ap: 9th. 1696
Thee Amen.
Performed y^e 16th following at Whitehall.
Thee Amen.
Thee Amen.
Organ
yea y^e multitude of y^e
Thr: Bass:
The Lord is King y^e earth may be glad be glad there=of
Isles may be glad be glad thereof The Lord is King y^e Earth may be glad be glad thereof
Isles may be glad be glad thereof The Lord is King the Earth may be glad thereof
yea y^e

yea y^e multitude of y^e Isles may be glad thereof. The multitude of y^e Isles may be
yea the multitude of y^e Isles may be glad thereof The
multitude of y^e Isles the- multitude of y^e Isles may be glad thereof ye multitude of y^e
glad may be glad ye multitude of ye Isles may be glad thereof,
multitude of ye Isles may be glad may be glad may be glad thereof yea y^e
Isles may be glad — may be glad Isles may be glad there of yea y^e
yea y^e multitude of y^e Isles may be glad thereof.
multitude of y^e Isles — may be glad thereof.
multitude of y^e Isles may be glad thereof. Organ.
Verse solo:
Sion heard of it and re= joy Sion heard of it
and re= joy = ced- and y^e Daughters of Juda were glad were glad, y^e daughters of-

111.
The daughters. &c
For
Vers: Tenor Solo.
Juda were glad because of thy Judgm^ts O Lord, For thou thou Lord art higher than all all that are
in the Earth, for thou thou Lord art higher art higher than all all that are in y^e Earth,
Thou art ex=alted ex=alted ex=alted ex= al===ted far above all Gods
Thou art ex= see below y^e 2 last lines.
Tenor
yea y^e multitude of y^e Isles y^e multitude of y^e
The Lord is King y^e earth may be glad be glad thereof, yea y^e multitude of y^e Isles y^e
Isles may be glad thereof multitude of y^e Isles may be glad may be
Isles of y^e Isles may be glad thereof. the multitude of y^e Isles may be
multitude of y^e Isles may be glad thereof. the multitude of y^e Isles may be glad
Turn over quick.
Thou art exalted exalted ex=alted ex=al ted far a=bove all Gods
as above.

112
Organ Cornet.
glad — ye multitude of ye Isles may be glad thereof.
glad may be glad — may be glad thereof
Vers solo:
may be glad thereof may be glad thereof
Cornett:
O ye yt love the Lord see see yt ye hate ye thing yt is evil.
Cornet
O ye yt love the Lord see see see ye ye hate ye thing yt is evil
ye Lord pre-
Cornett
-serveth preserveth ye souls of his Saints
The Lord preserveth preserveth pre-
Cornett
Cornett.
-serveth ye souls of his Saints
He shall de- liver them

Cornett
shall deliver them
from y^e hand y^e
hand of the un = godly
he shall deliver y^m
shall de = liver them
from y^e hand y^e
hand of the ungodly
Cornett
Cornet
he shall deliver them,
shall de = liver them from y^e hand y^e hand of
the un = godly.
There is sprung up a Light for y^e righteous
Cornett
Light for y^e Righteous
& joyfull Gladness
& joy - - - = full Gladness for such as

Cornett
are as are for such as are true hearted, There is sprung up a light a light a light for yͤ
Cornett.
righteous a Light for yͤ Righteous & joy — full joyfull gladness for such as are true
hearted for such as are for such as are as are true hearted
Vers: 3 voc:
Rejoyce rejoyce re= joyce in yͤ Lord o ye Righteous re= joyce rejoyce re= joyce in the
Re= joyce rejoyce re= joyce in yͤ Lord o ye Righteous re= joyce rejoyce re= joyce in the
Rejoyce rejoyce re= joyce in yͤ Lord o ye Righteous re= joyce rejoyce re= joyce in the
Lord o ye Rightrous and give thanks give thanks for a remembrance
Lord o ye Rightrous and give thanks give thanks for a remembrance
Lord o ye Rightrous and give thanks give thanks for a re= membrance and give

and give thanks give thanks for a re= membrance of his holi= =ness give thanks give
and give thanks give thanks for a re= membrance & give thanks give
thanks give thanks for a re = mem = brance of his holiness, and give thanks give
thanks for a Remembrance of his ho= =li= ness give thanks for a re= membrance of his
thanks for a Remembrance of his ho= =li= ness and give thanks for a remembrance of
thanks for a Remem = brance of his holi= ness & give thanks for a re= mem brance of his
ho=li=ness Re= joyce rejoyce re= joyce in the Lord o ye Righteous rejoyce re =
his holiness Re= joyce rejoyce re= joyce in the Lord o ye Rightrous rejoyce re=
holiness Re= joyce rejoyce re= joyce in the Lord o ye Righteous rejoyce re =
Re= joyce rejoyce re= joyce in the Lord o ye Righteous rejoyce - re =
-joyce re=joyce in ye Lord o ye Righteous, and give thanks give thanks for a remembrance of
joyce rejoyce in the Lord o ye Righteous and give thanks give thanks for a remembrance of
joyce rejoyce in the Lord o ye Righteous and give thanks give thanks for a rembrance of
=joyce rejoyce in the Lord o ye Righteous & give thanks for a remembrance of -

his ho=li=ness, Rejoyce re=joyce in ye Lord o ye Righteous, and give thanks give thanks give
his ho=liness Re=joyce rejoyce in ye Lord o ye Righteous and give thanks give thanks give
his holiness Re=joyce rejoyce in ye Lord o ye Righteous , & give thanks give thanks & give
his holiness Re=joyce rejoyce in ye Lord o ye Righteous, & give thanks give thanks & give
thanks for a Remembrance of his holiness of his hol=iness
thanks for a Remembrance of his holiness of his ho=li=ness
thanks for a Remembrance of his holiness of his ho=liness
thanks give thanks for a Remembrance of his holiness of his ho=liness
Janonimous

Psal: 50. Vers: 1.
116
117.
The Lord ev'n y^e most mighty God hath spoken, The Lord ev'n y^e most mighty God hath
spoken, y^e most mighty y^e most mighty God hath spoken, & called y^e World from ye Ri----sing
up ye Ri----ing up of ye Sun unto ye going down unto ye go----ing
down thereof unto ye going down unto ye go---ing down there--of.
out of Sion hath God ap-peared, out of Sion hath God ap-peared in perfect
Beauty Our God shall come & shall not keep silence Our God shall come and
shall not keep Silence, & shall not keep Silence; there shall go before him, there shall go be-
-fore him a consu---ming Fire & a mighty Tem--pest shall be stirred up round

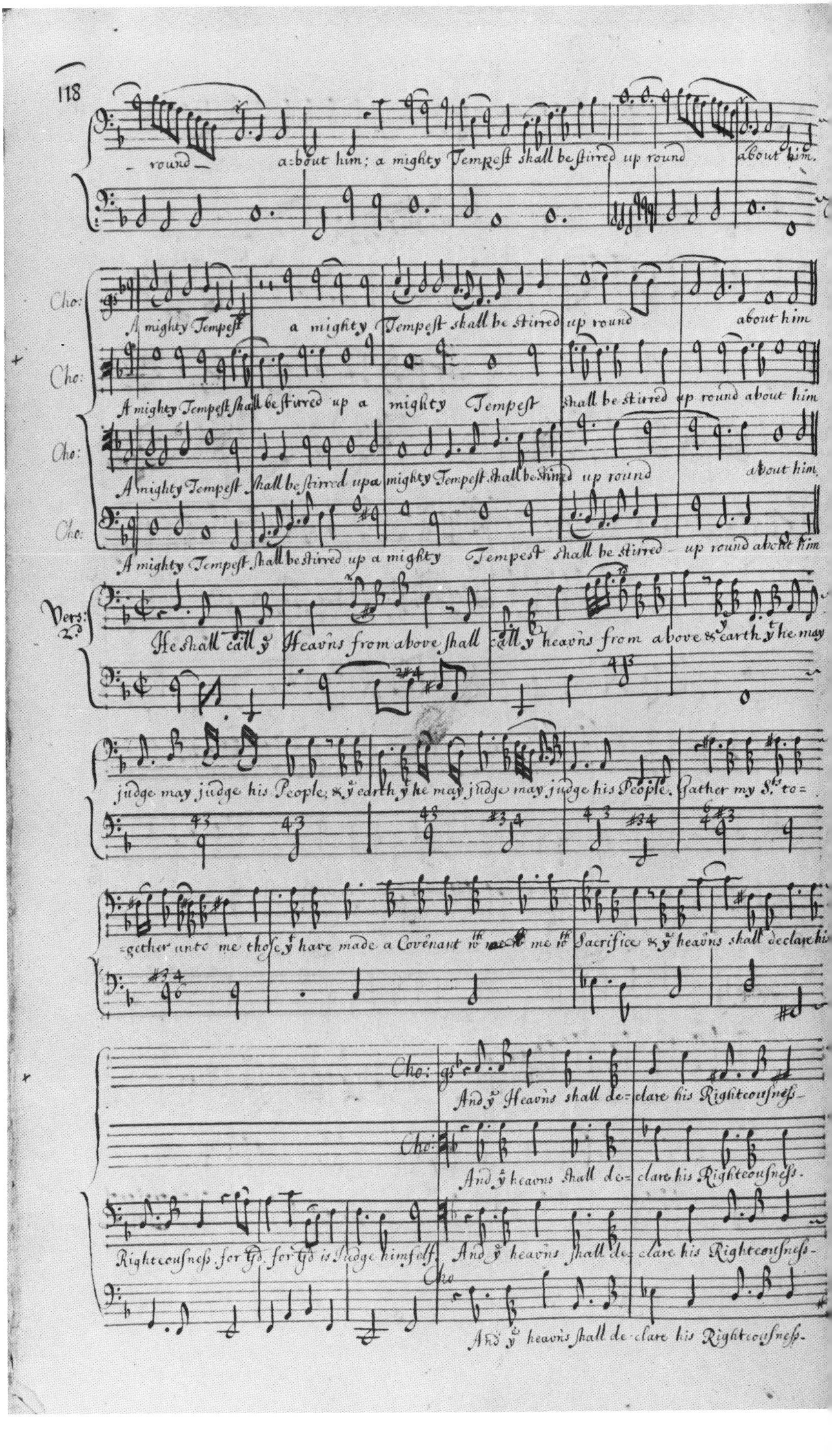
118
- round - a:bout him; a mighty Tempest shall be stirred up round about him.
Cho: A mighty Tempest a mighty Tempest shall be stirred up round about him
Cho: A mighty Tempest shall be stirred up a mighty Tempest shall be stirred up round about him
Cho: A mighty Tempest shall be stirred up a mighty Tempest shall be stirred up round about him.
Cho: A mighty Tempest shall be stirred up a mighty Tempest shall be stirred - up round about him
Vers: 2.d
He shall call ye Heavens from above shall call ye heavens from above & earth yt he may
judge may judge his People; & ye earth yt he may judge may judge his People. Gather my Sts to=
-gether unto me those yt have made a Covenant wth me wth Sacrifice & ye heavens shall declare his
Cho: And ye Heavens shall de- clare his Righteousness-
Cho: And ye heavens shall de- clare his Righteousness.
Righteousness for God, for God is Judge himself. And ye heavens shall de- clare his Righteousness-
Cho: And ye heavens shall de- clare his Righteousness.

shall declare his Righteousness, for God is Judge himself.
shall declare his Righteousness for God is Judge himself.
shall declare his Righteousness for God is Judg himself.
Vers: 3d
Hear o my People & I will -
Verse. 3d.
shall declare his Righteousness for God is Judg himself.
speak; I will testify against thee o - - Israel, for I - - - am God I - - - am God even thy
God; I will not I will not reprove thee. because of thy Sa- - - - - - - - crifices or for
thy burnt Offerings because they were not alway before me, I will take no Bullock out -
of thine house, nor He-Goat out of thy Folds for all all, for all all ye beasts of ye Forest
are mine & so are ye Cattle upon a thousand hills upon a thou- - - - - - - - sand thousand
Hills. If I be hungry I will not tell thee, For all ye world is mine, & all ye therein is

120
thinkest thou ye I will eat Bulls-Flesh thinkest thou ye I will eat Bulls Flesh
drink ye blood of Goats, or drink ye blood of Goats: thinkest thou ye I will eat Bu
Flesh or drink ye blood of Goats or drink ye blood of Goats
Offer
Cho: Offer unto God thanks-giving
Cho. Offer unto God thanks-giving Vers:
unto God thanksgiving Offer unto God thanksgiving. And pay thy vows unto ye m
Cho: Offer unto God thanksgiving
Cho: And pay thy vows unto ye most high ye most high.
Cho: And pay thy vows unto ye most high.
High ye most High Cho: And pay thy Vows unto ye most High ye most high, and call upon m
Cho: And pay thy vows unto ye most high ye most high.
in ye Time of Trou-ble & call upon me in ye time of Trouble call upon me in ye Time

121
Cho
And call upon me in ye time of Trouble & call upon me
Cho: And call upon me in ye time of Trouble in the
Trouble so will I hear Thee
Cho: And call upon me in ye time of Trouble & call upon me
And call upon me in ye time of Trouble in ye time of
in ye time of Trouble so will I will I hear Thee & thou shalt praise me shalt praise me
Time of Trouble so will I hear Thee and thou shalt praise me so
in ye Time of Trouble so will I will I hear thee & thou shalt
Trouble so will I hear Thee & thou shalt praise
So will I hear thee & thou shalt praise me so will I hear Thee & Thou
will I hear thee and thou shalt praise me So will I hear Thee & Thee
praise me so will I hear thee & Thou shalt praise Me so will I
me shalt praise me so will I hear thee & thou shalt praise me so will I hear
and Thou shalt praise Me
thou shalt praise me shalt praise Me
Dr Blow. comp: 1687.
hear Thee and Thou shalt praise Me
Thee & thou shalt praise, shalt praise Me

Sing unto God: Psa: 68. 4 last verses.

Sing sing unto God sing unto
God o — — — ye Kingdoms o — — — — ye Kingdoms of ye Earth o sing — —
— — — — Praises o sing — — — — Praises sing — sing praises s
Cho: Halleluia halleluia halleluia halleluia hal-lelu-
Cho: Halleluia halleluia halleluia halleluia hal-le-lu
— — ing Praises unto ye Lord Halleluia Halleluia Halleluia Halleluia Hal-lelu-
Cho: Halleluia halleluia halleluia halleluia halle-lu —
Vers: 2d. Who sitteth in ye heavns o-ver all Who sitteth in ye heavns o-ver
all lo he doth send out his Voice yea & that a mighty mighty mighty Vo
lo he doth send out his Voice Yea & that a mighty mighty mighty Voice

123
yea & that a migh-----ty Voice Ascribe ye ye Power to
God over Israel ascribe ye ye Power to God o--ver Israel his worship & strength is
in ye Clouds his worship & strength is in ye Clouds as-cribe ye ye Power to
God over Israel his worship & strength is in ye Clouds his worship & strength is
Cho:
Alleluia Alleluia Alleluia Alleluia Al--lelu--ia.
Cho:
in ye Clouds Alleluia Alleluia Alleluia Alleluia Al-le-lu--ia.
Cho:
Alle-lu---ia.
Vers:3
O God O------God, wonderfull wonderfull art
thou in thy holy Places wonderfull wonderfull art thou o----God,

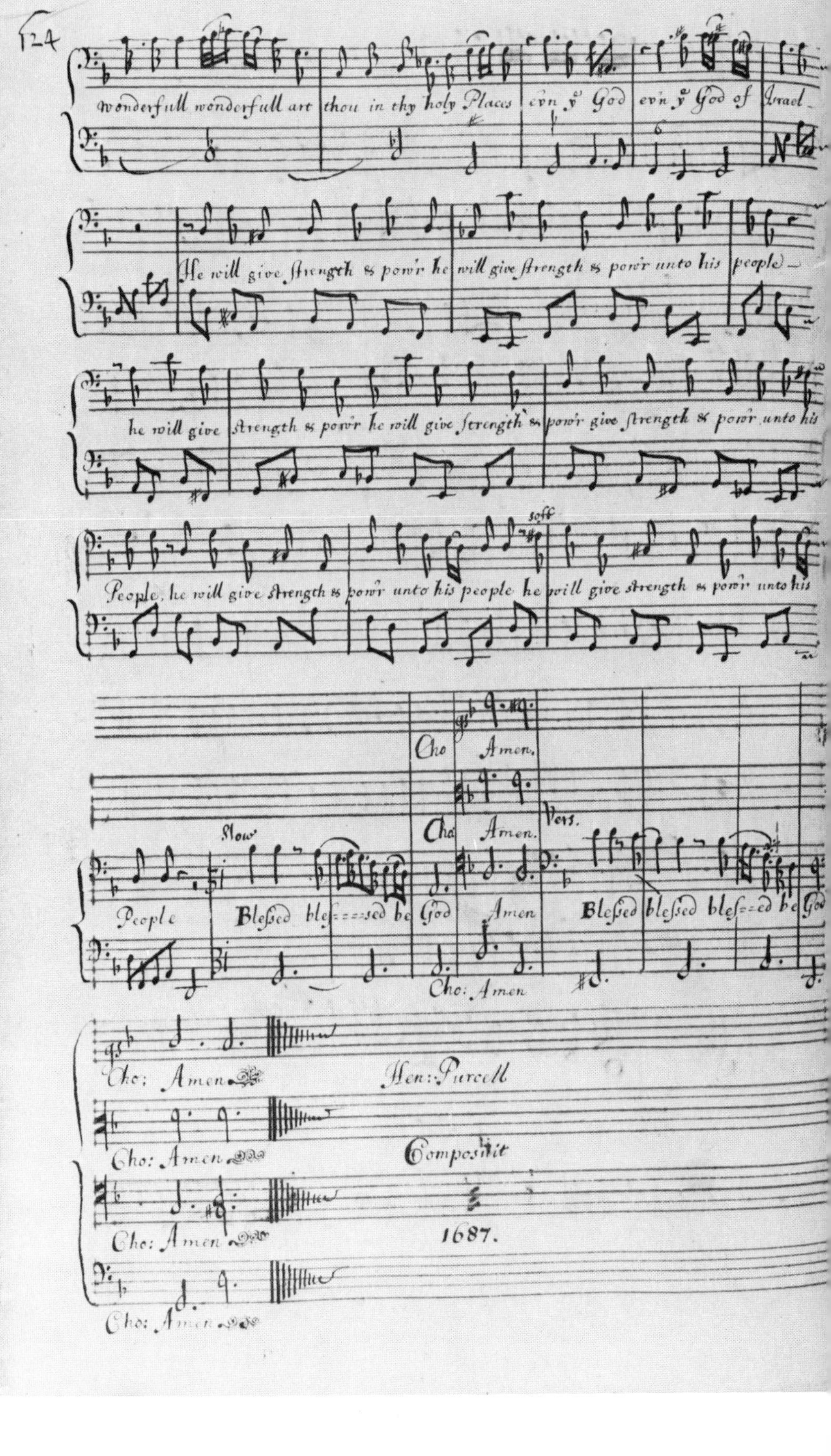
124
wonderfull wonderfull art thou in thy holy Places evn ye God evn ye God of Israel
He will give strength & pow'r he will give strength & pow'r unto his people
he will give strength & pow'r he will give strength & pow'r give strength & pow'r unto his
People, he will give strength & pow'r unto his people he will give strength & pow'r unto his
soft
Cho Amen.
Cho Amen.
Vers.
Slow
People Blessed ble====sed be God Amen Blessed blessed ble===ed be God
Cho: Amen
Cho: Amen
Hen: Purcell
Cho: Amen
Composuit
Cho: Amen
1687.
Cho: Amen

My Song. &c
Vers:
125
My Song shall be alway of ye lo-ving Kindness of ye Lord,
My Song shall be alway of ye lo-ing Kindness of ye Lord with my
mouth will I ever be shewing forth thy Truth wth my mouth will I ever be shewing forth thy
Truth from one Genera-tion to ano-ther from
one Genera-tion to ano-ther
O Lord O Lord ye very heavns shall praise thy won-drous Works
O Lord ye very heavns shall praise thy won-drous works, & thy
Truth in ye Congregation of ye Saints, & thy Truth in ye Congregation of ye Saints.

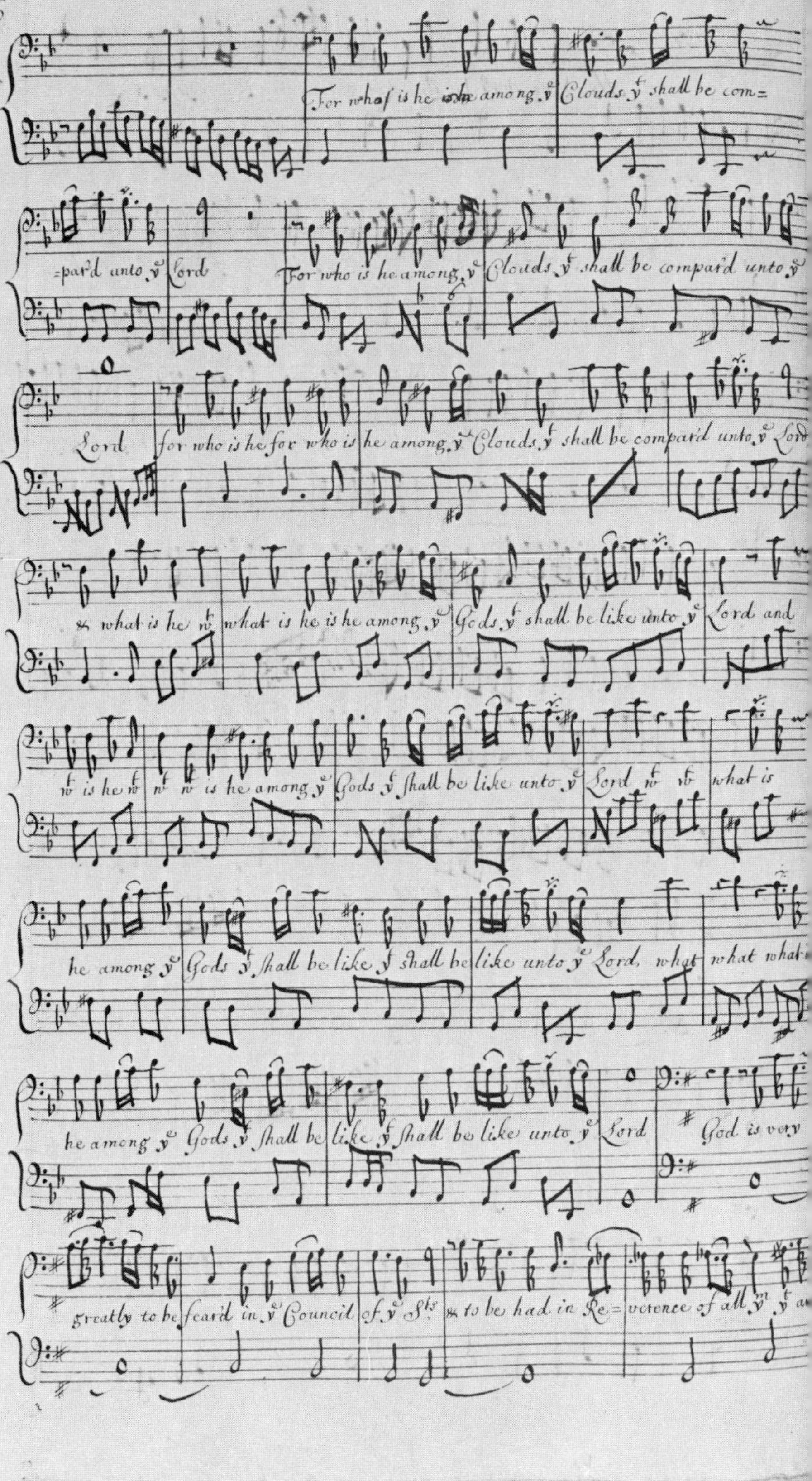
For what is he among ye Clouds yt shall be com=
=pard unto ye Lord For who is he among ye Clouds yt shall be compar'd unto ye
Lord for who is he for who is he among ye Clouds yt shall be compar'd unto ye Lord
& what is he wt what is he is he among ye Gods yt shall be like unto ye Lord and
wt is he wt wt wt is he among ye Gods yt shall be like unto ye Lord wt wt what is
he among ye Gods yt shall be like yt shall be like unto ye Lord, what what what
he among ye Gods yt shall be like yt shall be like unto ye Lord God is very
greatly to be fear'd in ye Council of ye Sts & to be had in Re= verence of all ym yt a

round about him God is very greatly is very greatly to be feard & to be had in
Reverence of all them y^t are round are round about him
Cho:
Alle-lu-ia Al-le-lu-ia, Al-le-lu-ia, Al-le-luia, Al-le-lu-ia Al-le-lu-ia.
Alle-luia Al-le-lu-ia Alle-luia Alleluia Alleluia Allelu-ia.
Alle-luia Alleluia Alle-luia Alle-luia Al-le-luia Alle-lu-ia.
Alle-luia Alle-luia Alle-luia Alle-luia Alle-luia Alle-lu-ia.
Lord God of Hosts who who is like unto Thee Ld God of
Hosts who who who is like unto Thee, Thy Truth most migh-ty Lord is on every
Side, thy Truth most migh-ty Lord most migh-ty Lord is on every Side
Turn over to quick Time

Faster
Thou rulest ye Ra=========ging of ye Sea Thou rulest ye Rag========
ging of ye Sea
Thou stillest ye waves
of when they arise=
Thou stillest ye Waves thereof ye stillest ye waves
of wn they arise
Thou stillest ye Waves thereof Thou
stillest ye Waves thereof ye Waves
thereof wn they a===rise.
Slow
Thou hast a migh==ty mighty migh=ty Arm Thou hast a migh=ty
mighty migh=ty Arm: strong is thy hand strong is thy hand & high & high is
right hand
Thou hast a migh=ty mighty Arm. strong is thy hand strong is t

129.
Hand & high & high- is thy right hand. Righteousness & Equity are ye Ha-bi-
-tation of thy seat. Righteousness & Equity are ye Ha-bi-ta- tion of thy
Seat. Mercy & Truth shall go before thy Face, Mercy & Truth, Mercy & Truth shall
go be- fore thy Face.
Allelu-ia
Allelu-ia
Al- lelu-ia al- le- lu- ia alle- lu- ia alle-
lu- ia al- le-lu-ia al- le lu-ia al-
Cho: Alle &c Alleluia Alle: Alle: Alle: Alleluia
Cho: Alleluia
le- lu ia al- le- lu- ia
Alleluia

130 Verse. O Lord thou art my God.
solus.
O Lord Thou art my God I will exalt thee exalt thee,
O Lord thou art my God I will - exalt Thee I will praise thy name for thou hast
don won=====derfull Things I will praise thy name for thou thou hast don
won==derfull Things O Lord thou art my God I will exalt thee for yu hast don
wonderfull won=================derfull Things For thou hast been a-
Strength to ye poor Thou hast been a strength to ye poor, a strength to ye needy in his dis-
-tress a Refuge from ye Storm from ye Storm A Refuge fro ye
quick
quick
Storm A Shadow from ye Heat when ye Blast of ye
Slow

131.
terrible ones is as a great Storm — against y^e Wall.
When y^e blast of y^e terrible ones is as a great Storm
When y^e blast of y^e terrible ones is as a great storm as a great Storm When ye blast of y^e
When ye blast of ye terrible ones is as a great Storm is as a great Storm as a great Storm
When ye blast of ye terrible ones is as a great Storm is as a great Storm when y^e
when ye blast of ye terrible ones is as a great Storm as a great Storm against ye Wall.
terrible ones is as a great Storm as a great storm a great Storm against ye wall
when ye blast of ye terrible ones is as a great Storm against ye wall.
Vers: 2d blast of ye terrible ones is as a great Storm against ye wall.
He shall bring down down y^e noise of Strangers he he shall bring down do-
-wn y^e noise of Strangers The branch of y^e terrible ones shall be brought low,
The branch of y^e terrible ones shall shall be brought low. He will

132
swallow up Death will swal=low up Death in Vict=ory.
swal=low up death death in Victory
For ye Lord God
For ye Lord God will wipe away Tears from off all Faces will wipe awa
Tears from off all Faces For ye Lord ye Lord For ye Lord ha
spoken it For ye Lord ye Lord hath spoken it For ye Lord
Lord for ye Lord hath spo=ken it
shall be said in that day And it shall be said in that day lo
lo! this is our God we have waited for him have waited for him he w

133.
save us will save us & he will save will save us; This is ye Lord we have waited for
him have waited for him we will be glad we will be glad & rejoice rejoyce
quicker
in his Salvation we will be glad & rejoice — — — in
his salvation in his salvation, we will be glad & rejoice re=joyce in his salva=======ti-on.
Cho
Cho.
We will be glad & rejoice & rejoice rejoice in his Salvation.
We will be glad & re=joice will be glad & re=joicein his salvati-on.
Verse
We will be glad & re=joice will be glad & rejoice in his Salvati-on.
And rejoice
We will be glad & rejoyce will be glad & rejoycein his Salvati=on.
Cho: We will be glad
Cho: We will be glad.
vers
Cho: We will be glad, & rejoice—
Cho:
Cho: We will be glad,

134
Cho:
Cho:
Cho:
Cho:
We will be glad,
We will be glad,
Verre
We will be glad, And rejoice
We will be glad
Cho: We will be glad & re=
Cho: We will be glad & re=
Cho: We will be glad & re=
Cho: We will be glad & re=
=joice and re=joice will be glad & re=joice and rejoice in his sal=:::va
=joice and re=joice will be glad & re=:::joice we will be glad &
=joice and re=joice we will be=glad & rejoice & re=joice we will be glad & re
joice will be glad & rejoice re=::::joice we will be glad & rejoice & re
=:::vation in his salvati=:on.
=joice & rejoice in his salvati=:on.
=joice & rejoice in his salvati=:on.
=joice & rejoice in his salvati=:on.
Composed by
Dr. Jo: Blow
June 19
1688.

Vers: solus. The Lord is King. Psa: 97.
135
Lord is
King
The Lord is King ye Earth may be glad=
there=
of
The Lord is King ye Eearth may be glad - - - - - there=
=of yea ye multitude of ye Isles may be glad -
there=of= yea the
Multitude of ye Isles may be glad
thereof may be glad -
there= =of.
Clouds and ~
darkness are round -
about him
Clouds & darkness are round -
about him
Righteousness &c -

Judgment, Righteousness & Judgment are ye Ha= bi- tation of his
Seat, Righteousness & Judgment are ye Ha= bi- ta= tion of – his
Seat. There shall go before him a consu= ming Fire there shall go be=
=fore him a consum= ing Fire & burn up his Enemies, & burn up his Enemies his
Enemies on every Side; his Lightning gave Shine unto ye World gave Shine unto ye
World The Earth saw it & was afrayd, ye Earth saw it & was afray
Flat 3d & 6.
The hills mol= ted like Wax ye hills mol=
= ted like Wax at ye Presence of ye Lord at ye Presence of ye Lord of

ye whole Earth at ye Presence at ye Presence of ye Lord of ye whole Earth.
Cho: The heavns have declared ye heavns have declared his Righteous=ness.
Cho: The heavns have de=clared ye heavns have de=clared his Righteous=ness, & all the
Cho: The heavns have de=clared ye heavns have de=clared his Righteousness.
The heavns have de=clared ye heavns have declared his Righteousness.
& all ye people have seen have seen his Glory & all ye people have seen his
People have seen his Glory have seen his Glory & all ye people have seen have seen his Glo=
& all ye people have seen have seen his Glo= = = = = =
& all ye
Glo= = = ry have seen his Glory & all ye people have seen have seen his Glo= =ry.
=ry & all ye people have seen & all ye people have seen his Glo= = ry have seen his Glo= ry.
= = = ry & all ye peo= ple have seen have seen his Glo= = ry.
people have seen his Glory & all ye people have seen his Glo= = ry.
O ye ye love ye Lord see ye ye hate ye thing wch is evil

138
O ye yt love ye Ld see yt ye hate ye thing wch is e=vil The Lord preserveth ye
Souls of his Saints The Lord preserveth ye Souls of his Saints and de=
=livreth ym from ye hand of ye ungodly & delivreth ym & delivreth them from
== ye hand of ===== ye ungodly. There is
sprung up a light for ye Righteous There is sprung up a Light for ye
Righteous & a joy========= full Gladness a joy============ full
Gladness for such as are true hearted. There is sprung up a Light for ye
Righteous & a joy========= full Gladness for su

as are true hearted.
Re=joyce rejoyce rejoice —
Re=joyce rejoice rejoice
Rejoice rejoice rejoice
in ye Lord ô yee Righteous ô
ye
Cho: Alleluia alle=luia alleluia alle=luia alle=lu==ia
Cho: Alleluia alle==luia alleluia alle=luia alle=lu==ia
Vers:
Cho: Alleluia alle=luia alleluia alle=luia alle==lu==ia
rejoice, rejoice re=
Righteous. Alleluia alleluia alleluia alle==luia allelu== == ia.
joice
& give thanks for a re=membrance & give thanks for a re=
Cho: Alleluia Alle=luia Allelu==ia.
Cho: Alleluia Alle=luia Allelu==ia.
=membrance of his holynes. Cho: Alleluia Alleluia Alle=lu=ia And give
Cho: Alleluia Alleluia allelu===ia

140
Thanks for a Remembrance & give thanks for a remembrance of — his
Alleluia alleluia alle-luia alleluia alle-luia alleluia alleluia alle-
Alle-luia alleluia alle-luia alleluia alle-luia alleluia alle-
Alle-luia alleluia alle-luia alleluia alle-luia alle-luia alle-
holines Alleluia alleluia alle-luia alleluia alle-lu
-lu-ia
-lu-ia
-lu-ia
ia
Composed by
Mr Hen: Purcel.
1688.

Lord remember David.
141.
Organ
Lord remember remember David & all his troubles
Lord re= member remember David
Lord remember re= member David & all his troubles.
& vowd a vow un=
how he sware unto ye Lord and vowd a
& all his Troubles.
how he sware unto ye Lord and
= to the Almigh= = = = = = = = ty God of Jacob.
Cho: Lord rememb. rememb. David,
Vow unto ye Almigh= = = = = = = = = ty God of Jacob.
Cho: Lord re= memb. rememb. David.
vowed a Vow unto ye Almigh= = ty God of Jacob.
Cho: Lord re= memb. rememb. David.
Cho: Lord rememb. rememb. David.
& all his Troubles.
Vers: Lord rememb. re= memb. David & all all his troubles how he
Vers: Lord remember re= member David & all his troubles.
Vers: Lord remember re= memb. David & all all his troubles.
& all his Troubles.

swear unto ye Lord & vowed a Vow unto ye Almighty God of Jacob and vowed a Vow
how he sware unto ye Lord & vowed a Vow unto ye Almighty God
how he sware unto ye Lord and vowed a Vow & vowed a Vow un=
unto the Almigh- - - - ty God of Jacob he sware unto the Ld & vowed a vow un=
of Jacob he sware unto ye Lord & vowed a vow unto ye Almighty God of Jacob and=
=to ye Almighty God of Jacob & vowed a vow un=
=to the Almighty God of Jacob he sware unto ye Lord & vowed a Vow & vowed a Vow un=
vowed a vow unto the Al- mighty ye Almighty God of Jacob and vowed a Vow un=
to the Almighty God of Jacob he sware un=to ye Lord and vowed a vow un=
=to ye Almigh= = = ty God of Jacob.
=to ye Almighty God of Jacob.
Solo,
to ye Almigh= = ty God of Jacob. Slow I will not suffer mine eyes to sleep,

I will not Suffer will not Suffer mine eyes to sleep nor the Temples nor the
Temples of my head to take any Rest I will not suffer mine Eyes to sleep nor ye Temples
of my head to take any Rest untill I find out a place for ye Temple of the Lord an
habitation for ye mighty God of Jacob, untill I find out a Place for the
Temple of ye Lord an habitation for the mighty
God of Jacob.
We will go in= to his Tabernacle
4 voc:
We will go into his Tabernacle will go into his Taber= na= =cle we
We will go into his Taber= nacle will go into his Ta= =ber= nacle
We will go in=

We will go in = to his Tabernacle and fall fall low fall low on o^r knees and fall fall
will go into his Taber= nacle and fall fall low, and fall fall-
and fall fall low we will go in= to his Tabernacle,
to his Tab^r nacle will go into his Ta = = = =b^r nacle we will go into his Tab^r na= = cle
low We will go into his Taber= nacle and fall fall low on o^r knees and
low fall low on o^r knees We will go in = to his Tabernacle and
and fall fall low on o^r knees and fall fall low on o^r knees & fall fall low and
and fall fall low on o^r knees before his footstool before his Footstool & fall fall low
fall fall low on o^r knees before his footstool.
fall fall low on o^r knees before his Footstool.
Solo:
fall fall low on o^r knees before his Footstool. A-Rise o Lord into thy resting place, a
feell low on our knees before his Footstool.
rise o L^d o L^d into thy resting place thou & y^e Ark of thy strength thou & y^e ark
of thy strength arise o L^d into thy resting place, thou & y^e ark of thy strength, thou and y^e

2 Voc:
Let thy Preists be clothed with Righteousness be
ark of thy Strength Let thy Preists be clothed with Righteousnes be clothed with
clothed with Righteousness & let thy Saints sing sing sing sing wth Joyfull=
Righteousness & let thy Sts sing sing sing wth Joyfull
=ness Let thy Preists be clothed wth Righteousness and let thy Saints
=ness Let thy Preists be clothed be clothed wth Righteousness & let thy Saints sing
sing with Joyfullness & let thy Sts sing sing wth Joyfull=ness.
sing with Joyfullness & let thy Sts sing sing sing wth Joyfull=ness.
Lord grant ye King a long Life Lord grant the
Lord grant ye King a long Life Lord grant the
Lord grant ye King a long Life Lord grant the
Lord grant ye King a long Life Lord grant the

146
King a long Life. That his years may endure his yeers may en-dure throughout all
King a long Life. That his yeers may en-dure his yeers may endure throughout all
King a long Life. That his yeers may en-dure his yeers may endure throughout all
King a long Life
Cho:
Gene-rations Lord grant ye King a long Life That his years may en
Generations Lord grant ye King a long Life. That his yeers may en
Lord grant ye King a long Life. That his yeers may en-
Cho:
Generations Lord grant ye King a long Life.
-dure his yeers may en-dure his yeers may en-dure through-out
-dure his yeers may en-dure through-out all Ge-ne-rations that his
dure his yeers may en-dure through-out all Gen-e-rations that his
That his yeers may en-dure his yeers may en-dure that his yeers may en-
That his yeers may en-dure may en-dure

all
Ge = = = = ne= rations through=out all. Gene=rations throughout all
years may en= dure that his. years may en= dure thro= = out all Gene=rations thro=out all
years may en= dure his years may en= dure through= out all Ge=ne= rations thro= out all
dure through= out all Gene= = = rations thro= out all — Gene= rati=ons thro=out all —
that his years may en= dure thro= out all Gene= rations thro= out all —
Gene= = rations A= = men.
Dr Blow.
Gene= = rations A= = men.
1698.
Gene= = rations A= = men.
Gener= ations A= = men.
Gene= = rations A= = men.
Blessed is he, blessed is he yt considereth ye poor, ye Poor and needy. —
Blessed is he &c. is he ye considereth ye poor ye poor & needy. —
Blessed is he &c. is he yt considereth ye poor ye poor and needy —

148
Blessed is he, Blessed is he ÿ considereth ÿ poor & Needy. ÿ Lord shall deliver him in ÿ Time in ÿ The time of Trouble, ÿ Lord shall de=li=ver him in ÿ time of Trouble ÿ Ld shall deliver him in ÿ Time of Trouble
Blessed is he Blessed is he ÿ con=sidereth ÿ poor & Needy ÿ Ld shall de=li=ver him in ÿ Time of Trouble de=liver him in ÿ time of Trouble ÿ Ld shall de=li=ver him shall de=li=ver him in ÿ time of Trouble ÿ Ld shall de=li=ver him in ÿ Time of Trouble
Blessed is he Blessed is he ÿ con=sidereth ÿ poor & Needy. ÿ Ld shall de=liver him in ÿ time of Trouble ÿ Ld shall de=li=ver him ÿ Ld shall deliver him in ÿ time of Trouble ÿ Ld shall de=li=ver him in ÿ Time of trouble.
The Ld preserve him preserve him & keep him a=live & keep him a-
=live ÿ Ld pre=serve him ÿ Lord pre=serve him pre=serve him and keep him a=live

That he may be
blessed
that he may be
bless=
sed up = on
earth,
and de = liver not thou him
will of his
Enemies.
The Lord comfort him the
The Lord comfort him y
Lord comfort
comfort him the
The Lord comfort him y
Lord comfort
comfort him y
Lord comfort him when he lieth sick upon his Bed. Make thou all his Bed
Lord comfort him when he lieth sick upon his Bed. Make thou all his Bed.
Lord comfort him when he lieth sick upon his Bed.
Make thou all his

180

make thou all his Bed in his Sickness make thou all his Bed make thou all his
make thou all his Bed in his sickness make thou all his Bed. make thou all his
Bed make thou all his Bed in his Sickness make thou all his Bed,
Bed all all all all all all his Bed in his Sickness.
Bed all, all all all all all his Bed in his Sickness.
make thou all his Bed all all all all make thou all his Bed in his Sickness. Glo = = = ry be to y
Glo = ry be to y
Father Glo = = = = = = = ry be to y Son Glo - - - - ry be to y holy Ghost.
Glo = - - ry be to y Father Glo
Father Glo - - - - - ry be to y Son Glo - - - - - ry be to y holy Ghost

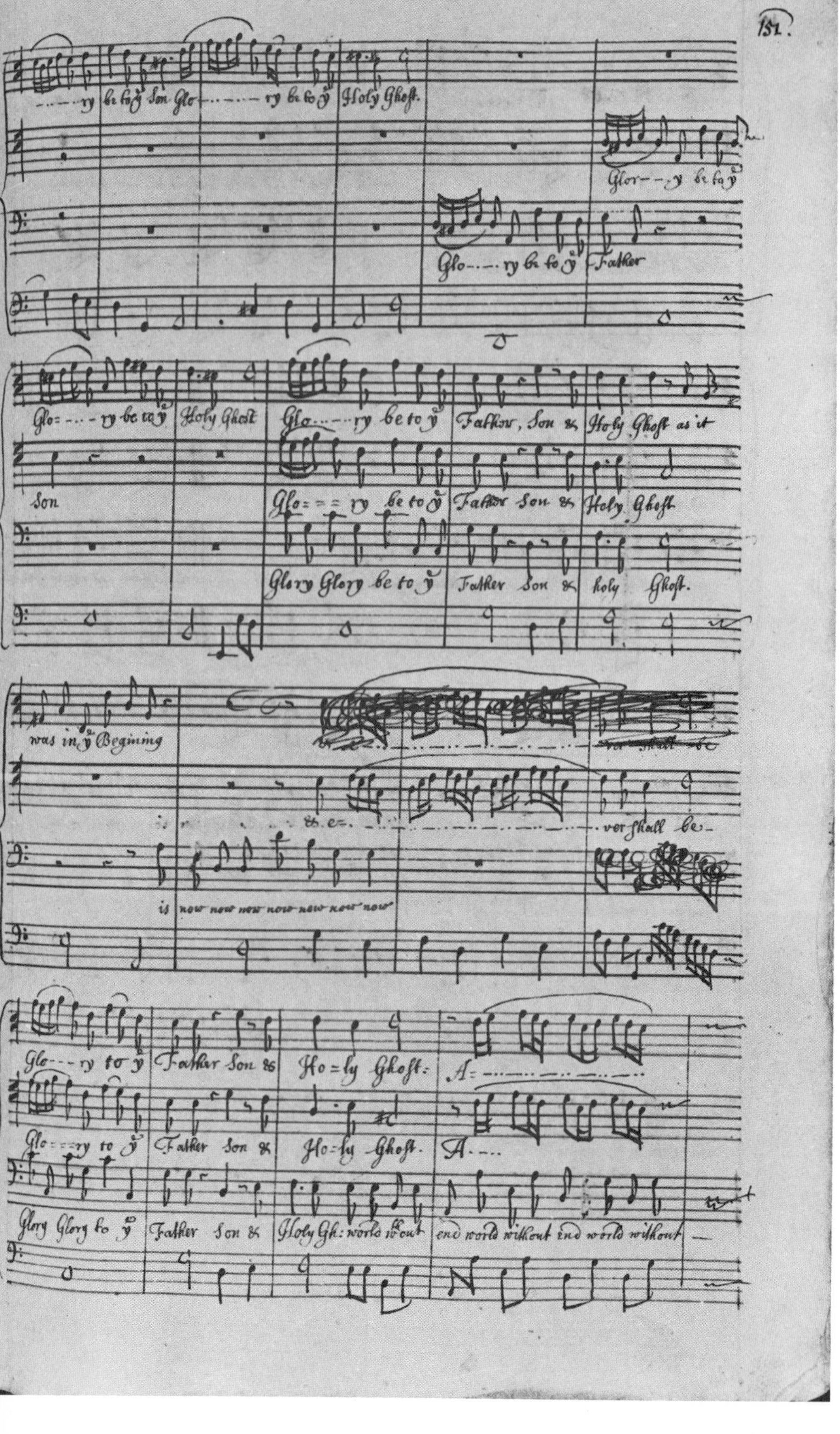
151.
ry be to ye Son Glo ry be to ye Holy Ghost.
Glor y be to ye
Glo ry be to ye Father
Glo ry be to ye Holy Ghost Glo ry be to ye Father, Son & Holy Ghost as it
Son Glo ry be to ye Father Son & Holy Ghost.
Glory Glory be to ye Father Son & holy Ghost.
was in ye Begining
is now now now now now now now
ver shall be
Glo ry to ye Father Son & Ho ly Ghost. A
Glo ry to ye Father Son & Ho ly Ghost. A
Glory Glory to ye Father Son & Holy Gh: world without end world without end world without

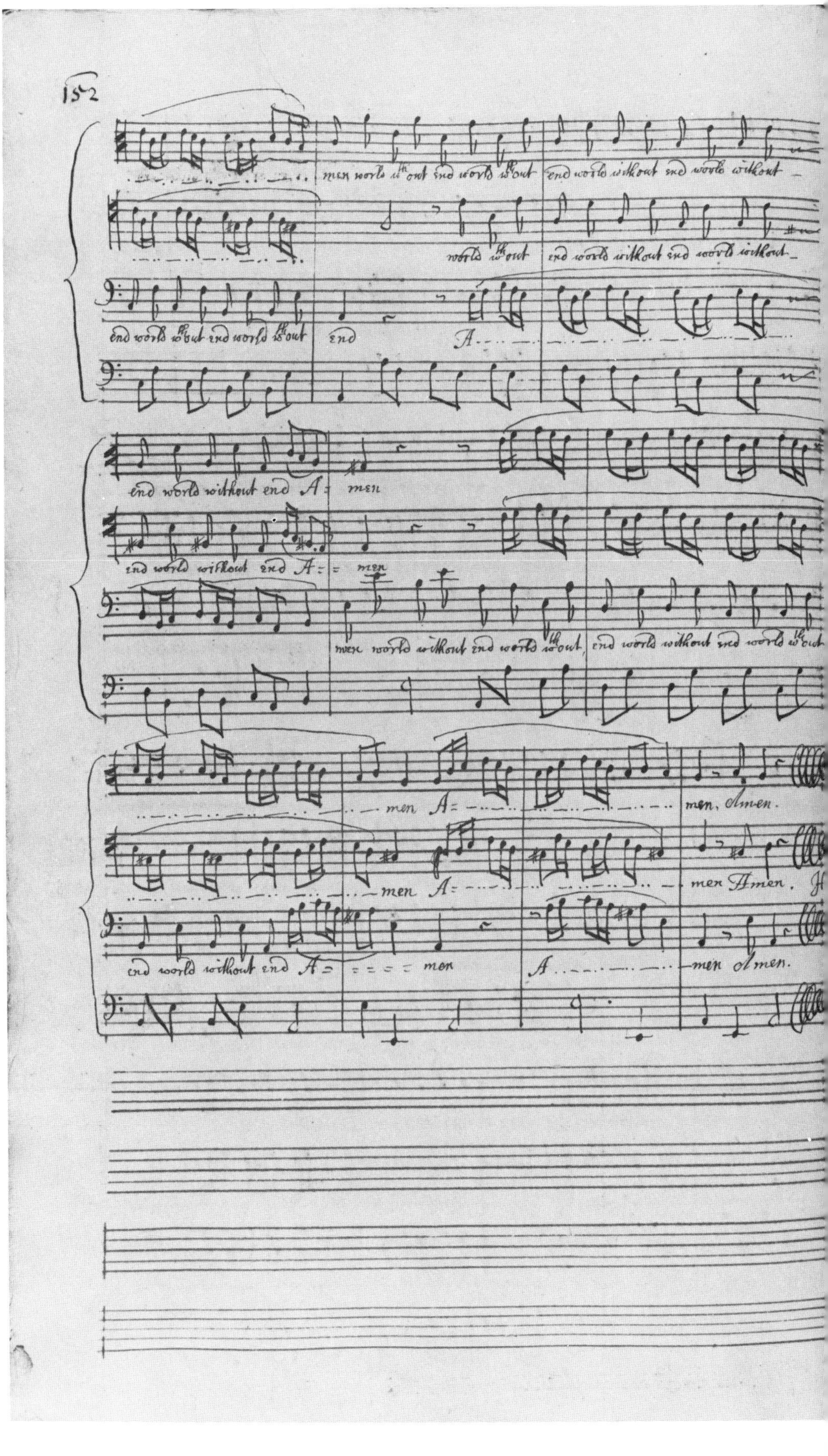
152
men world without end world without
end world without end world without
world without
end world without end world without
end world without end world without
end
A
end world without end A
men
end world without end A
men
men world without end world without
end world without end world without
men A
men, Amen.
men A
men Amen.
end world without end A
men
A
men Amen.

Not unto us o Lord
8 notes higher
Organ
Vers: 3 voc
Not unto us ô Lord not unto us but unto thy name unto thy name give the praise for thy loving mercy and for thy truths sake
Not unto us ô Lord not unto us but unto thy name un-to thy name give the praise for thy loving mercy thy loving mercy and for thy truths sake,
Not unto us ô Lord not unto us but unto thy name un-to thy name give the praise for thy loving mercy thy loving mercy and for thy truths sake
Ritor.
Vers: Med: Decani
Not unto us o Lord Not unto us but unto thy name
Med: Cantoris
Vers: Decani
Not unto us o Lord not unto us. But unto thy
Vers Cantoris
Not unto us O Lord not unto us, But unto thy
Vers Not unto us O Lord Not unto us, But unto thy name
Decani.
Vers: Cantoris
Not unto us ô Lord not unto us But unto thy
Vers: Decani
Not unto us ô Lord not unto us, But unto thy name
Verse Cantoris
Not unto us o Lord not unto us But unto thy
Verse not unto us ô Lord not unto us but unto thy name

Ritor
give y^e praise for thy loving mercy &c for thy truths sake.
name give y^e praise for thy loving mercy for thy loving mercy &c for thy truths sake.
name give y^e praise for thy loving mercy for thy loving mercy &c for thy truths sake.
give ye praise for thy loving mercy thy loving mercy &c for thy truths sake.
name give ye praise for thy loving mercy for thy loving mercy and for thy truths sake.
give ye praise for thy loving mercy thy loving mercy and for thy truths sake.
name give ye praise for thy loving mercy for thy loving mercy and for thy truths sake.
give ye praise for thy loving mercy thy loving mercy &c for thy truths sake.
Ritor
Vers: 3 voc
Wherefore shall y^e heathen say where is now their
wherefore shall y^e heathen say where is now their God as for our God he is in
wherefore shall y^e heathen say where is now their God as for o^r God he is in
God as for o^r God he is in heavn

155
heavn, he hath don whosoever pleased him he is in Heavn, he hath don
heavn, he hath don whosoever pleased him he hath don whosoever pleased him
he hath don whosoever pleased him as for our God he hath don whosoever pleased him
whatsoever pleased him whoso=ever pleased him. Ritorn
whatsoever soever pleased him.
whatso=e= =ver pleased him.
Ritor
Verse
The Lord hath been mindfull of us and he shall bless us
The Lord hath been mindfull of us and
The Lord hath been mindfull of us and he shall bless us
The Lord hath been mindfull of us, and
The Lord hath been mindfull of us, and he shall bless us
The Lord hath been mindfull of us and
The Lord hath been mindfull of us and he shall bless us
The Lord hath been mindfull of us and

156
and en=crease you more and more
he shall bless us
and en=crease you more &c more and en
&c en=crease you more and more
he shall bless us
and en=crease you more &c more &c en
and en=crease you more and more
he shall bless us
and en=crease you more &c more &c en
and en=crease you more and more
he shall bless us.
and en=crease you more &c more &c en
=crease you more and more,
Ritor
=crease you more and more
soft
=crease you more and more, and encrease you more &c more
=crease you more and more
soft
=crease you more and more and en=crease you more &c more
=crease you more and more,
=crease you more and more and in=crease you more &c more.
Ritor
crease you more and more

The dead shall not praise y^e o
The dead shall not praise thee o God nor all they that go down in = to the Silence
The dead
46
Lord nor all they that go down in = to, y^e Silence but we
but we -
Shall not praise thee o God nor all they that go down in to the Silence but -
46
will praise y^e Lord will praise y^e Lord from this time forth for evermore but we
will praise y^e Lord will praise y^e Lord from this time forth for ever more but we -
we will praise y^e Lord will praise y^e Lord for evmore but we will praise y^e
will praise y^e Lord from this time forth for ever = more but we will praise y^e Lord
will praise y^e Lord from this time forth for ever = more but we will praise y^e
Lord from this time forth for e = = = = ver = more but we will praise y^e

158
Ritorn.
From this time forth from this time forth for ever=more
Lord fro this time forth for e=====ver=more
Lord fro this time forth for e=====ver=more
Ritor.
Vers: Decani
Alle=lu=ia Alle=lu==ia
Cantoris
Alle=luia, Alle=
Decani
Alle=luia Alle=lu=ia
Alle=luia Alle=
Cantoris
Alle=lu=ia Al=le=lu==ia
Decani
Alle=luia Alle==lu=ia
Alle=luia Alle=
Cantoris
Alle=lu=ia Alle=lu=ia
Decani
Alle=lu=ia Al=le lu==ia
Alle=lu=ia Alle
Cantoris
Alle lu=ia Al=le lu=ia
Vers:

159.
Ritor:
Vers:
Cho:
Alleluia
Mr Lock.

Thy Beauty o Israel

Thy Beauty ô Israel is slain upon ye high Places
Thy Beauty ô Israel is slain upon ye high places
How are ye mighty faln
How are ye mighty faln
How are ye mighty faln
Tell it not in Gath lest the
Tell it not in Gath in Gath
Tell it not in Gath Tell it not in Gath
Daughters of ye Philistines re:joyce Tell it not in Gath publish it not in ye streets of
Tell it not in Gath pub=lish it not in ye streets of
Tell it not in Gath pub=lish it not in ye streets of
Ascalon Lest ye daughters of ye un cirumcised tri=umph
Ascalon lest ye Daugh=ters of ye uncirumci=sed tri=umph
Ascalon Lest ye daughters of ye uncircum=cised triumph ye mountains o

Gilboa, let there be no dew no dew neither let there be Rain up=on you nor Feilds of
Offerings For there the Sheild of the migh= = = = = = = = = = = = = = = ty y
migh= = = ty was vile=ly cast a=way The Sheild of Saul of Saul
as if he had not been a=nom=ted wth Oil.
Cho:
Cho:
Tell it not in Gath pub=lish it not in ye streets of Ascalon
Tell it not in Gath pub=lish it not in ye streets of Asca=lon lest ye daughters of ye uncircum=
Tell it not in Gath pub=lish it not in ye streets of Asca=lon Lest the Daughters of
Tell it not in Gath publish it not in ye streets of Ascalon, Lest ye Daughters of ye un
Tell it not in Gath least ye Daughters of ye uncircumcised tri= = = = =umph=
=ci= = = = = = =sed tri= = =umph Lest ye daughters of ye uncircumcised triumph
ye uncircum cised tri= = = =umph least they lest they triumph.
=circumci= = =sed triumph Lest the daughters of ye uncircumcised Tri=umph.

2d Tenor
Verse
2 From the Blood of the slain. From ye Fat of ye mighty, the Bow of Jonathan
turned not back, and the Sword of Saul returned not empty.
Saul & Jonathan were lovely & pleasant in their Lives &
Saul & Jonathan were lovely & pleasant in their Lives and
Saul & Jonathan, were Lovely & pleasant in yr Lives and
in their deaths they were not divided they were not divided, and in their
in their deaths they were not divided they were not divided, and in their
in their deaths they were not divided not divided and in their
deaths they were not divided they were not divided.
deaths they were not divided they were not divided.
deaths they were not divided they were not divided.
vers Teno

Verse
First Tenor.
163.
Ye Daughters of Isra=el. weep over Saul weep over Saul weep over Saul who
clothed you in Scarlet who put on Ornaments of Gold who put on ornaments of
Gold upon your Appar==el. who put on ornaments of Gold upon —
yo Ap=par===ell.
How are ye mighty faln! how are ye mighty faln in ye midst of the Battle in the
How are ye mighty faln! how are ye mighty faln in ye midst of the Battle in
How are ye mighty faln! how are ye mighty faln in ye midst of ye Battle in ye midst
How are ye mighty faln! how are ye mighty faln in ye midst of ye Battle - in the
midst in ye midst of the Battle.
ye midst ye midst of ye Battle.
in the midst of the Battle.
Thy Beauty ô Israel is slain upon ye high places
midst the midst of the Battle.

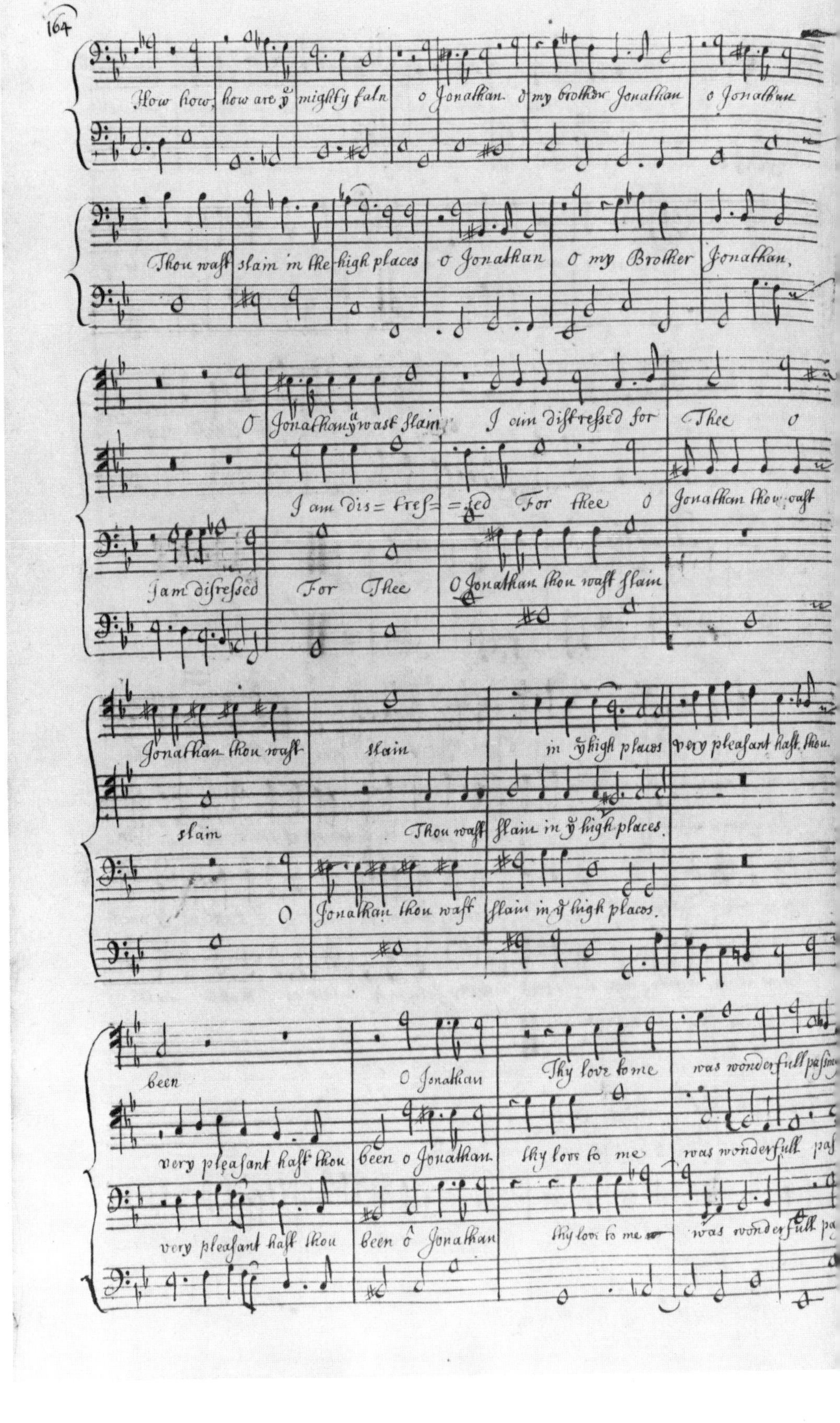
164
How how, how are ye mighty faln O Jonathan O my brother Jonathan O Jonathan
Thou wast slain in the high places O Jonathan O my Brother Jonathan,
O Jonathan thou wast slain I am distressed for Thee O
I am dis=tres==sed For thee O Jonathan thou wast
I am distressed For Thee O Jonathan thou wast slain
Jonathan thou wast slain in ye high places very pleasant hast thou
slain Thou wast slain in ye high places.
O Jonathan thou wast slain in ye high places.
been O Jonathan Thy love to me was wonderfull passing
very pleasant hast thou been O Jonathan thy love to me was wonderfull pas
very pleasant hast thou been O Jonathan thy love to me was wonderfull pa

Love passing ÿ | Love the Love | of women. Cho: How are ÿ mighty faln!
-sing ÿ Love pas- | -sing ÿ Love the, | Love of women. Cho: How are the mighty faln!
-sing ÿ Love pas- | sing ÿ Love ÿ | Love of women. Cho: How are the mighty faln!
Cho: How are ÿ mighty faln.
how are ÿ mighty | faln & ÿ weapons of ÿ | War are pe-ri- | shed
how are ÿ mighty | faln & ÿ weapons of ÿ | war are pe--ri- | shed & the weapons of the
how are ÿ mighty | faln & ÿ weapons of ÿ | war are pe--ri- | shed & ÿ weapons of the
how are ÿ mighty faln ... and ÿ weapons of the
and the weapons of ÿ | war are pe-- | --rished.
war are pe--ri- | shed and the wea- | -pons of ÿ war are | perished.
war are pe--ri- | shed and ÿ weapons ÿ | weapons of ÿ war are | perished.
war are per-i- | shed & ÿ weapons of the | war are pe---rished.

166
Be not wroth very sore o Lord nei= = = ther re=member Iniqui= ty.
Be - not wroth very sore o Lord
Be - not wroth very sore o

167.
are thy people Si=on. is a wilderness Jerusalem a Desolation
see we are thy people. Si=on is a wilderness Jerusalem a Desolation.
we are thy people. Si=on is a wilderness Jerusalem a Desolation
-seech thee we= are thy people. Sion. is a wilderness Jerusalem a Desolation.
are thy people.
oh holy & oh beautifull house
Si=on is a wilderness Jerusalem a Desolation oh holy & oh beautifull
Si=on is a wilderness Jerusalem a Desolation oh holy-
Sion is a wilderness Je=rusalem a Desolation oh
Si=on is a wilderness Jerusalem a Desolation
oh holy and oh beautifull, house is burnt up wth
house, Oh holy and oh beau=ti=full house
& oh beautifull house oh holy and oh beautifull house is burnt
holy and our beautifull house where oh Fathers praised thee,
oh holy and oh beautifull house where oh Fathers praised thee

168

Fire is burnt up with Fire burnt up up with Fire
will thou refrain thy self for these things o Lord will thou refrain thy
up is burn up with fire will thou refrain thy self for these things O Lord will thou hold thy
is burnt up with Fire will thou re-frain thy self
is burnt up with Fire will thou refrain thy self
self will thou hold will thou refrain thy self will thou hold thy peace
self will thou hold thy peace will thou hold thy peace o Lord
peace will thou refrain thy self will thou hold thy peace will thou re-
will thou hold thy peace for these things o Lord will thou hold thy peace will
will thou hold thy peace will thou re-
will thou refrain thy self will thou hold thy peace and Af-flict us very sore
will thou hold thy peace will thou hold thy peace & af-flict us very sore
-frain thy self will thou hold thy peace. o Lord will thou hold thy peace & aff-lict us very sore
thou hold thy peace o Lord will thou hold thy peace o Lord & aff-lict us very sore
frain thy self will thou hold thy peace and af-flict us very sore

I was glad
I was glad
I was glad w^n they said unto me, let us let us
I was glad, I was glad I was glad w^n they said unto me I was glad let us let us go let us
I was glad I was glad I was glad w^n they said unto me I was glad let us let us let us
I was glad I was glad I was glad when they said unto me let us
go into ye house of ye Lord I was glad I was glad I was glad w^n they said unto me
go into ye house of the Lord I was glad I was glad w^n they said unto me let us go let us
go into ye house of ye Lord I was glad I was glad I was glad w^n they said unto me let us
go into ye house of ye Lord I was glad I was glad when they said unto me let us go,
let us go let us go into the house of ye Lord. O^r feet shall stand within thy
go into ye house of ye Lord into ye house of the Lord. O^r feet shall stand within thy
go into ye house let us go into ye house of the Lord. O^r feet shall stand within thy
let us go into the house of the Lord. O^r feet shall stand within thy
gates O Jerusalem, For thither ye Tribes go up ev'n ye Tribes of y^e
gates O Jerusalem. For thither y^e Tribes go up y^e Tribes go up ev'n y^e Tribes of y^e
gates O Jerusalem For thither y^e Tribes go up ev'n y^e Tribes of y^e
gates O Jerusalem. For thither y^e Tribes go up ev'n y^e Tribes of y^e

170
unto the Testimony of Israel. To give thanks to give thanks unto the name of the Lord
Thanks to give thanks unto the name of the Lord For there are set thrones of Judgment even the
Thrones of the house of David. O pray for the Peace of Jerusalem pray pray for the
peace of Jerusalem. They shall prosper that love Thee. They shall

171
pry. love — Thee They shall prosper that love thee they shall pros=
They shall pros= = per that love ye they shall pros= per they shall
They shall prosper ye love ye they shall pros= per that
pros= per ye love Thee. They shall prosper
per that love thee they shall. prosper shall prosper that love thee. Peace be within thy
prosper that love thee they shall. pros= per that love thee Peace be within thy
love thee they shall pros= per they shall prosper ye love thee. Peace be within thy
They shall pros= per they shall prosper yt love thee. Peace be within thy
walls, & pros= perity, & pros= perity within thy Pa=laces & prosperity pros= perity with=
walls & pros= perity & pros= perity within thy Palaces & prosperity pros= perity with=
walls and pros= perity and pros= perity within thy Palaces & prosperity pros= perity with
walls & pros= perity & pros= perity within thy Palaces & prosperity pros= perity with
=in thy Pa=la=ces. Glo= = =ry be to the
=in thy Pa=la=ces. Glo= = =ry be to the Father
=in thy Pa=la=ces. Glo= = =ry be to ye Father
=in thy Pa=la=ces. Glo= = =ry be to ye Father & to the

172
Father and, to the Son and to the holy Ghost
and to the Son and to the ho = = = ly Ghost As it was in the begining is
and to the Son & to the holy Ghost, As it was in ye begin=
Son & to the holy Ghost,
the begining is now and ever shall be world without end A
now and ever shall be and e = = ver shall be world without
=ing is now & ever ever shall be, world without end, A
it was in the begin=ing is now and ever shall be
A = = = = men world without End A = men A
end A = men world without end A = men A men A
men world without end A = men
without End A = = = men world without end A = men A = =
men A men A = men.
men A = men A = men A = = mm A = men.
Mr F: Pigge

Praise the Lord O Je=rusalem, praise thy God thy God o Sion,
Praise the Lord O Je=rusalem praise thy God thy God o Sion
Praise the Lord O Je=rusalem, praise thy God thy God o Sion For Kings shall
Praise the Lord O Je=rusalem, praise thy God thy God o Sion For
& Queens thy nursing Mothers, Kings shall be thy nursing
& Queens thy nursing Mothers
be thy nursing Fathers,
Kings shall be thy nursing Fathers For Kings shall be thy
Fathers For Kings shall be thy nursing Fathers and Queens
& Queens thy nursing Mothers Kings shall be thy nursing Fathers and Queens
& Queens thy nursing Mothers For Kings shall be thy nursing Fathers and
nursing Fathers For Kings shall be thy nursing Fathers
& Queens thy nursing Mothers, & Queens & Queens thy nursing Mothers.
& Queens & Queens thy nursing mothers, & Queens & Queens & Queens thy nursing Mothers
Queens & Queens & Queens thy nursing mothers, & Queens & Queens thy nursing mothers.
& Queens & Queens thy nursing mothers, & Queens & Queens thy nursing mothers.

Turn over

174
As we have heard So have we seen in ye City of our God. As we have heard So have we
As we :||:
As we have
As we have. heard So have we seen in ye City of our God. As we have heard So have we
As we have :||:
As we have :||:
Seen in ye City of our God. God upholdeth ye same for ever
God up=
Be thou exalted
Seen in ye City of our God. God up= holdeth ye same for ever. Be thou ex
God up=
Be thou ex= al= =ted Lord in thine own Strength So will we
Lord in thine own Strength be thou exalted Lord in thine own Strength So will we
= alted Lord be thou exalted Lord in thine own Strength So will we
Be thou exalted Lord be thou exalted Lord in thine own Strength. So will we
Sing, So will we Sing. So will we Sing will we Sing and praise thy Power.
Sing. So will we Sing. So will we Sing will we Sing and praise thy Power
Sing. So will we Sing So will we Sing will we Sing and praise thy Power
Sing will we Sing and praise thy Power.
So will we Sing So will we Sing.

175
Alle=luia Alle=luia Alle=luia Alle=luia, Alle=luia Alle=luia, Alle=
luia, Alle=luia, Alle=luia, Alle=luia, Alle=luia.
Alle:
Alleluia
soft
Mr. Jer: Clark.

176
Slow
Mr Tudway:
Vers: 3 voc
Is it true?
Is it true!
Is it true, is it true that God will
Is it true
Is it true is it true yt God will dwell wth men
That God will dwell will dwell wth men u=
dwell wth men,
That God will dwell will dwell wth men upon ye Earth, yt God will dwell will dwell wth men upon ye Earth.
That God will dwell wth men wth men u= pon ye Earth yt God will dwell wth men wth men upon ye Earth.
=pon ye Earth: That God will dwell wth men u=pon ye Earth, That God will dwell wth men u=pon ye Earth.
Rit:
Vers: Slo
Be= hold Be= hold the heavns,
Be= hold the heavns & ye Heavn of Heavns are not able to con= tain thee

how much more, how much more un able is this house how much more un=
=able is this house how much more un= a= = =ble is this house how much more un
a= =ble is this House?
Rit:
Ver: 3 voc: But have thou re=
Grace. But have thou re=
But have thou re=
=spect un=to ye Pray'r of thy Servants but have thou respect un= to ye prayr of thy Servants O
=spect unto ye Pray'r of thy Servants but have thou respect un= to the prayr of thy Servants O
=spect unto ye Prayr of thy Servants but have thou respect un to ye prayer of thy Servants O
Lord our God O Lord our God who pray before thee who pray before Thee.
Lord our God o Lord our God who pray before thee who pray be= fore Thee.
Lord our God O Lord our God who pray before thee who pray be fore Thee.
Turn over. –

Vers; 2 voc:
Grave
That thine Eyes may be open towards this House Day
Grave That thine Eyes may be open towards this House Day and Night That thine eyes may be
and Night may be open towards this house day and Night even towards y^e place where=
open towards this house day and night day and night even towards y^e place where=
= of thou hast said y^t thou wouldst put thy name there y^t thou wouldst put thy name there even
of thou hast said- y^t thou wouldst put thy name there y^t thou wouldst put thy name there even
towards y^e place where= of thou hast said y^t thou wouldst put thy name there thou wouldst put thy
towards y^e place where= of thou hast said y^t thou wouldst put thy name there thou wouldst put thy
3 voc Hear thou therefore y^e Sup= =plications of thy Servants
name thy there Grave Hear thou therefore y^e Supplications of thy Servants
name there Hear thou therefore y^e Supplications of thy Servants
#3 4 4 3

hear thou therefore y^e Sup= =plications of thy Servants which they pray which they pray in this place, and
hear thou therefore y^e Sup=pli=ca=tions of thy Servants which they pray which they pray in this place, and
hear thou therefore y^e sup=pli= cations of thy Servants which they pray which they pray in this place, and
hear thou in y^e place of thy ha=bi= tation, Evn in heavn Evn in heavn Ritor
very slow
hear thou in y^e place of thy habi= tation Evn in heavn Evn in heavn -
hear thou in y^e place of thy habi= tation Evn in heavn Evn in heavn. Ritor
very slow.
Evn in heavn, & when thou hearest be mercifull & when thou=
Evn in heavn & when thou hearest be mercifull & when thou
Evn in heavn & when thou hearest be mercifull & when thou
hearest thou hearest be mercifull be mercifull.
hearest thou hearest be mercifull be mercifull.
hearest thou hearest be mercifull be mercifull.

180
vers 3 voc:
Arise ô Lord Arise ô Lord and come in to thy Rest arise o
Arise ô Lord o Lord arise ô Lord and come in to thy Rest arise ô Lord
Arise ô Lord ô Lord Arise ô Lord o Lord and come in to thy Rest Arise o Lord o
Lord ô Lord and come in: to thy Rest. Thou Thou & y Ark thou
arise ô Lord & come in to thy Rest. Thou Thou & y Ark Thou & y Ark of thy
Lord & Come & come in to thy Rest. Thou Thou & y Ark- Thou & y Ark-
Thou Thou & y Ark of thy Strength Thou & y Ark Thou & y Ark of thy
Strength, Thou and y Ark of thy Strength Thou & y Ark thou Thou & y Ark of thy
Thou Thou & y Ark of thy Strength. Thou & y Ark thou Thou & y Ark of thy
Strength Ritor. Cho: Arise ô Lord arise ô Lord ô
Strength Cho: Arise ô Lord arise ô Lord ô
Strength Cho: Arise ô Lord, arise ô Lord ô
Cho: Arise ô Lord arise ô Lord ô

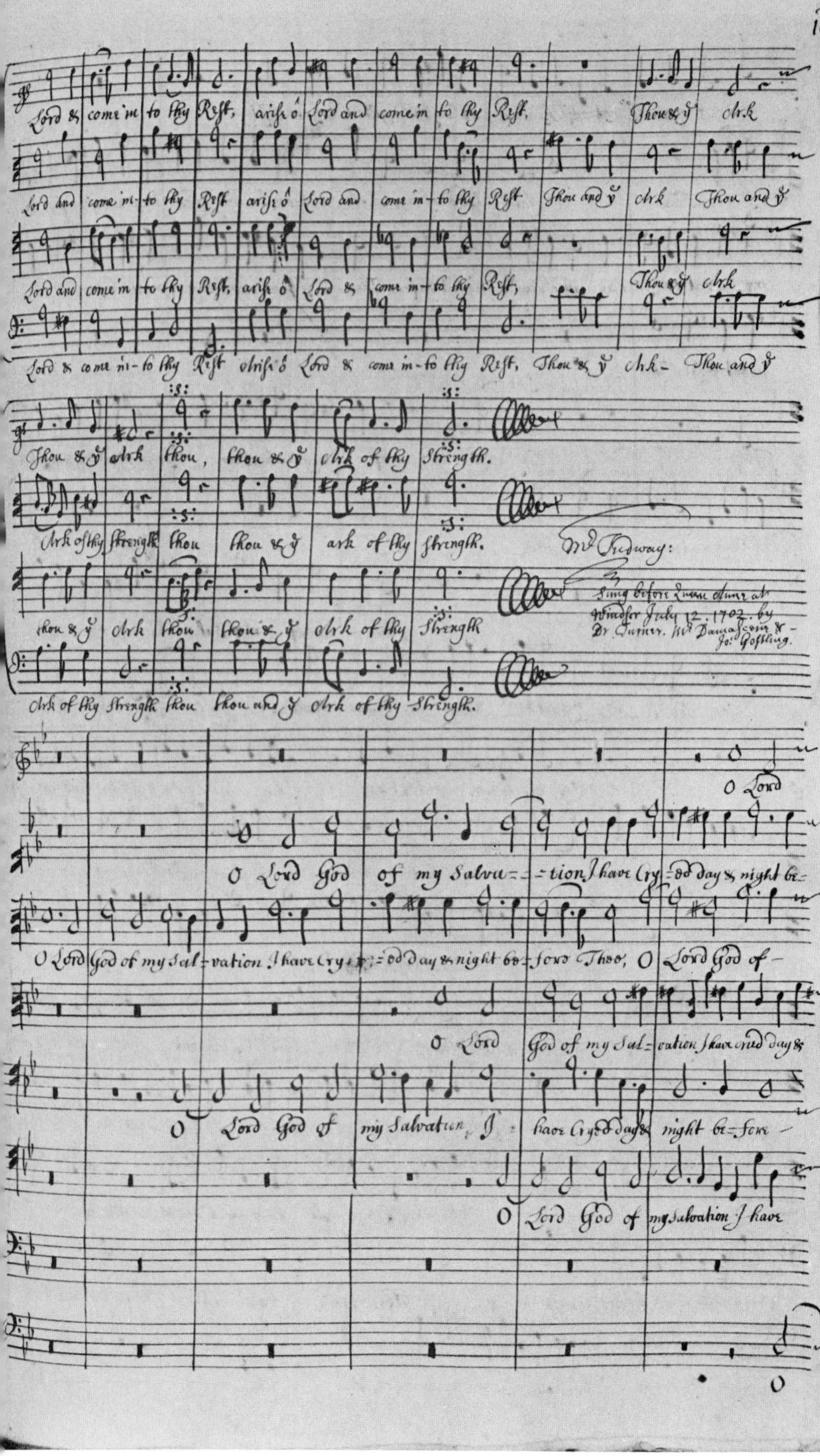

181.
Lord & come in to thy Rest, arise O Lord and come in to thy Rest, Thou & ye Ark
Lord and come in to thy Rest arise O Lord and come in to thy Rest Thou and ye Ark Thou and ye
Lord and come in to thy Rest, arise O Lord & come in to thy Rest, Thou & ye Ark
Lord & come in to thy Rest arise O Lord & come in to thy Rest, Thou & ye Ark Thou and ye
Thou & ye Ark thou, thou & ye Ark of thy Strength.
Ark of thy Strength thou thou & ye ark of thy strength.
thou & ye Ark thou thou & ye Ark of thy Strength
Ark of thy Strength thou thou and ye Ark of thy Strength.
Mr Tudway:
Sung before Queen Anne at Windsor July 12. 1702. by Dr Turner. Mr Damascene & Jo: Gostling.
O Lord
O Lord God of my Salvation I have cry'd day & night be-
O Lord God of my Salvation I have cry'd day & night before Thee, O Lord God of
O Lord God of my Salvation I have cried day &
O Lord God of my Salvation I have cry'd day & night before
O Lord God of my salvation I have

God of my sal- vation I have cry- ed day & night be- fore Thee,
- fore Thee O Lord God of my Sal- vation I have cryed day & night befor Thee
my Salvation I have cryed day & night before Thee I have cryed day & night befor Thee be-
night befor Thee
Thee O Lord God of my Salvation I have cryed day & night be
cryed day & night be- fore Thee,
O Lord God of my Sal- vation I have cryed
Lord God of my Salvation I have cryed day & night. O Lord God of
O Lord God of my Salvation I have cryed day & night have cryed day & night be
I have cryed day & night before Thee I have cryed day & night before Thee. I have cryed day & night be- fore Thee I have cryed day & night be
O Lord God of my Sal- vation I have cryed day & night- have cryed day and
- fore Thee, I have cryed day & night I have cryed day & night have cryed day & night
Lord God of my Salvation I have cryed day & night have cryed day & night be- fore
day & night before ye have cryed day & night before Thee, I have cryed day & night be-
my Salvation I have cryed day & night before Thee I have cryed day & night be-

Vers: 6. voc:
O let my Prayer enter into thy Presence,
O let my prayer enter into thy Presence.
let my prayer enter in= = =to thy Presence.
let my prayer enter in= = to thy Presence
O let my
into thy Presence
inclinc thine Ear unto my Calling inclinc thine Ear thine Ear unto my
O let my Prayer enter in= to thy Presence, O let my Prayer enter into thy Presence
O Let my prayer enter into thy Presence,
inclinc thine Ear unto my Calling
O Let my
let my prayer En= ter in to thy Presence
prayer enter in= = = = to thy Presence,

184
Calling. O let my prayer enter into thy Presence incline thine Ear
incline thine Ear unto my Calling incline thine ear un- -to my Calling incline thine
- - - ling. in- -cline thine ear unto my Cal- -ling incline thine ear un- -to my calling in
prayer enter into thy Presence, incline thine ear unto my Calling incline thine ear unto my calling,
incline thine ear unto my Calling incline thine Ear
let my prayer enter into thy Presence. Incline thine ear unto my Calling Incline thine ear unto my-
unto my Calling incline thine Ear unto my Calling. Cho: For my Soul is full of Troubles;
Ear incline thine Ear un- -to my Calling incline thine Ear un- -to my Calling. Cho: For my Soul is full of Troubles;
-cline thine ear unto my Calling in- -cline thine ear unto my Calling un- -to my Calling. Cho: For my Soul is full of Troubles;
Cho: For my Soul is full of Troubles;
In- -cline thine ear incline thine Ear un- -to my Calling. Cho: For my Soul is full of Troubles;
Incline thine ear unto my Calling incline thine Ear un- -to my Calling. Cho: For my Soul is full of Troubles;
calling in- -cline thine ear unto my Calling un- -to my Calling. Cho: For my Soul is full of Troubles;
For my Soul is full of Troubles;

& my life draweth nigh unto Hell.
& my life draweth nigh unto Hell. & my life draweth nigh unto Hell.
I am so fast in Prison I- am so fast in Pri-
I am so fast in Prison & my life draweth nigh unto-
& my life draweth nigh unto Hell- I am so fast in Prison, & my life draweth nigh
& my life draweth nigh unto Hell I am so fast in Prison
& my life draweth nigh unto Hell
I am so fast in-
I am so fast in Prison I am so fast in Prison yt I cannot I cannot get Forth.
I am so fast in Prison yt I cannot get forth yt I cannot I can-not get Forth.
-son yt I cannot get forth I cannot get forth yt I cannot get forth, I- cannot get Forth.
Hell. I am so fast in Pri-son yt I cannot get forth that I can-not get Forth.
Dr Blow.
unto Hell, yt I cannot get forth yt I can-not get forth I cannot get Forth.
I am so fast in Prison yt I cannot get forth I cannot get Forth.
I am so fast in Prison yt I cannot I cannot get Forth.
Prison yt I cannot get forth yt I cannot I cannot get forth yt I - cannot I cannot get Forth

186
Man yt is born of a Woman hath but a short time to live & is full of Misery
Man yt is born of a Woman hath but a short time to live & is full of Misery
Man yt is born of a Woman hath but a short time to live & is full of Misery he cometh
Man yt is born of a Woman hath but a short time to live & is full of Misery.
he cometh up and is cut down, & is cut down he cometh up & is cut down &
he cometh up & is cut down cut down, he cometh up and is cut down cut down he
up and is cut down & is cut down he cometh up & is cut down cut - down he cometh up &
he cometh up & is cut down he cometh up & is cut - down he cometh up & is cut -
is cut down like a Flowr he fleeth as it were a Shadow & ne'r continueth
cometh up & is cut down like a Flowr he fleeth as it were a Shadow. & ne'r con=
is cut down like a Flowr he fleeth as it were a Shadow & ne'r con= tinueth -
down & is cut down like a Flowr he fleeth as it were a Shadow and
& ne're con= tinueth ne're con= tinueth & ne're continueth ne're continueth in one Stay. Cho: He
= tinueth & ne're continueth, & ne're continueth ne're continu= eth in one Stay in one Stay. Cho: He
& ne're continu= eth ne're continu= eth, & ne're continueth in one Stay. Cho: He
ne're continueth, ne're continueth & ne're con= tinueth ne're con= tinueth in one Stay. Cho: He

flesh as it were a Shadow & nere continueth & nere con= tinueth nere con tinueth &
flesh as it were a Shadow & nere con= tinueth & nere continueth & nere continu=
flesh as it were a Shadow. & nere con= = tinueth, & nere continu= eth nere continu= eth,
= flesh as it were a Shadow. & nere continueth, nere continueth, & nere con.
nere continueth, nere continueth in one Stay. Vers: In ye midst of Life we are in Death,
= eth nere contin-u = eth in one Stay in one Stay. Vers
& nere contin — u= eth in one Stay. verse
tinueth nere con= tinueth in one Stay In ye
of whom may we seek for Succo but of Thee O Lord In ye mids of Life we are in Death
In ye midst of Life we are in Death, of whom may we seek for
In ye midst of Life we are in Death.
mids of Life we are in Death of whom may we seek for Succo — In ye
of whom may we seek for Succo but of thee O
succo but of Thee O Lord of whom may we seek for Succo but of thee O
Of whom may we seek for Succo, of whom — may we seek for Succo But of Thee O
midst of Life we are in Death. Of whom may we seek for Succo But of Thee O

Lord who for o^r Sins art just= ly displeas= =ed.
Vers: & Cho: Yet o Lord o Lord most mighty o
holy, o holy & most mercifull Savi= o^r deliver us not into y^e bit= = = ter Pains
of eternal death
Vers:
Thou knowest Lord y^e Secrets of o^r hearts

189.
Shut not thy mercifull Ears thy mercifull Ears un= to ye prayrs un=
Shut not thy mercifull Ears thy mercifull Ears un= to ye prayrs un= to ye prayrs un=
Shut not thy mercifull Ears thy mercifull Ears unto ye Prayrs. Shut not thy mercifull
Secrets of our hearts. Shut not thy mercifull Ears un= to ye prayrs un=
to ye Prayrs but Spare us Lord most holy, O God most mighty o holy & most mercifull Savio & most
to ye Prayrs &c
Ears unto ye Prayrs &c
to ye Prayrs but Spare us Lord most holy o God most mighty o holy & most mercifull Savio & most
Vers & Cho:
mercifull Savio thou most worthy Judg thou most worthy Judg E= ter= nal. Suffer us not at ye last
mercifull
mercifull
Vers: & Cho:
mercifull
Suffer us not at ye last
hour at ye last hour for any Pains of Death to fall to fall a way from Thee.
Mr Purcell.
hour at ye last hour. for any Pains of Death to fall away from thee to fall away from Thee
hour at ye last hour for any Pains of Death to fall to fall to fall a= way a way from Thee.
hour at ye last hour for any pains of Death to fall to fall a= way from Thee.

190 Sing O heavens
Organ Trumpet Stop.
Sing O heavens
Sing O heavens.
Sing O heavens.
Sing O heavens.
Sing O heavens
Sing sing Sing O heavens.
& be joyfull. & be joy full be
& be joyfull & be joy be joy full be
& be joyfull & be joy full be
joyfull O Earth be joyfull be joy full O Earth be
joyfull O Earth & be joyfull be joy full O Earth be
joyfull O Earth be joy full be joy full be joyfull O Earth be
Joy full be joy full O Earth break forth into Singing O
joy full O Earth, break forth into Singing O
Joyfull be joy full O Earth, break forth into Singing O

mountains break forth into Singing O Mountains
break forth break forth into Singing break
Mountains break forth into Singing O Mountains
break forth break forth into Singing break
Mountains break forth into Singing O Mountains.
break forth break forth into singing break
forth into Singing O Mountains.
For y Lord hath comforted hath comforted his
forth into Singing O mountains.
For y Lord hath Comforted hath
forth into Singing O Mountains,
people the Lord hath com for ted his peo ple, for y
comforted his people hath Com for ted his peo ple for y Lord hath Comforted for y
For y Lord hath Comforted his
Lord hath comforted hath com forted his People & will have mercy have mercy &
Lord hath comforted hath com forted his People & will have mercy have mercy &
people hath comforted hath com forted his people have mercy have mercy &

Rit:
will have mercy will have mercy upon his afflic=ted.
will have mercy will have mercy upon his afflicted.
will have mercy will have mercy upon his af=flicted.
Slow
But Si==on said, but Si=..........on said ỹ Lord ỹ Lord hath forsaken
Slow - But Si==on said but Si=..........on said ỹ Lord ỹ Lord hath forsaken
me & my Lord my Lord hath for-gotten me and my Ld my Ld & my Lord hath forgotten
me and my Lord & my Ld hath for-gotten me, and my Lord my Lord hath forgotten
me
Can a woman forget her sucking Child that she should not have Com=
me
#3 ♭6 4 ♭3 #3 #343

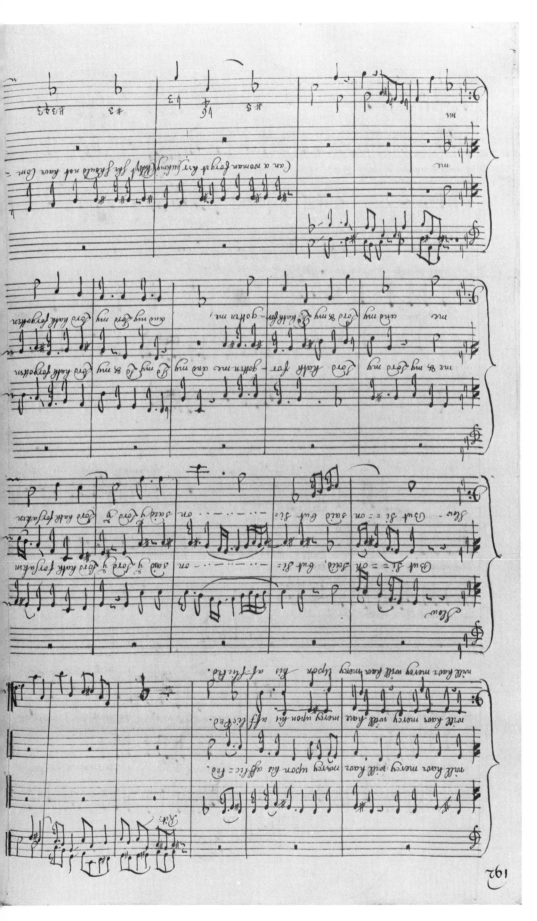

-passion, yt she should not have Com- passion ony Son ye Son of her womb, yea yea yea they may for-
yea yea yea they may for-
yea yea yea they may for
=get yet will not I yet will not I for=get thee yea they may for- get yet will not
get, yet will not I yet will not I for get- thee yea they may for get —
get yet will not I yet will not I forget thee yea they may for= get
I yet will not I for get thee yea they may forget yet will not I yet will not
Yet will not I yet will not I for- get thee yea they may forget, yet will not I yet will not
yet will not I not I for- get thee yea they may for- get yet will not I not
Trumpet Stop
Rit
I for-get Thee Sing o heavns
I for= get Thee Sing o heavns
I for-get Thee, Sing o heavns

Sing O heavns
Sing Sing O heavns,
Sing Sing Sing O heavns
& be
joyfull & be Joy full be joyfull O Earth.
joyfull, & be Joy full be Joy full be joyfull O
Joyfull, & be Joy full be joyfull O Earth.
be joyfull be joy full O Earth be joy full be
& be Joyfull be joy full O Earth. be joy
be joy- full be joyfull be joyfull O Earth be Joyfull be joy
Cho: Break forth break forth into Singing O mountains break forth into
joy- full Earth, Cho: Break forth break forth into singing O mountains break forth into
joyfull O Earth, Cho: Break forth break forth into Singing O mountains break forth into
joyfull O Earth, Cho: Break forth break forth into Singing O mountains break forth into

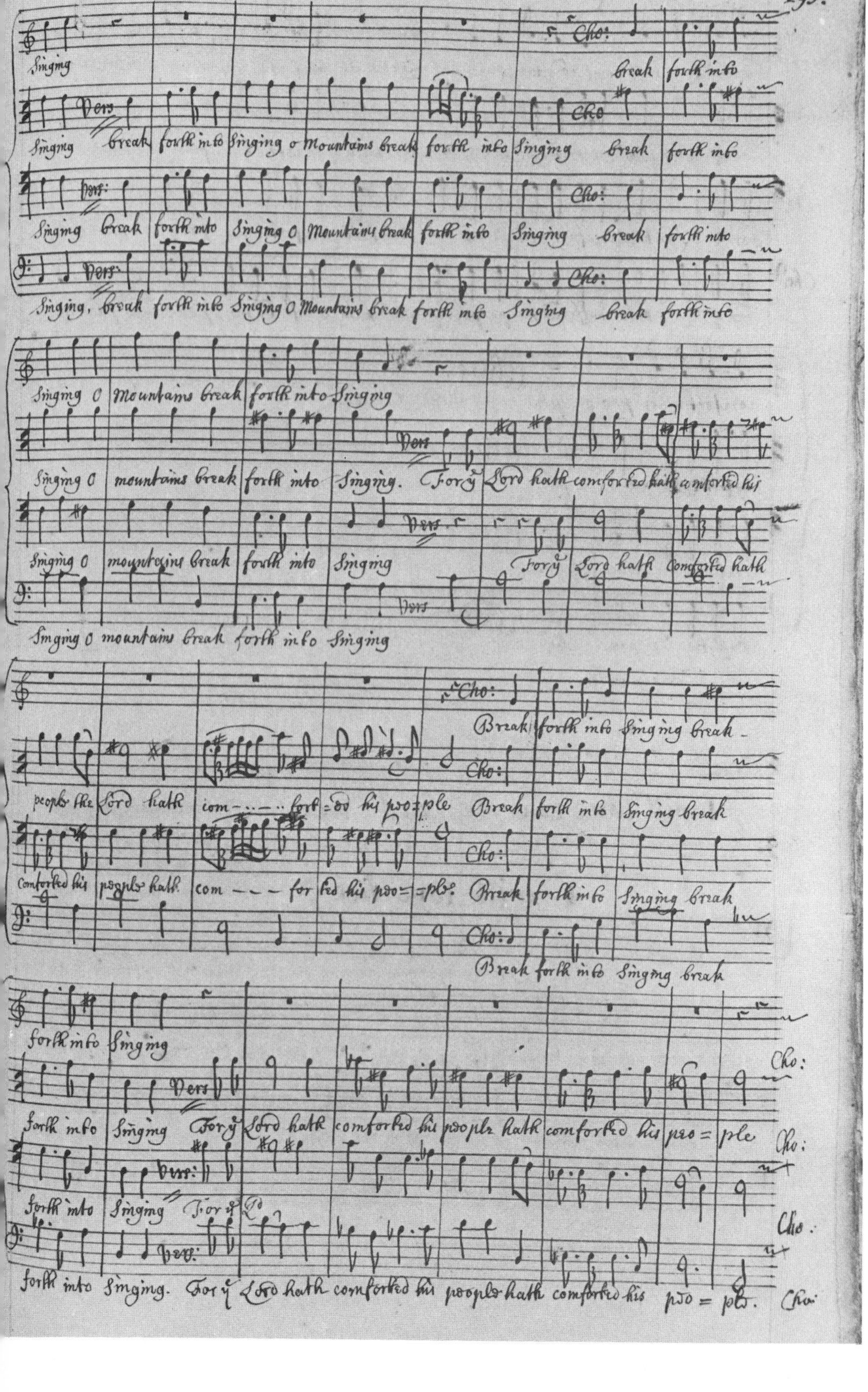
Singing
Vers Cho
Singing break forth into Singing o Mountains break forth into Singing break forth into
Vers: Cho:
Singing break forth into Singing O Mountains break forth into Singing break forth into
Vers Cho:
Singing, break forth into Singing O Mountains break forth into Singing break forth into
Singing O Mountains break forth into Singing
Vers
Singing O mountains break forth into Singing. For ye Lord hath comforted hath comforted his
Vers
Singing O mountains break forth into Singing For ye Lord hath comforted hath
Vers
Singing O mountains break forth into Singing
Cho:
Break forth into Singing break-
Cho:
people the Lord hath com------fort=ed his peo=ple Break forth into Singing break
Cho:
comforted his people hath com --- for ted his peo==ple: Break forth into Singing break
Cho:
Break forth into Singing break
forth into Singing
Vers Cho:
forth into Singing For ye Lord hath comforted his people hath comforted his peo=ple Cho:
Vers:
forth into Singing For ye Lord Cho:
Vers:
forth into Singing. For ye Lord hath comforted his people hath comforted his peo=ple. Cho:

196.
I will love thee &c
Mr Clark.
For ye Lord hath comforted his people, ye Lord hath comforted his peo- - -ple hath
For ye Lord hath Comforted his people ye Lord hath comforted his peo- - -ple hath
For ye Lord hath comforted his people ye Lord hath comforted his peo- - -ple hath
For ye Lord hath comforted his people ye Lord hath comforted his peo- - -ple hath
comforted his peo- -ple
Mr Fudway.
comforted his peo- -ple.
comforted his peo- -ple.
comforted his peo- -ple.
I will love thee O Lord my Strength will love Thee O
I will love thee O Lord my Strength will
Lord will love thee will love thee O Lord my Strength ye Lord is my Strong
Love thee O Lord will

Rock & my Defence my Saviour my God my God & my might in whom I will trust
Lord is my stony Rock & my Defence my Saviour my God & my might in whom I will trust my
The horn also of my Salvation my Buckler y Horn also of my Salvation
Buckler The horn also of my Salvation y Horn also of my Salvation
and my Refuge.
and my Refuge.
Solo:
I will call upon the Lord I will call upon y Lord who is
worthy to be praisd So shall I be safe be safe from mine Enemies
So shall I be safe, So shall I be safe be safe be safe from mine Enemies.

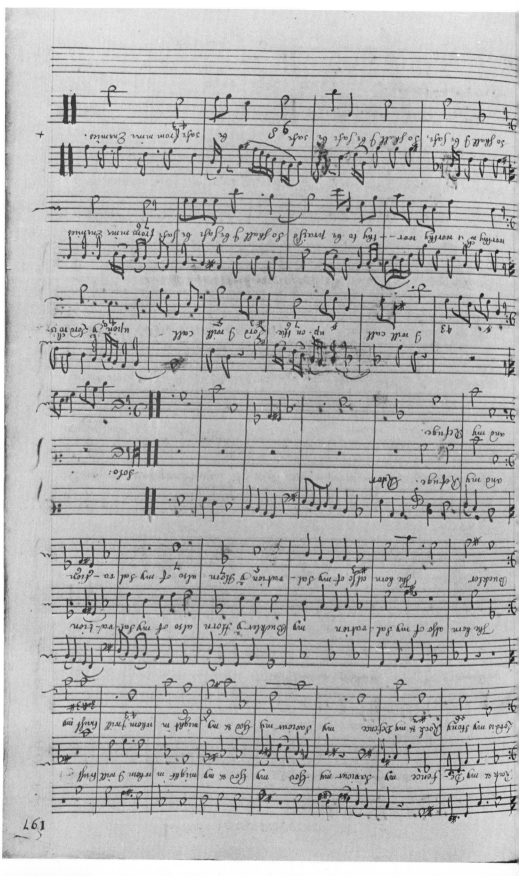

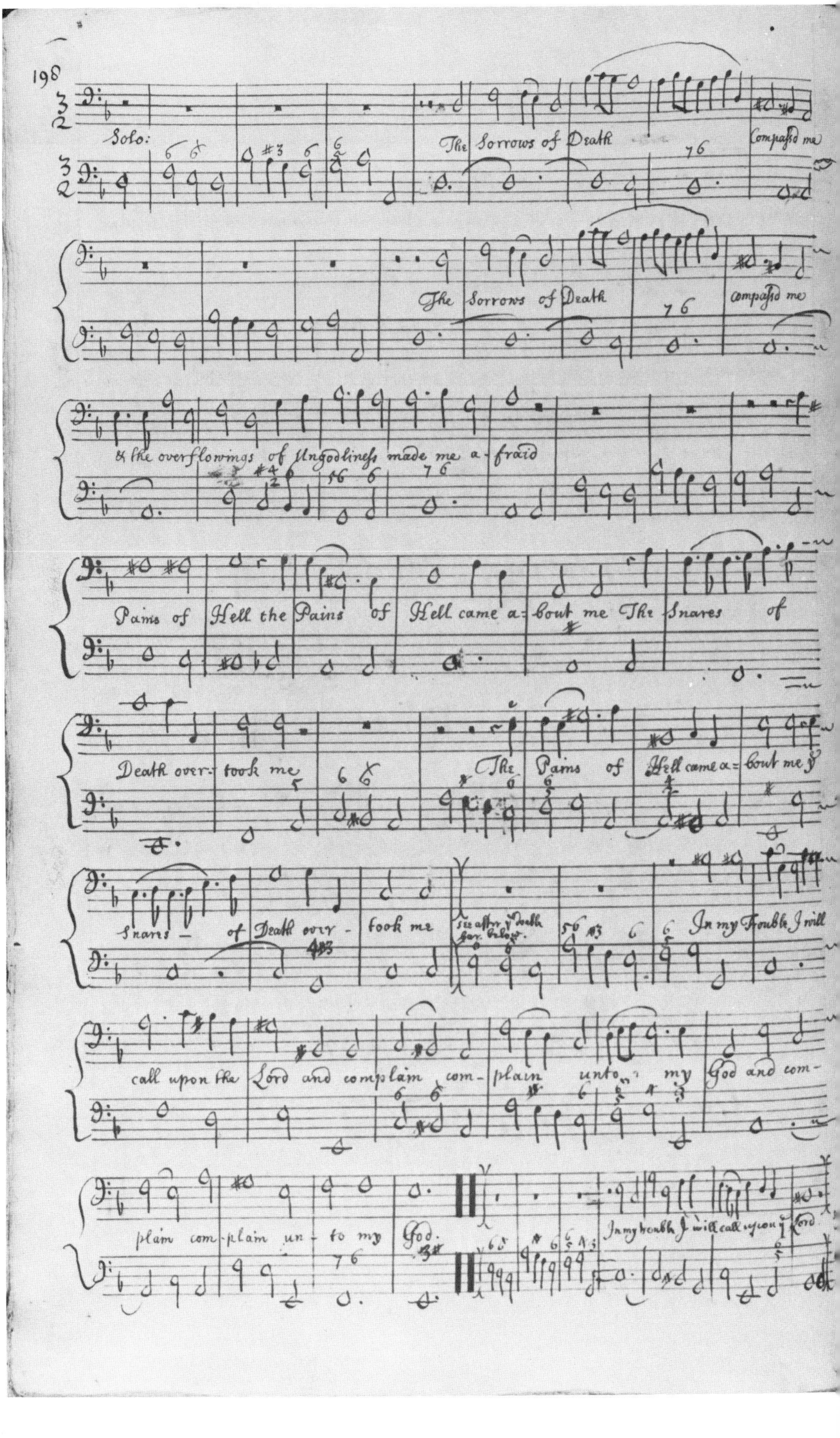
198
Solo:
The Sorrows of Death Compass'd me
The Sorrows of Death compass'd me
& the overflowings of Ungodliness made me a-fraid
Pains of Hell the Pains of Hell came a-bout me The Snares of
Death over-took me The Pains of Hell came a-bout me
Snares of Death over-took me
In my Trouble I will
call upon the Lord and complain com-plain unto my God and com-
plain com-plain un-to my God.
In my trouble I will call upon ye Lord

199
Vers 2 voc: So shall he hear my voice So shall he hear my voice out of his holy Temple, and my Com=
So shall he hear my voice So shall he hear my voice out of his holy Temple
plaint shall come shall come shall come be- fore him It shall enter ev'n unto his Ears
& my com plaint shall come shall come shall come be- fore him. It shall enter ev'n unto his ears.
Cho:
Cho: The Earth Trem-bled & quaked The Earth trembled & quaked,
Cho: The earth trem... bled & quaked The earth trem- bled & quaked The very foun-
Cho: The earth tremb- led & quaked The earth tremb- led & quaked The very foun-
Cho: The Earth tremb- led & quaked The Earth tremb- led & quaked
The very foundations of ye
dations of the hills shook & were re- moved removed were re- moved removed be-
dations of ye hills shook & were removed re- moved were re- moved be-
ye very foundation of ye hills shook & were re- moved re- moved be

hills shook and were re- mov'd remov'd because he was wroth.
cause he was wroth, & were re- mov'd be- cause he was wroth.
cause he was wroth, & were remov'd because he was wroth.
Vers 2 voc.
cause he was wroth & were remov'd be- cause he was wroth.
The Lord also Thun- dred out of Heaven and y highest gave his Thunder, the highest gave his
The Lord al- so- Thun- dred out of Heaven. And the highest gave his Thunder y
Thun- der hail stones & Coals of Fire
highest gave his Thunder hailstones & Coals of Fire

The Lord al-so Thun— — — —dred out of
The Lord al-so Thun— — —dred out of
heavn, & ye highest gave his Thunder the highest gave his Thunder hailstones & Coals of Fire.
heavn, and the highest gave his Thunder gave his Thunder hailstones & Coals of Fire.
Ritor:
Slow He shall send down from on
Slow He shall send down from on
high to fetch me, and shall take me out of ma- - ny waters because I have kept ye ways of ye
high to fetch me and shall take me out of many waters be-cause I have kept ye ways of ye
Lord and have not forsaken and have not for-saken for-saken my God.
Cho:
Lord and have not for-saken and have not for-saken for-saken my God.
Cho:

202
Cho:
He shall send down from on high to fetch me, & shall take me out of many-
Cho:
He shall &c
Cho:
He shall send down from on high to fetch me & shall take me out of ma-ny-
Cho:
He shall &c.
waters be-cause I have kept the ways of the Lord and have not for-saken for-
waters be-cause I have kept the ways of ye Lord and have not for-saken for-
-saken my God and have not for-saken for-saken my God.
Mr Jer: Clark.
saken my God and have not for-saken for-saken my God.

Thanksgiving Anthem Aug: 23. 1705

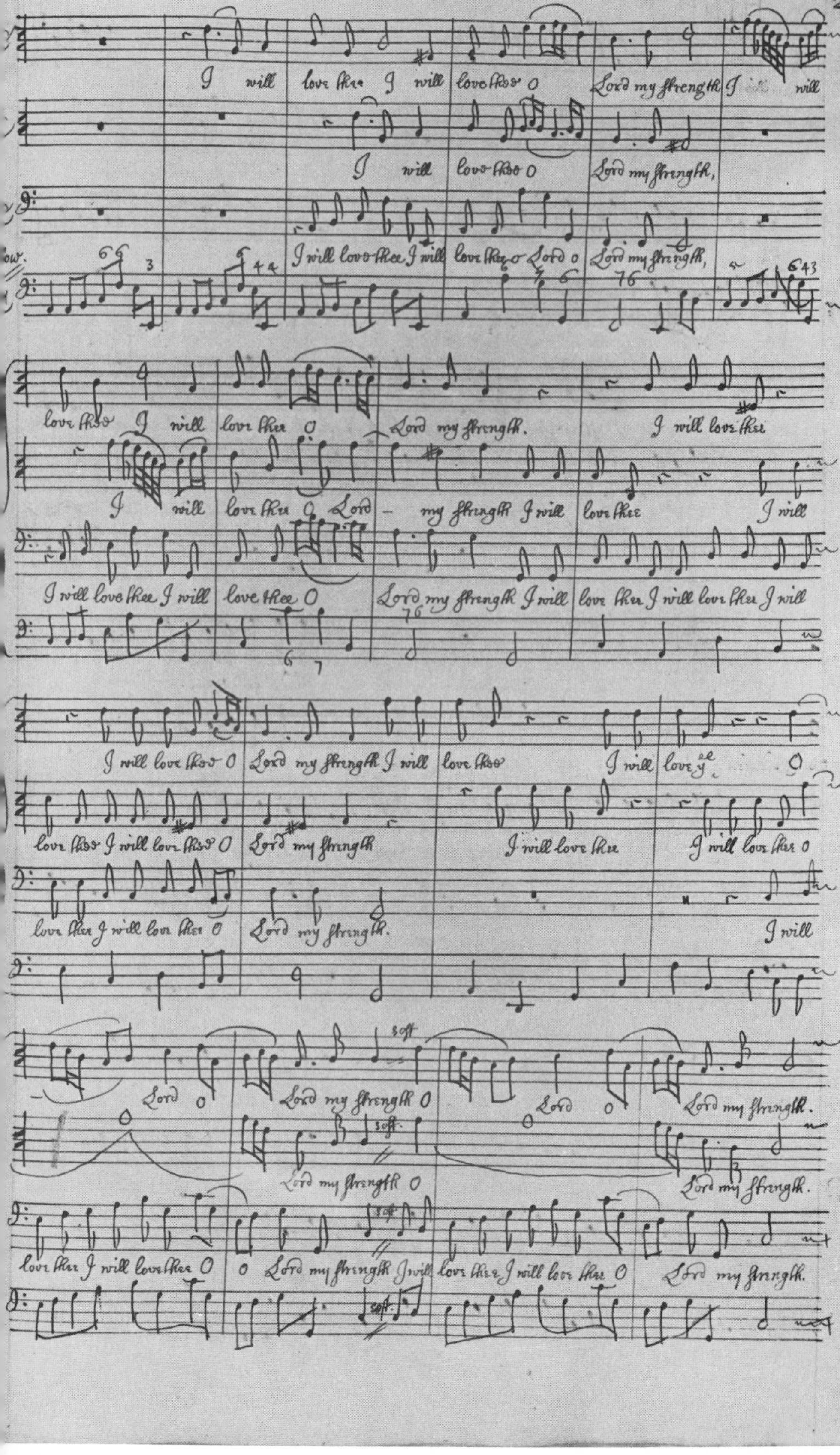
I will love thee I will love thee O Lord my strength I will
I will love thee O Lord my strength,
I will love thee I will love thee O Lord O Lord my strength,
love thee I will love thee O Lord my strength. I will love thee
I will love thee O Lord - my strength I will love thee I will
I will love thee I will love thee O Lord my strength I will love thee I will love thee I will
I will love thee O Lord my strength I will love thee I will love ye O
love thee I will love thee O Lord my strength I will love thee I will love thee O
love thee I will love thee O Lord my strength. I will
Lord O Lord my strength O Lord O Lord my strength.
Lord my strength O Lord my strength.
love thee I will love thee O O Lord my strength I will love thee I will love thee O Lord my strength.
soft

Trumpet Stop:
It is God yt Girdeth me wth strength of war
It is God yt girdeth me wth strength of war & maketh my way perfect
faster
faster
faster
faster. I will follow I will follow I will follow I will follow I will follow upon mine Enemies.
I will follow I will follow I will follow upon mine Enemies.
I will follow upon mine Enemies.
Cho:
Cho:
Cho:
Cho:
I will follow I will
I will follow I will follow up — on mine
I will follow I will follow up — on mine Enemies I will follow I will
I will follow I will follow up — on mine Enemies I will follow I will follow

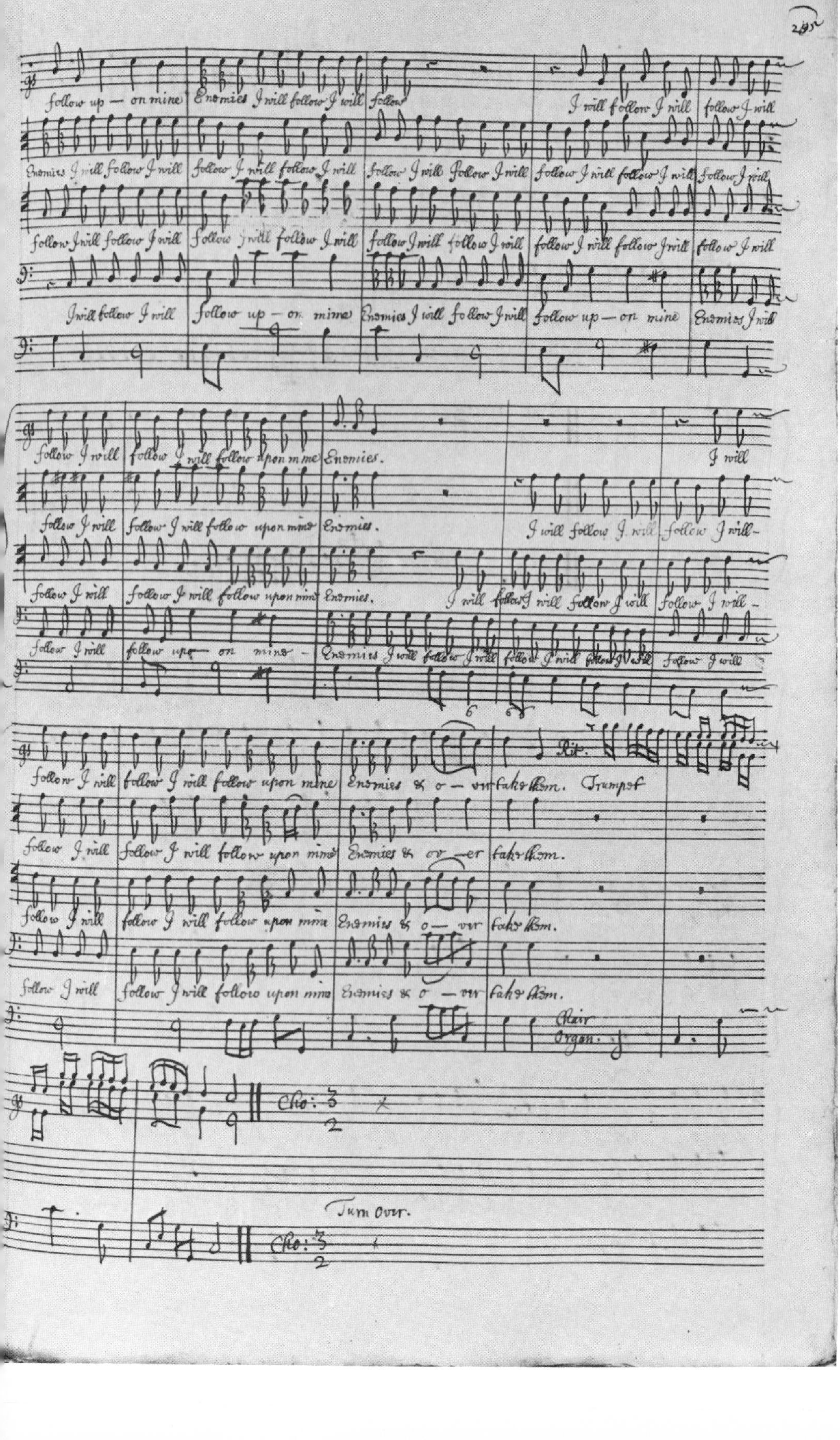

follow up — on mine Enemies I will follow I will follow I will follow I will follow I will
Enemies I will follow I will follow I will follow I will follow I will follow I will follow I will follow I will follow I will follow I will
follow I will follow I will follow I will follow I will follow I will follow I will follow I will follow I will follow I will
I will follow I will follow up — on mine Enemies I will follow I will follow up — on mine Enemies I will
follow I will follow I will follow upon mine Enemies. I will
follow I will follow I will follow upon mine Enemies. I will follow I will follow I will
follow I will follow I will follow upon mine Enemies. I will follow I will follow I will follow I will
follow I will follow up — on mine — Enemies I will follow I will follow I will follow I will follow I will
follow I will follow I will follow upon mine Enemies & o — ver take them. Trumpet
follow I will follow I will follow upon mine Enemies & o — ver take them.
follow I will follow I will follow upon mine Enemies & o — ver take them.
follow I will follow I will follow upon mine Enemies & o — ver take them.
Rit.
Chair Organ.
Cho: 3 2
Turn over.
Cho: 3 2

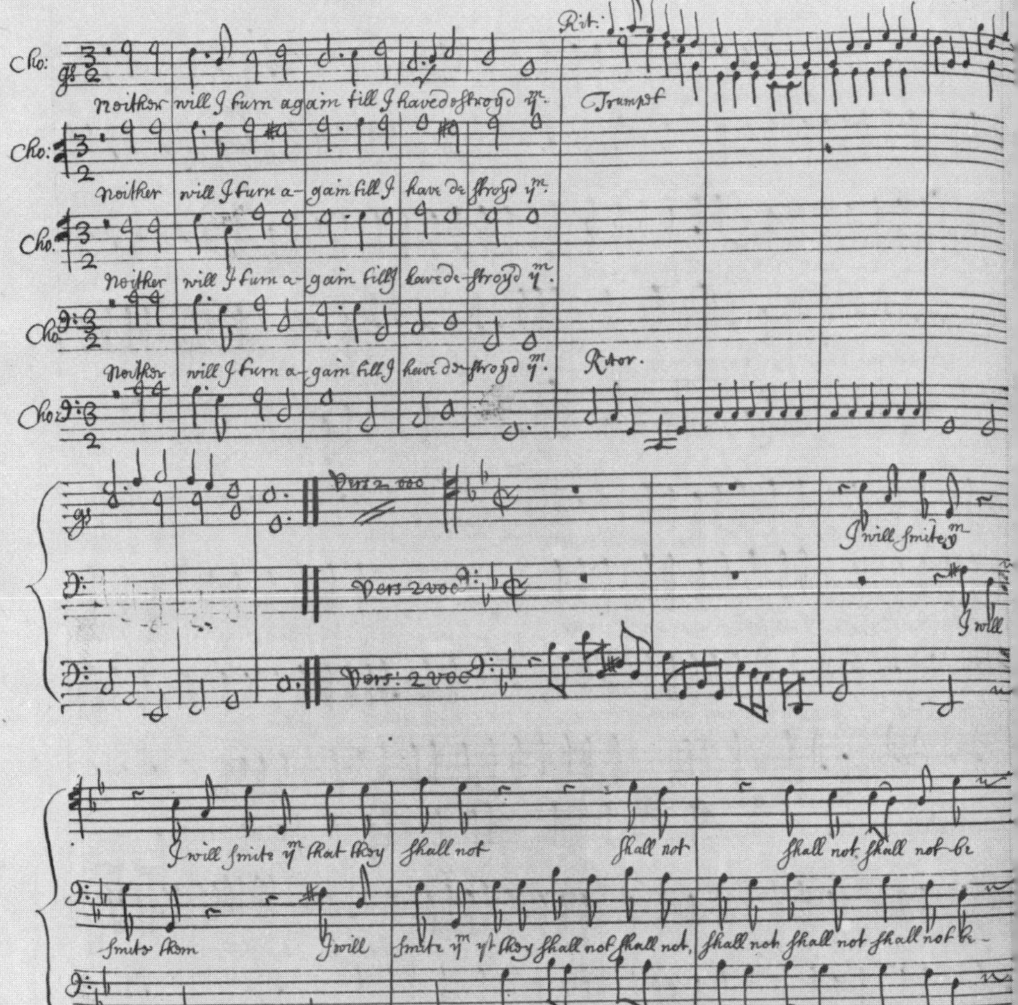
Cho:
Neither will I turn again till I have destroy'd them.
Rit:
Trumpet
Ritor.
Vers: 2 voc:
I will smite them
I will smite them that they shall not shall not shall not, shall not be
smite them I will smite them yt they shall not shall not, shall not shall not shall not be-
a-ble to stand
able to stand
shall not shall not shall not be- able be able to stand but fall but fall, but fall fall under my feet

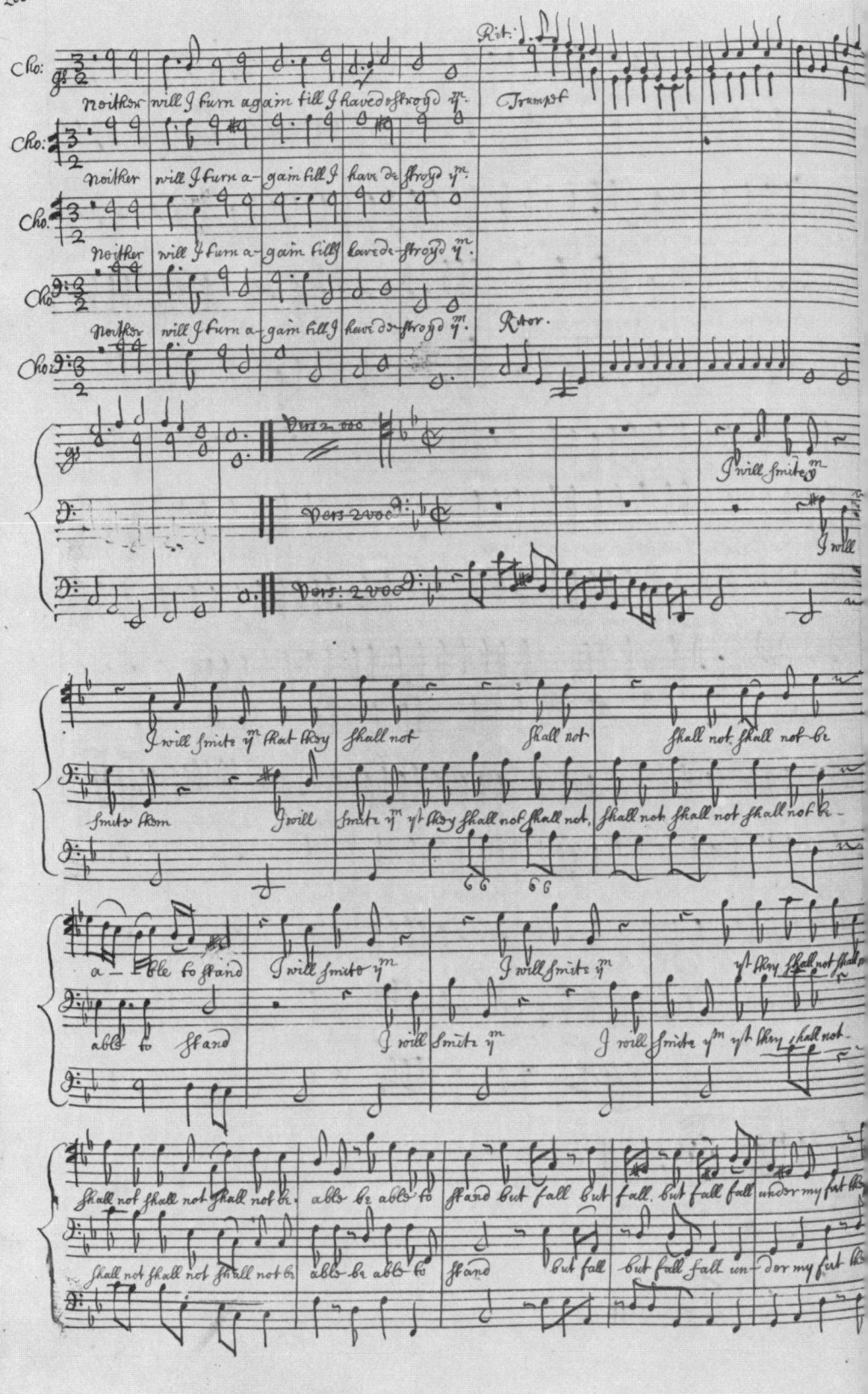

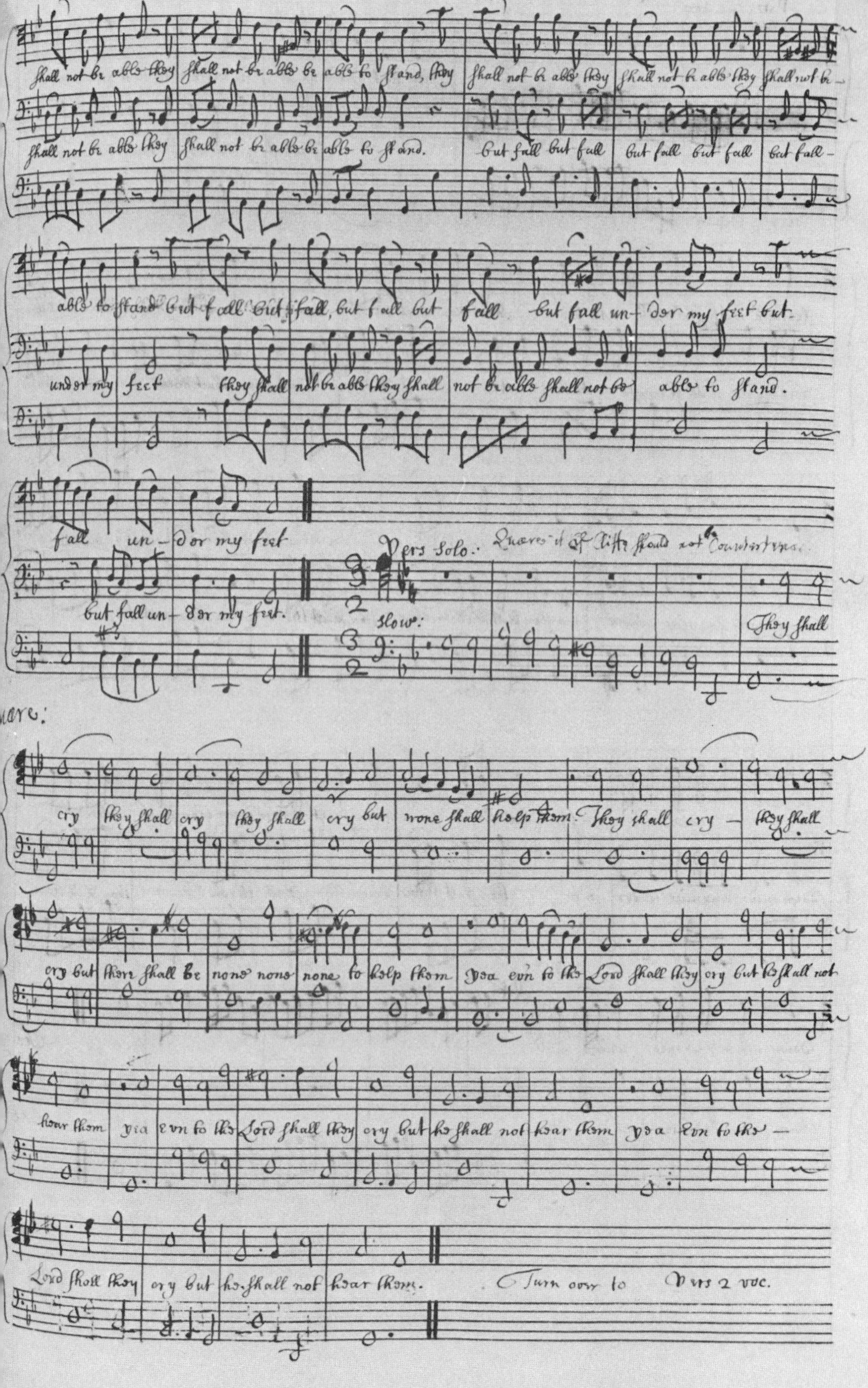
shall not be able they shall not be able be able to stand, they shall not be able they shall not be able they shall not be-
shall not be able they shall not be able be able to stand. but fall but fall but fall but fall but fall-
able to stand but fall but fall, but fall but fall but fall under my feet but
under my feet they shall not be able they shall not be able shall not be able to stand.
fall under my feet
but fall under my feet.
Vers solo. Quare if of Tiffs should not Countertenor.
slow.
They shall
…ore:
cry they shall cry they shall cry but none shall help them. They shall cry - they shall
cry but there shall be none none none to help them yea even to the Lord shall they cry but he shall not
hear them yea even to the Lord shall they cry but he shall not hear them yea even to the -
Lord shall they cry but he shall not hear them.
Turn over to Vers 2 voc.

Vers: 2. voc.
Thou hast girded me wth strength thou hast girded me wth
thou hast girded me wth strength thou hast
strength with strength unto the Battle thou shalt throw down thou shalt throw down thou shalt throw
girded me with strength unto the Battle thou shalt throw down thou shalt throw down thou shalt throw
down mine Enemies under me thou shalt throw down thou shalt throw down thou shalt throw
down mine Enemies under me thou shalt throw down thou shalt throw down thou shalt throw
down mine Enemies under me thou shalt throw down thou shalt throw down thou shalt throw
down mine Enemies under me thou shalt throw down thou shalt throw down thou shalt throw
Down mine Enemies under me
down mine Enemies under me.
Rit
Chor
Cho.

Chorus
Chorus
For this cause will I give
For this Cause will I give Thanks to Thee O Lord
Chorus
For this Cause will I give Thanks to Thee O Lord will I give
Chorus
For this cause will I give Thanks to
Organ
Thanks to Thee For this cause will I give Thanks to
will I give Thanks to Thee. For this cause will I give
Thanks to Thee will I give Thanks will I give Thanks.
Thee will I give Thanks to Thee will I give Thanks.
Thee O Lord For this
Thanks to Thee O Lord O Lord to Thee O Lord for this
For this Cause will I give thanks to Thee for this Cause will I give thanks for this
Cause will I give Thanks to Thee for this
cause will I give thanks to Thee O Lord And sing praises to thy
cause will I give thanks to Thee O Lord And sing praises to thy name, & sing
cause will I give thanks to Thee O Lord and sing praises to thy name and sing praises to thy
cause will I give thanks to Thee O Lord And sing praises to thy name & sing

Name and sing praises to thy name and sing praises to thy name to thy name.
praises to thy Name and sing praises to thy name un- to thy name
name and sing praises to thy Name & sing praises to thy name un- to thy name
praises to thy name & sing praises to thy name sing praises to thy name.
Vers slow
The Lord, ye Lord liveth The Lord liveth The Lord the Lord liveth The Lord
Vers: The Lord liveth The Lord liveth The Lord the Lord liveth
Vers slow The Lord liveth The Lord liveth The Ld ye Lord liveth
Cho:
Vers:
liveth & blessed blessed be my strong helper, And blessed blessed be my strong helper.
And blessed blessed be my strong helper.
Solo:
Ritor
praise—ed be ye God of my Salvation And prai—sed praise

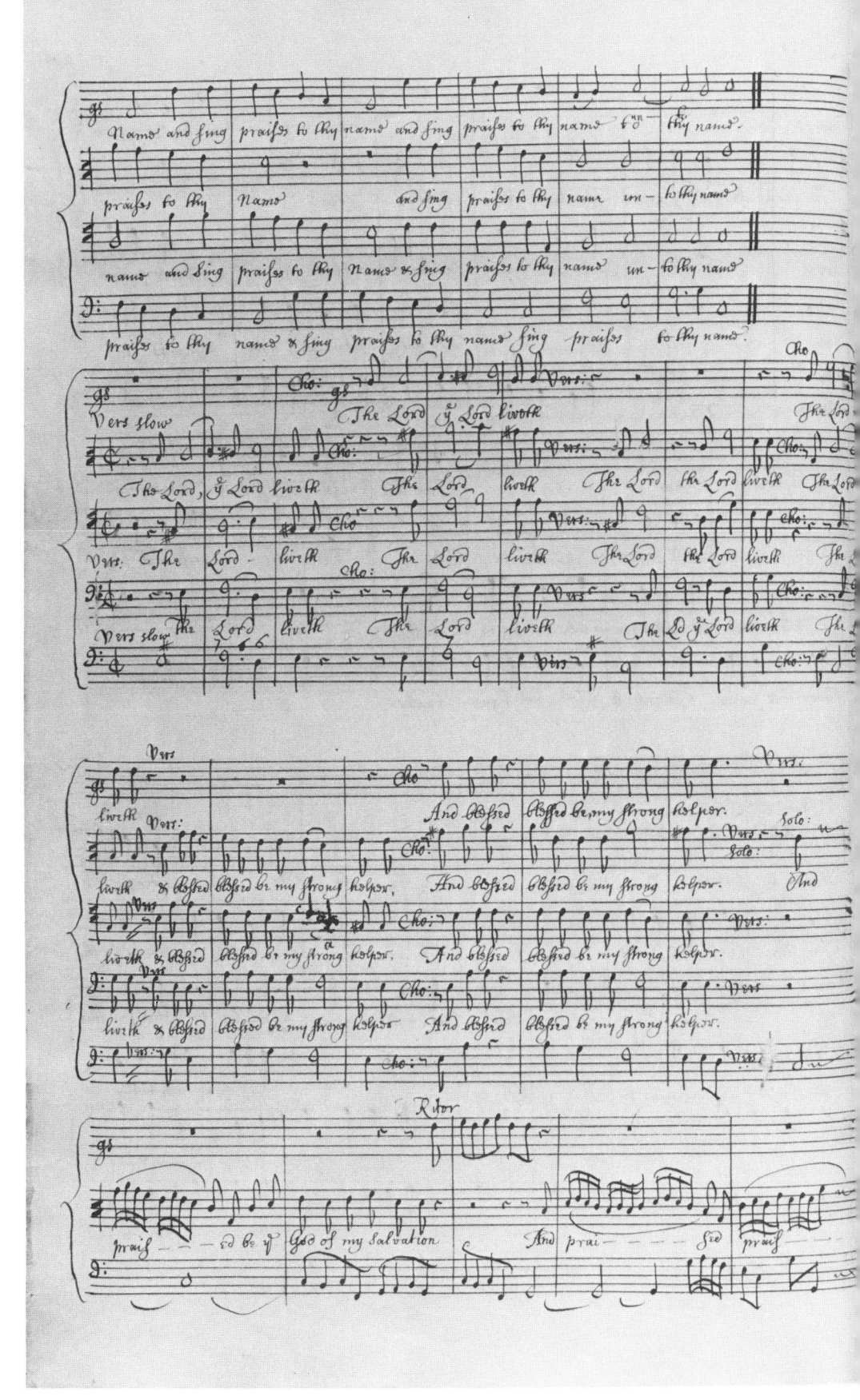

Ritor
sod be the God of my salvation
Alle
luia alle-luia alle-luia alle=luia alle-lu-ia alle=luia
soft
loud
Alle-luia alle
luia
Alle-luia alleluia al-le-lu ia al-le-luia al-le-luia alle luia
Alle-
luia alle-luia alle lu-ia al-le lu ia
Alle luia alleluia al-le-luia all-e luia alle-luia alle luia
alle-
luia alleluia alle-lu-ia al-lelu-ia

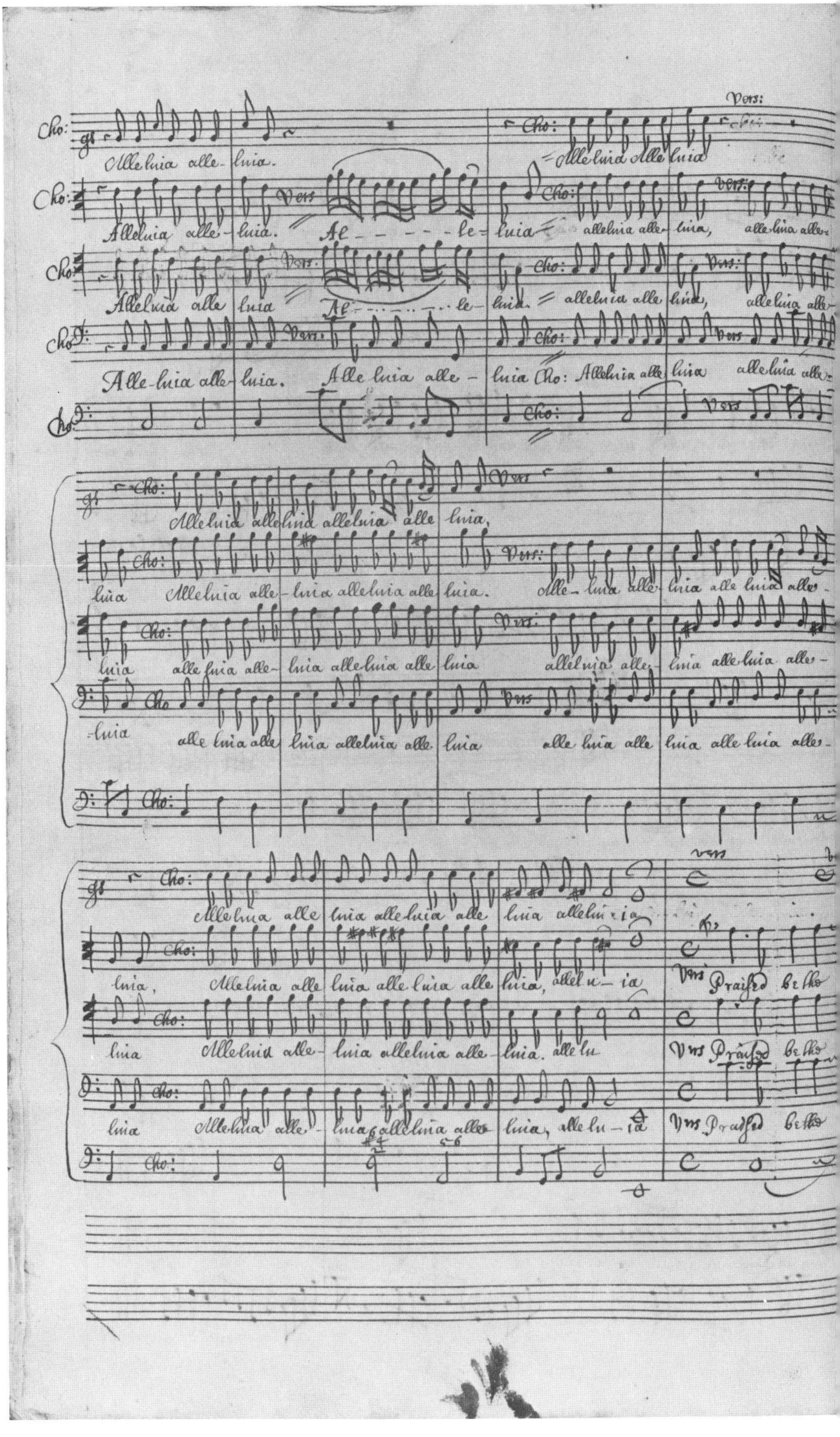
Vers:
Cho:
Allelnia alle-lnia.
Allelnia Allelnia
Alle-lnia alle-lnia.
Alle lnia alle-
lnia Cho: Allelnia alle lnia
Allelnia alle lnia alle lnia,
Vers
Praised be tho

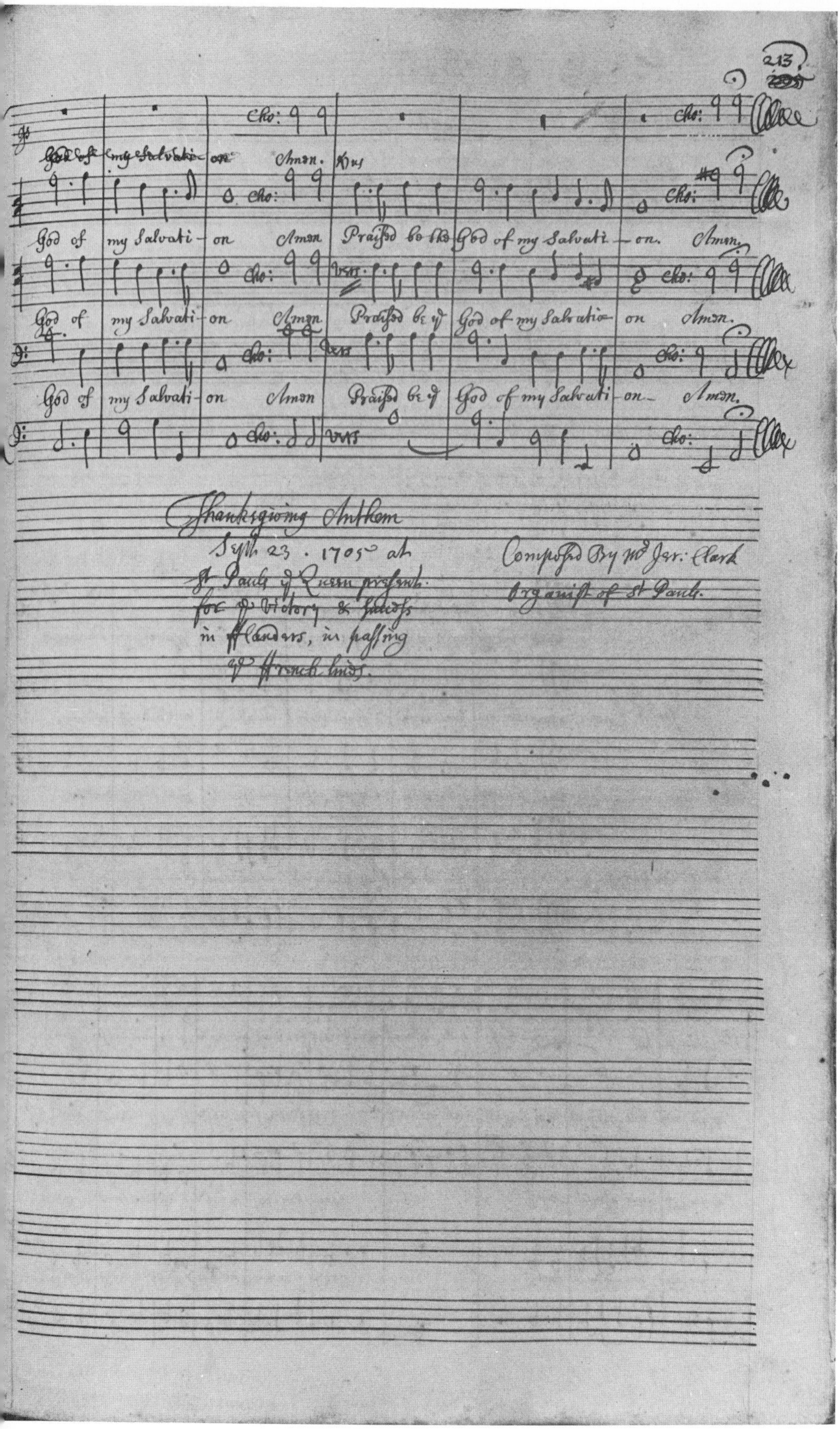
213
God of my Salvati- on Amen. Vers
God of my Salvati- on Amen Praised be the God of my Salvati- on. Amen.
God of my Salvati- on Amen Praised be y God of my Salvatio- on Amen.
God of my Salvati- on Amen Praised be y God of my Salvati- on- Amen.
Cho:
Thanksgiving Anthem
Sept. 23 . 1705 at
St Pauls y Queen present.
for y Victory & Success
in Flanders, in passing
ye French lines.
Composed By Mr Jer: Clark
Organist of St Pauls.